THE PAPACY IN THE MODERN WORLD 1914–1978

Pope Benedict XV

The Papacy in the Modern World
1914–1978

J. Derek Holmes

Burns & Oates · London

First published by Burns & Oates, 2/10 Jerdan Place, London SW6 5PT
in Britain and associated territories in 1981
and in the USA by the Crossroad Publishing Co., New York

ISBN (UK) 0 86012 076 7

ISBN (USA) 0 8245 0047 4

Printed in Great Britain at
The Camelot Press Ltd, Southampton

for Search Press Ltd.,
2/10 Jerdan Place, London SW6 5PT

Contents

Contents

List of Illustrations

Acknowledgements for the illustrations are due to the following:

Mansell Collection: plates 1, 3, 6, 11, 12
Keystone Press: plates 4a, 5, 8a, 9, 10 13, 15
The Author and Ushaw College Library: plates 2, 7a, 7b, 8b
French Embassy: plate 4b
William Collins Sons & Co. Ltd.: plate 14

Author's Preface

The dangers of commenting on the recent past are well known. The lack of much original material coupled with the need to see events from a more distant perspective creates obvious pitfalls and I must leave it to others to decide how far I have succeeded in avoiding them. Nevertheless the importance of the contemporary Papacy and the keen interest shown in the institution – not only by Roman Catholics – is such that there is an obvious demand for historical studies – however inadequate these might ultimately prove to be – as a necessary prelude to any deeper reflection on the wider significance of the popes in the twentieth century.

With the exception of papal encyclicals, conciliar decrees and the documents of the Holy See during the War, this account is inevitably based on secondary material and it seemed somewhat pretentious to attempt to annotate it. However, those sources from which I have quoted or used directly are marked with an asterisk in the bibliography. I must also express my deep gratitude to the Rev. T. W. Van Luenen, former secretary of Cardinal de Jong, who gave me valuable information, to Dr John Coulson for his help and collaboration, and to the Editors of the *Clergy Review* and the *Tablet* who so kindly allowed me to use material which first appeared in those periodicals.

I eventually decided to avoid commenting more directly or in greater detail on the initial pattern of events immediately following the election of Pope John Paul II since my preliminary remarks apply with even greater force in the case of a living pope.

Ushaw College   *J. Derek Holmes*

Pope John XXIII as a sergeant in the army medical service, Bergamo, 1915

Chapter I

Benedict XV and the First World War

When Pope Benedict XV died in 1922 at the age of sixty-seven, he was dismissed by the left-wing press in Italy as 'Cold, mediocre, obstinate'; 'Tomorrow history will have already forgotten him'; and similar verdicts were expressed over the next few decades by other critics, Catholic and non-Catholic alike. Benedict was a pope who was totally misunderstood during his own lifetime and a man whose real merits have only slowly and recently been appreciated by historians and commentators. He was – like truth itself – one of the first victims of war, while his premature death meant that his successor was given the credit for many of his most promising initiatives. However there were a few contemporaries who recognized his virtues and who appreciated the reasons for his unpopularity. One commentator wrote in 1922: 'Alone among the statesmen of Europe he tried to find a common ground between the belligerents. Alone among those in authority, in any Christian sect, he seemed to think that peace remained, even in war time, the leading doctrine of his Master. For that he received the scorn and abuse of all the warring nations'.

Yet it is difficult to see how far the Cardinals who elected Benedict were influenced by the outbreak of war. The First World War had been raging for almost a month when, on the day on which Pius X died, the German forces occupied Brussels. The Russians had attacked East Prussia and Poland, while the British had won the Battle of Heligoland. At the same time the Germans had annihilated the Russian army at Tannenberg, the British and French were retreating and the French Government had been forced to move from Paris to Bordeaux. The belligerents included Germany and Austria-Hungary, where Catholics were numerous and well-organized, and countries such as France and Russia, England and Italy which, for various historical, political or religious reasons, did not sympathize with the international authority of the Papacy or the promotion of Catholic interests throughout the world. However, only a quarter of the Cardinals at the Conclave then belonged to the belligerent nations, and the war had broken out so quickly and recently, that it was not unreasonable to expect that it might just as quickly be brought to an end.

The Cardinals were probably more influenced in their choice of Benedict by their divisions between those who were in favour of continuing the more

1

conservative and intransigent policies associated with Pius X or Merry del Val and those who felt that the claims of 'orthodoxy' and discipline had been carried too far during the preceding pontificate. Giacomo Della Chiesa, who had spent many years in the diplomatic service of the Holy See, was greatly influenced by his former superior Rampolla del Tindaro, Leo XIII's Secretary of State. Della Chiesa had been personal secretary to Rampolla and had accompanied the Cardinal when he went as Nuncio to Spain and then acted as Under-Secretary of State at the Holy See. However, during the pontificate of Pius X Della Chiesa was appointed to the archbishopric of Bologna because of differences in approach, and he was not raised to the cardinalate for several years. Della Chiesa's appointment as Archbishop of Bologna and the long delay before he received the red hat has inevitably been compared with the later and similar appointment of Giovanni Battista Montini to the archdiocese of Milan.

Della Chiesa undoubtedly had reservations about the policies associated with Pius X and Merry del Val, particularly over academic issues and relations between the Holy See and the French Government. He gave positive encouragement to the development of theological studies after the years of integrist reaction, while his appointment first of Ferrata and then of Gasparri as Secretaries of State indicated his intention of reflecting the spirit of Leo XIII rather than that of Pius X. Ferrata was the former Nuncio in Paris while Gasparri had been Professor of Canon Law at the Catholic Institute in Paris for some twenty years. Benedict also wrote a note in his own hand to tell the President of the French Republic of his election before informing other Governments. These and similar initial moves reflected his genuine sense of Christian charity and his determination to work for peace among the nations and reconciliation between the Church and the Powers of this world. He ordered that his coronation should take place quietly in the Sistine Chapel, in a subdued fashion, as a sign of his concern for the sorrows caused by war. The new pope also immediately investigated the financial state of the Vatican in order to set aside a large sum of money for immediate distribution to those in need.

On the eve of the Conclave, in August 1914, the Archbishop of Bologna had written to his Vicar General: 'I would be sorry if any parish priest took sides for one or other belligerent. I have done my best to propose that we pray God for the cessation of the war without dictating to the Almighty the way in which this terrible scourge may cease'. Two days after his coronation, Benedict published an exhortation to Catholics throughout the world in which he made it clear that he intended to intervene in every way possible in the hopes of bringing the conflict to an end: '. . . we are firmly resolved, so far as it is in our power, to leave nothing undone which can conduce to the more speedy ending of this calamity'; and he was openly demanding peace negotiations within two months of the outbreak of war.

During the Great War, the Holy See could not support either side and was inevitably forced to adopt a neutral policy. The Pope himself subordinated everything to the moral and evangelical condemnation of war and, in an effort to stop the bloodshed, consistently tried to contain the conflict, to prevent its further escalation and to end the War. The Pope's policies were not welcomed by the Allies, especially in 1915 and 1917, when Italy and the United States were about to enter the War, or by the Central Powers who felt that they were more deserving of papal support than the Protestant or secularist countries opposing them. But Benedict had an instinctive and Christian horror of war and as Pope would never allow chaplains to appear in military uniform within the precincts of the Vatican. At the time his attitudes were completely misinterpreted and misunderstood by countries dominated by the passions of nationalism and militarism and in due course he was denounced by the opposing sides as Maledetto XV, the 'Boche Pope' and the *Franzosenpapst*.

In his first message to the world on 8 September 1914, the new Pope described war as 'the scourge of the wrath of God'; he repeated this message in his first encyclical, *Ad Beatissimi*, which was published on 1 November 1914: 'Truly those days seem to have come upon us of which Our Lord foretold: Ye shall hear of wars and rumours of wars . . . For nation shall rise against nation and kingdom against kingdom. The terrible spectre of war dominates everywhere and there is hardly any other thought in men's minds. Great and flourishing nations are there on the fields of battle. What wonder is it, then, if, being well furnished as they are with those horrible weapons that the progress of military science has invented, they inflict tremendous carnage on each other. There is no limit to the ruin and slaughter: every day the earth is steeped in fresh blood and covered anew with dead and wounded. And who would believe that such peoples, armed against each other, are all descended from the same progenitor, have the same nature and belong to the same human society? Who would think they could be brothers, sons of a single Father in Heaven? And in the meantime, while huge armies fight on both sides, nations, families, and individuals groan under the sorrows and miseries attendant on war; day by day the ranks of the widows and orphans swell; trade languishes because of destroyed communications, the fields are abandoned, the arts suspended, the rich are in difficulties, the poor in abject misery, and all in distress'.

In 1914 the Pope asked Cardinal Mercier to use the money collected for 'Peter's Pence' in Belgium to alleviate the distress of the Belgian people and the Belgian victims of war. In December of the same year the Pope proposed the exchange of all prisoners who were incapable of further military service and directly approached the belligerent countries in a futile attempt to secure a truce on Christmas Day. He hoped, as he said, that such an armistice might have 'consoled so many mothers and so many wives with the certainty that in the few hours consecrated to recollection of the divine birthday their loved ones would not have fallen under the enemy's lead'. In January 1915 the Pope also proposed that women and children, youths under seventeen and adults over fifty-five, medical practitioners, ministers of religion and those disqualified from military service should be returned to their homes. Between March 1915 and November 1916 almost two and a half thousand German and almost nine thousand French disabled prisoners were repatriated. Meanwhile more than 3000 Belgians were allowed to return home and no less than 20,000 interned French civilians were released within a month. A German newspaper commented: 'The thanks of millions go out to him. His request has even succeeded in obtaining an extension of the prescriptions of the law of nations, and that at a time when these are outraged ten times over in one day. The voice of a compassionate man has achieved what the statesmen could not'. Benedict was later successful in obtaining the release of Italian prisoners of war suffering from tuberculosis and the exchange of German and French fathers of large families. He also secured the release of those British subjects interned in Germany who were medically unfit for active service.

The Pope's official letters published in the Roman *Acta* reveal his preoccupation with the sufferings caused by war and his determination to do everything he could to relieve the distress of the sick and the wounded, the imprisoned, the deported and the interned at whatever cost to himself or to the Church. During the First World War the Holy See engaged in charitable and humanitarian works on a vast scale as a 'second Red Cross'. The Pope spent his own personal fortune as well as the ordinary revenue of the Holy See and it is estimated that the Vatican spent about eighty-two million gold *lire* on charitable works during the war. Large gifts of money and food supplies, medicines, clothing and literature were sent — sometimes in neutral ships controlled by the Holy See — to France, Belgium and Luxemburg, northern Italy, Germany and Poland, Serbia and Montenegro, Ruthenia and Lithuania.

The Vatican, in collaboration with the International Red Cross, became a clearing-house for tracing and exchanging prisoners, searching for missing persons and re-establishing family contacts, and even occasionally for securing the return of the remains of those who had been killed. The

Pope ordered bishops of the dioceses where prisoners were held to appoint chaplains to look after their spiritual and material interests and especially to help them to communicate with their families. He encouraged the formation of Catholic agencies in Germany and Switzerland for the care of prisoners and personally obtained hospital treatment for sick and wounded prisoners in Switzerland. Although Benedict condemned the confiscation of ecclesiastical property for military use, he willingly handed over Catholic hospitals, colleges and seminaries for the use of the civil authorities. The Pope showed special concern for children and for refugees, for the victims of bombardment and particular individuals caught up in the fighting. In July 1915 he secured the release of over a hundred French hostages and in September 1916 at the Pope's request the Kaiser freed and pardoned Arthur Verhaegen, the Leader of the Belgian Catholic Labour Party. Benedict also persuaded the Kaiser to reduce to imprisonment the sentence imposed on several leading Belgians who had been condemned to death and achieved the same result in the case of three German citizens condemned by the French authorities.

Benedict composed his famous prayer for peace, which he ordered to be recited throughout the world, at the beginning of 1915: 'Dismayed by the horrors of a war which is bringing ruin to peoples and nations, we turn, O Jesus, to Thy most loving Heart as to our last hope. O God of Mercy, with tears we invoke Thee to end this fearful scourge. O King of Peace, we humbly implore the peace for which we long. From Thy Sacred Heart Thou didst shed forth over the world divine Charity, so that discord might end and love alone might reign among men. During Thy life on earth Thy heart beat with tender compassion for the sorrows of men; in this hour made terrible with burning hate, with bloodshed and with slaughter, once more may Thy divine Heart be moved to pity. Pity the countless mothers in anguish for the fate of their sons: pity the numberless families now bereaved of their fathers; pity Europe over which broods such havoc and disaster. Do Thou inspire rulers and peoples with counsels of meekness, do Thou heal the discords that tear the nations asunder; Thou who didst shed Thy Precious Blood that they might live as brothers, bring men together once more in loving harmony. And, as once before to the cry of the Apostle Peter: *Save us, Lord, we perish*, Thou didst answer with words of mercy and didst still the raging waves, so now deign to hear our trustful prayer, and give back to the world peace and tranquillity'. The French Government originally forbade the public recitation of the Pope's prayer and he was widely accused of attempting to destroy the morale of the men fighting at the front.

On 28 July 1915, the first anniversary of the outbreak of war between

Austria and Serbia, Benedict XV once again appealed to the leaders of the nations: 'In the holy name of God, in the name of our heavenly Father and Lord, by the Precious Blood of Jesus, the price of man's redemption, we conjure you whom divine providence has placed over the nations at war, to put an end at last to this horrible slaughter, which for a whole year has dishonoured Europe. It is the blood of brothers that is being poured out on land and sea. The most beautiful regions of Europe, this garden of the world, are strewn with corpses and with ruin. Where but a short time ago there flourished the industry of manufactures and the fruitful labours of the fields, the guns now thunder fearfully and in their destructive fury they spare neither village nor city, but spread havoc and death everywhere. You bear before God and man the tremendous responsibility of peace and war. Give ear to our prayer, to the fatherly voice of the Vicar of the Eternal and Supreme Judge, to whom you must render an account alike of your public conduct as of your own private actions. The abundant wealth with which God the Creator has enriched the lands that you rule enables you to continue the struggle, but at what cost? Let the thousands of young lives extinguished every day on the battlefield make answer; the ruins of so many towns and villages, of so many monuments raised by the piety and genius of your forefathers. And the bitter tears shed in secret at home, or at the foot of altars where suppliants pray – do not these also repeat that the price of the long protracted struggle is great, too great? . . . Nor let it be said that this vast conflict cannot be settled without the violence of arms . . . Recollect that nations do not die: humiliated and oppressed, they chafe against the yoke imposed on them, preparing revolt and transmitting from generation to generation a tragic heritage of hatred and revenge'.

In the Pope's Christmas message for 1915 he spoke of the world as 'a hospital and a charnel-house'. In the following March he referred to the 'suicide of civilized Europe'. In July he described the recourse to arms as 'the darkest tragedy of human hatred and human madness'. In September he told the German bishops that he was 'supremely bound in conscience to counsel, suggest, inculcate nothing else but peace' and to support the cause of mankind rather than men. Meanwhile he promised to 'continue by every means in our power to alleviate, at least in part, the awful accumulation of miseries which are the sad consequence of the war'.

Benedict consistently denounced the War as a barbarous and useless means of trying to deal with national conflicts and he repeatedly appealed to the nations to establish a just peace without regard to military victory or defeat. Catholics throughout the world were genuinely divided on the points at issue. At the end of 1914 the German bishops declared in a pastoral letter: 'We are innocent of the outbreak of war; it was imposed on us; this we can testify before God and men'. So the Pope did not denounce those Catholics who were involved in the War but appealed to their governments to end the conflict and to settle their differences by peaceful means. War, he argued, simply resulted in destruction and tragedy, pestilence and famine, without guaranteeing the peace and future security even of the victorious nations. He never referred to the classical distinction in Catholic theology between just and unjust wars, and would seem to have regarded the traditional ecclesiastical teaching as inadequate to deal with contemporary circumstances and even calculated to prolong the struggle. And unlike other Christian leaders – such as the seventy-six leading German Catholics who described the war as 'the new springtime of religion' – he refused to believe that the War provided an opportunity for religious and moral revival.

The Holy See was accused of following the Central Powers when the Secretariat of State tried to prevent Italy and the United States from entering the war on the side of the Allies, but the Pope publicly expressed his sympathy for Belgium, refused to support the Irish fight for independence, condemned the sinking of the *Lusitania* and personally rebuked Kaiser Wilhelm II for the use of poison gas. The Pope openly condemned the bombardment of unfortified towns – especially aerial bombardments – and the deportation of civilians when these crimes were committed by either side. When the Germans began to deport Belgian and French civilians in June 1916 the Pope issued a strong protest which had an immediate effect.

Benedict was especially criticized by the Allies for failing to condemn the German violation of Belgian neutrality, but the violation of Belgian neutrality was one of the instances when the Pope did adopt a definite standpoint on the basis of incontestable and officially recognized facts. The Secretary of State made it clear in a letter to the German authorities that the Pope's general condemnation of injustice covered the invasion of Belgium which was a violation of international law, and the Pope himself endorsed Gasparri's declaration: 'The violation of the neutrality of Belgium, on the admission of her [Germany's] own Chancellor, contrary to international law, *was certainly one of those injustices which the Holy Father in his Consistorial Allocation of 22 January "Strongly reprobates"*'. The Prussian Minister to the Holy See sent a formal protest, French journalists thanked the Pope for having, alone of the neutral powers, condemned the violation of Belgian neutrality and the Pope himself remarked: 'The Belgian Government has sent Us its most cordial thanks. Some would have had the Pope to be more explicit. It is impossible . . . a German assured us lately that he had himself seen the priests of Belgium in the act of firing upon the German soldiers. . . . We don't believe it, but before making a public pronouncement we ought, in the position We hold, to have mathematical exactness in our assertions'. The Holy See also protested at the detention of Cardinal Mercier and the restrictions imposed on other Belgian bishops and the Pope himself personally gave 25,000 *lire* for the relief of suffering in Belgium and appealed to Catholics throughout the world to help their Belgian co-religionists.

The Pope's main aims were to end the War and to mitigate its horrors while it continued and he could only hope to achieve these aims by keeping open every means of communication with both sides. To have condemned either side for particular acts of injustice might have jeopardized that impartiality which the Pope felt he needed. As he said on one occasion: 'To proclaim that for nobody is it lawful on any plea whatever to offend justice, belongs chiefly, beyond all question, to the Roman Pontiff who is by God appointed the supreme interpreter and defender of the eternal law. And We do proclaim it without qualification, condemning every injustice by whatever side it may have been committed. But to involve the authority of the Pope in the actual contests of the belligerents, would surely be neither appropriate nor useful. Certainly anybody who judges carefully cannot fail to see that in this enormous struggle the Apostolic See, though filled with the greatest anxiety, must remain perfectly impartial. . . . Were he to do otherwise, not only would he not help at all the cause of peace, but, worse, he would create aversions and enmities to religion and would expose to grave disturbances the tranquillity and internal concord of the Church'. If the Pope had not remained impartial, he would have been restricted and inhibited in his charitable endeavours. He would not have been able to secure the exchange of wounded prisoners or the liberation of civilian captives and the appointment of apostolic visitors to investigate conditions in prison camps.

The exhortations and denunciations of the Pope proved particularly annoying to the Italian Government. Italy had entered the war on 24 May 1915 in the hopes of gaining the Trentino from Austria, and in spite of the efforts of the Pope, who had done everything possible to preserve Italian neutrality. As he wrote: 'The voice of the friend and of the father, we say it with a heart crushed with grief, was not harkened to. The war continues to drench Europe with blood, and on land and on sea even means of offence which are contrary to the dictates of humanity and international law are not avoided. And as if that was not enough, the terrible conflagration has extended even to our beloved Italy, making one fear for it also that sequel of tears and disasters which is the accompaniment of every war, even when it is successful'.

The Pope's pathetic appeals to the King of Italy begging him to end the 'useless slaughter' were bitterly condemned by the Italian nationalists as jeopardizing national morale and unnecessarily defeatist.

Anti-clericals were among the leading supporters of Italy's entry into the War and several of them suggested that the privileges granted to the Holy See by the Law of Guarantees should be suspended for the duration of the War. In the event the provisions of the Law were not modified and they continued to be applied after Italy's declaration of war. During the War Pope Benedict was able to maintain good relations with the Italian Government by his tact and restraint without ever compromising the supra-national mission of the papacy or the strict neutrality of the Holy See. In fact the obvious sincerity of papal neutrality did much to discredit the old claims of the anti-clericals that the Vatican would seek to undermine the Italian State in the event of war.

An incidental result of the Italian declaration of war, and of the fact that the territorial sovereignty of the Vatican was not yet recognized, was that diplomatic representatives as well as German and Austrian churchmen no longer enjoyed unrestricted direct access to the Holy See. The outbreak of the Great War posed a threat to Catholic unity not only because of national divisions but because warfare interrupted communications between bishops and the Holy See. Meanwhile the conflicting countries effectively recognized the moral position of the Holy See by indiscreetly soliciting its support.

At the beginning of the War neither France nor Britain enjoyed diplomatic relations with the Vatican, and when Benedict was elected to the papacy most of the European nations were either unrepresented or had recently broken off diplomatic relations with the Holy See. It was therefore inevitable that representatives of the Central Powers who were constantly in attendance were suspected of having received undue consideration from Vatican officials bitterly opposed to British Protestants, French Freemasons and Italian anti-clericals. In fact allied sources accused the Pope of sympathizing with the Central Powers at a time when Austrian diplomats in Rome were complaining that Anglicans, Freemasons and atheists were better received at the Vatican than Catholics from the Central Powers. The importance of French Canada and Ireland prompted the British Government to send a temporary ambassador to the Holy See and as it became obvious that the Holy See was becoming of increasing significance during the War the French Government also sent an official observer.

In spite of the very bitter and vocal opposition to the Pope during the War, his courageous and disinterested work for peace and his efforts on behalf of the victims of war did much to enhance the international prestige of the papacy. In 1913 only fourteen states were represented at the Papal Court, but by the time of his death in 1922 twenty-five states, including almost every major country, had established regular diplomatic representation at the Holy See. Never before had so many and such influential foreign diplomats been accredited to the Holy See nor had so many Vatican representatives been accredited to foreign governments. The countries represented included France and Britain, Germany and Austria, Holland and Belgium, Spain and Portugal, Hungary and Czechoslovakia, Poland and Yugoslavia, Estonia and the Ukraine, Japan and Finland, as well as most of the countries of South America. When the Netherlands appointed an ambassador to the Vatican, the Dutch Prime Minister, a Protestant, declared in Parliament: 'Today no political centre wields more influence in the cause of peace than does the Vatican. The Pope is truly one of the great powers'. Pius XI continued the efforts of Benedict XV to establish or restore relations with secular governments in order that the Holy See might play a more effective part in international affairs. In 1870 only fifteen diplomatic representatives were accredited to the Holy See but by 1939 there were thirty-eight representatives. In 1870 there were only fifteen papal representatives throughout the world but in 1939 there were thirty-eight nunciatures and twenty-three apostolic delegations.

During the First World War the possibility of a peaceful compromise always seemed possible and this was only prevented by the tenacious determination of the warring nations to achieve the final victory. This very fact, that compromise was possible, was one of the reasons why the Pope's appeals for peace and attempts at mediation gave so much offence to those who were determined to secure a military victory. Secular governments firmly believed in the prospect of ultimate victory whereas the Pope believed that a peace conference could and should be called before one group of nations had been defeated or been utterly exhausted by the struggle. Benedict hoped for a 'stable and equitable' peace achieved through negotiation, a peace which would recognize 'the rights and just aspirations of peoples', rather than a peace imposed on the defeated 'who will prepare for revenge and transmit hatred from generation to generation'.

Benedict therefore not only condemned the War in general terms but took practical steps to promote peace negotiations. He unsuccessfully tried to persuade President Wilson to mediate, though in December 1916 the President did ask the belligerents to state their terms for peace. The Pope made his most important attempt to begin negotiations in 1917 when both sides were growing weary of war, when the possibility of a military solution appeared increasingly remote and the time seemed ripe for compromise.

The Pope privately formulated what he believed were the necessary conditions for the restoration of peace: Belgian sovereignty, the territorial
integrity of France, the preservation of Austria-Hungary though with concessions to Italy, the re-establishment of Poland, and a settlement in the
Balkans that would exclude Russia from Constantinople. He then directly
approached the German Government in an effort to discover whether
Germany would agree to the restoration of Belgian independence, and sent
Eugenio Pacelli as Nuncio to Germany with a personal letter to the Kaiser
asking for the conditions on which the German Government would be
willing to negotiate. The Nuncio in Munich, Pacelli, and the Nuncio in
Vienna spent months in negotiation and on 1 August 1917 the Pope
published his famous letter to 'the leaders of the belligerent peoples'.

Benedict pointed out that: 'Since the beginning of our Pontificate, in the
midst of the horrors of the terrible war which has burst upon Europe, we
have considered three things among others: To maintain an absolute impartiality towards all belligerents, as becomes him who is the common
father, and who loves all his children with an equal affection; to endeavour
continually to do the utmost good to all without distinction of persons,
nationality or religion, in accordance not only with the universal law of
charity, but also with the supreme spiritual duty laid upon us by Christ;
and finally, as is demanded by our pacific mission, to omit nothing, as far
as in our power lies, to contribute to hasten the end of this calamity by
trying to bring the peoples and their leaders to more moderate resolutions
in the discussion of means that will secure a "just and lasting peace"'.

The Pope then went on to outline the appeals he had made to end the
War and put forward specific proposals to serve as a basis for negotiation
and the establishment of a just and lasting peace. He proposed that the
restoration of the rule of law – the substitution of the moral force of right
for the material force of arms – should be achieved in three phases: the
suspension of fighting, a simultaneous and reciprocal reduction of arma-
ments – 'according to rules and guarantees to be established to the
extent necessary and sufficient for the maintenance of public order in each
State' – and the establishment of international arbitration, 'on lines to be
determined and with sanctions to be settled against any State that should
refuse either to submit international questions to arbitration or to accept its
awards'. At the same time occupied territories must be restored or
returned, remaining territorial disputes should be settled according to the
aspirations of the peoples concerned and the general welfare of mankind,
the free movement of peoples and common rights over the seas should also
be recognized, and demands for reparations or indemnities should be
renounced.

The official reactions of allied governments were extremely cautious and reserved while the replies of the Central Powers, encouraged by the outbreak of the Russian Revolution, were evasive. The German Chancellor deliberately frustrated the Pope's attempts to initiate negotiations by his delays and even by misleading the Reichstag. There was much opposition to the papal proposals in France where they were regarded as an attempt to save the Central Powers from defeat. Clemenceau denounced them as 'a peace against France' and 'a peace to the profit of the violators of justice'. The celebrated Dominican professor at the *Institut Catholique*, Père Sertillanges, declared in the presence and with the approval of Cardinal Amette: 'Holy Father, for the time we are unable to listen to your words of peace. Like the apparent rebel in the gospel, we are sons who reply "No, no"'. Meanwhile the entry of the United States into the conflict confirmed the Allies in their determination to defeat Germany, the Central Powers continued to hope for a decisive victory before the Americans could intervene, and within a few months the papal proposals had been forgotten.

The Holy See was excluded from participating in the Peace Conference by the terms of the Treaty of London which included a secret agreement between Italy and her allies barring the Vatican from the negotiations or the settlement: 'France, Great Britain and Russia pledge themselves to support Italy in not allowing the representatives of the Holy See to undertake any diplomatic steps having for their object the conclusion of peace or the settlement of questions connected with the present war'. This article was apparently intended to prevent the Holy See from attempting to secure a settlement of the Roman Question during the negotiations but it also effectively excluded the Holy See from the Versailles Conference, though there was a Vatican 'observer'.

During the War the Central Powers had encouraged suggestions for a settlement of the Roman Question in the hopes of winning the support of the Holy See and compromising its relation with the Italian Government. The Pope was not impressed with this clumsy manoeuvre, and when in July 1915 it was suggested that he was hoping to secure the restoration of his temporal power through the influence of Austria and her allies, the Secretary of State issued an immediate denial: 'The Holy See, as befits its neutrality, has no intention whatever of embarrassing the Government; it puts its trust in God and awaits a proper readjustment of its situation, not from foreign arms, but rather from the triumph of those sentiments of justice which, it hopes, are steadily gaining ground among the Italian people in conformity to its true interests'. This assurance that the Roman Question would not be exploited to the embarrassment of Italy was received with great satisfaction by the Italian Government and rendered the secret agreement in the Treaty of London superfluous and unnecessary.

At the same time Benedict was determined to safeguard the political independence of the papacy and the temporal rights of the Church and he protested against his situation as 'Prisoner of the Vatican' in his very first encyclical. 'And so, while earnestly desiring that peace should be concluded amongst the nations, it is also our desire that there should be an end to the abnormal position of the Head of the Church, a position in many ways harmful to the very peace of nations'.

The Pope was eager to make contacts with the Italian Government and was always careful to avoid offending Italian opinion. In December 1915 he again deplored the fact that the contemporary situation did not allow him 'that full liberty which is absolutely necessary for the government of the Church', while expressing his confidence that 'Those governing Italy are not wanting in good intentions to eliminate these inconveniences'.

Although Benedict has been justly described as 'a representative of the great universalist tradition, a worthy pupil of the school of Leo XIII and Rampolla', he recognized that the Italian policies of his predecessors had been superseded by events. When President Wilson visited Rome in 1919 Benedict did not uphold the principle previously laid down that the Vatican was closed to distinguished visitors who had called on the King of Italy. The Pope received the President even though representatives of Protestant sects in Italy had also arranged to meet with Wilson on the same afternoon. The Pope formally revoked the prohibition on Catholic rulers visiting the Italian King in his encyclical *Pacem Dei munus* in order 'not to prevent meetings so useful to peace by making it virtually impossible for Catholic heads of state to visit Rome'. The official ban on Catholics participating in the political life of Italy was finally and formally lifted during the pontificate of Benedict XV, who also allowed the formation of Don Sturzo's Popular Party. As one prominent Italian Senator and political commentator wrote after the Pope's death: 'Benedict XV was the first Pope since 1870 to show an acceptable inclination towards pacification and not to belie it by such words and deeds as to make it impossible. He was the first Pope who, either from natural sensitivity or from natural correctness of behaviour, did not contribute to making neighbourly relations with the Italian State an impossibility'.

Meanwhile it was suggested that the most effective way of securing an international guarantee for the independence and integrity of papal territory would be for the Holy See to join the League of Nations. It is difficult to surmise whether the moral significance of the Papacy might have been able to influence the development of the League. For a time, Benedict was an enthusiastic supporter of the League before its lack of universality and the exclusion of Germany caused him to become more critical and even disillusioned. Pius XI was to prove even more sceptical of the value of the League though he continued to collaborate in works of a religious, moral or humanitarian nature. In the event the Holy See renounced its right to apply for membership of the League in the subsequent Lateran Treaty.

Although the Holy See was not a member of the League of Nations, Benedict XV originally gave it his approval and blessing and he instructed the Catholic Union of International Studies to establish permanent links with the League so that the Church and the League would be able to collaborate on a number of specific points. In some ways the League of Nations was an attempt to establish 'the institution of arbitration' recommended by the Pope but his own demands for international cooperation and for proposals guaranteeing international security went much further. In any case the American Government refused to join the League and by the beginning of the 1920s the provisions of the peace settlement were already being challenged by the Polish invasion into Russia and the Italian claims to Fiume. Furthermore, the League of Nations was associated with the unjust provisions of the Treaty of Versailles.

Immediately after the War the Pope tried to win the support of Catholics for the 'equitable deliberations of the Peace Congress', but he became disillusioned with developments in Paris and began to support the cause of the vanquished on whom, as he rightly appreciated, the future peace of the world would ultimately depend. The demands for reparations, the refusal to adopt reciprocal disarmament or to restore former German colonies were directly opposed to the suggestions made by the Pope in 1917. At Versailles the defeated nations were not only excluded from the Conference until they were called in to sign a dictated peace, but subjected to a naval blockade which resulted in famine and starvation.

In the spring of 1919 the Pope called on German and French Catholics to forget their former hostilities. In the following December he strongly condemned national hatreds and the excessive nationalism of some ecclesiastical hierarchies. Benedict also conveyed German proposals on the settlement of reparations to the American Government in Washington and he protested against the naval blockade and the intolerable situation forced on Austria. He constantly recommended nations to lay aside their hatreds and to work charitably together for the relief of suffering.

On 23 May 1920 the Pope published his encyclical, *Pacem Dei munus*, in which he again expressed his anxieties: 'for if in most places peace of some sort is established and treaties signed, the germs of former enmities remain; and you well know . . . there can be no stable peace or lasting treaties . . . unless there be a return of mutual charity to appease hate and banish enmity'. He urged Catholics to do everything in their power to forgive former enemies and to assist the victims of war; not only individuals but nations and peoples must pursue policies and adopt attitudes of reconciliation. Finally Benedict encourages all states to 'unite in one league, or rather family of people, calculated both to maintain their own independence and safeguard the order of human society', to reduce wasteful military expenditure and to guarantee the independence and integrity of nations.

To some extent, Benedict's Christian pacifism was better appreciated after the War than it had been during the conflict. In July 1921 Catholic students, including representatives of the defeated as well as the victorious nations, established the 'Pax Romana' and in September 1923 the German bishops declared: 'We renounce all diets, all plans of hatred or revenge; we do not strive after any such reprisals. We content ourselves with that vengeance which St Paul calls the vengeance of heaven, and which consists in loving our enemies and praying for them'.

Hence, in spite of widespread criticisms and misunderstandings, the work of Benedict XV was not totally unappreciated even at the time. In 1918 the British Under-Secretary for Foreign Affairs had admitted to the House of Commons that: 'there are many occasions on which the Pope has interfered most benevolently, and in a way which has earned the gratitude of every person in this country. There are other cases to which I could refer, cases in which His Holiness obtained better terms for prisoners, the repatriation of prisoners, when he has rendered service in regard to hospitals and in regard to the graves of our soldiers in Italy. He has taken action with regard to matters of civilian relief, and so on, as to which we have had many diplomatic conversations in this country, and as to which we have always treated all his representations with the utmost respect, and we are grateful for the many things he has done to alleviate the conditions of our prisoners and others who have suffered during the war'.

On the death of the Pope in 1922 the President of the Reichstag declared: 'He used all the moral power of his office to alleviate human suffering, to banish hatred, and to reconcile the nations'. Lord Curzon also praised 'the late Pope, who during his too short tenure of his exalted office showed himself so consistent a friend of peace, and so firm an advocate of the moral brotherhood of mankind'. But such contemporary tributes were rare and only one monument was erected to honour Benedict during his lifetime. Less than a month before his death a monument was unveiled in Constantinople where Benedict had founded an orphanage for Armenian

His Eminence Cardinal Mercier, Archbishop of Malines.
Whose fearless denunciation of German atrocities made all Christendom ring.

Cardinal Mercier

children and had done so much for prisoners and other victims of the war. The inscription read: 'To the great Pontiff of the world tragedy, benefactor of peoples without distinction of race or creed'.

After the War the work of charitable relief under the patronage of the Pope had continued with even greater intensity. The Vatican continued to give substantial relief to the countries of Central Europe where economic and social problems were most acute. In 1920, for example, the Holy See distributed gifts of food, clothing and medicine as well as some seventeen million *lire* to ease distress in Poland, Lithuania and Rumania, the Ukraine and the Balkan States. Benedict himself, who on his deathbed remarked 'In all my life I have spent two and a half *lire* in medicines', personally gave two million *lire*. The problems of unemployment, famine and disease reached a climax in 1921 and the Pope repeatedly appealed for help and for volunteers to serve the starving and the destitute. Millions were dying of famine in Russia, while Germany and Poland, the Baltic and Balkan States, Greece, Turkey and China were inundated with refugees many of whom were also suffering from cholera and typhus.

One of Benedict's last acts was an urgent appeal for the relief of famine in Russia. He wrote to his Secretary of State: 'Immense numbers of human beings gripped by famine, mown down by typhus and cholera, wander despairingly over a country struck with barrenness, and return to the most crowded centres, where they hope to find bread and are driven back by armed force. From the basin of the Volga many millions of men faced with a most terrible death, are calling for the help of mankind . . . it concerns a people already extremely tried by the scourge of war, a people on whom the mark of Christ shines, a people that has always strongly desired to belong to the Christian family. Although separated from Us by barriers set up during long centuries, it is all the more close to Our fatherly heart in the measure of its misfortune. My Lord Cardinal, We feel it a duty to do all that Our poverty leaves in Our power to succour Our far-off children'.

The Pope appealed to the faithful and to governments throughout the world to support his efforts on behalf of the Russian people and he sent a telegram to the League of Nations: 'The tidings that reach us from Russia are continually worse, and the suffering is so great that only the union and collaboration of peoples and the governments can furnish a remedy. Therefore We turn through your Excellency to the representatives of the nations assembled and make Our warmest appeal to their feelings of humanity and brotherhood, in order that measures may be promptly taken to save the unhappy Russian people'. The League simply acknowledged the papal appeal and forwarded it to a committee of investigation.

The Russian Revolution had, at least in theory, put the Catholic Church

17

on the same legal level as the Orthodox Church and so initially seemed to allow for the possibility of evangelization among the Orthodox Slavs. Consequently both Benedict XV and Pius XI set aside large sums of money for the training of missionaries and a special Pontifical Oriental College was established in Rome. At the end of the War the Communists and the Holy See were interested in establishing diplomatic relations; the former as a means of securing international recognition and the latter in the interests of its missionary activities. Russian *émigrés* bitterly criticized the Holy See for having 'shaken the blood-stained hand of the Soviets'. However, the Communists insisted on securing Vatican recognition before giving any guarantees of religious freedom which, as the Roman authorities appreciated, would mean surrendering their strongest weapon at the very beginning of negotiations.

The ending of the civil war in Russia coincided with the failure of the harvest and widespread famine and the Pope immediately offered to send a relief mission with food and clothing. This mission was eventually accepted by the Russians on condition that it did not engage in apostolic activity and its members celebrated Mass in private. The papal mission established kitchens, hospitals and even clothing factories. Between September 1922 and February 1923 the mission fed some 25,000 people each day and was completely ignored by the Russian press. As conditions improved the Communist authorities became increasingly difficult and eventually forced the mission to leave. Nevertheless the Vatican still tried to come to terms with Moscow but the Communists kept increasing their demands and in 1927 suddenly announced that there could be no question of a Concordat and that all questions affecting the Church would be decided unilaterally. In May of that year the Soviet Government was officially recognized by Britain and the United States and no longer needed the recognition of the Holy See.

Benedict XV enjoyed an enviable reputation for his unselfish generosity throughout his life and he gave a great deal to private individuals as well as to groups of peoples and organizations. He also frequently replied to requests for money personally and often took pleasure in sending far more than the sum originally asked. On one occasion he not only provided the costs of treating three children for a skin disease but also gave 200,000 *lire* to enlarge the facilities of the clinic concerned. It is said that on the day of his death the Vatican Treasury contained little more than £10,000, not enough to pay the costs of the conclave, and that the Treasurer, Cardinal Gasparri, had to secure a loan.

The War and the economic dislocation that followed inevitably had a significant effect on the finances of the Vatican. During the War the expenses of the Holy See were increasing as its traditional means of support, Peter's Pence, was declining. Collections declined everywhere but especially in France, traditionally the most generous country, where the Pope's pacifism was so deeply resented. After the War Catholic areas in Germany and Austria which had previously proved to be so generous in supporting the Pope were themselves in need of financial help. Meanwhile the Holy See was not only spending vast sums of money on the victims of conflict and economic depression but supporting many of the religious institutions and congregations that had been ruined during the War. The Vatican became increasingly dependent on the contributions of individual wealthy Catholics and on the Church in North America. It has been estimated that American Catholics contributed at least half the total amount of Peter's Pence collected since the First World War. Although Pius XI was forced to be somewhat careful about money, he too was generous and gave over four million *lire* to the relief of suffering in Germany and Russia.

When economic distress resulted in violence during 1920, Benedict asked the wealthy to be 'generous in giving, be inspired by equity and charity rather than by strict justice'. But he also advised workers to 'be on your guard for your Faith which you put in danger when your protests are excessive'. Benedict based his social teaching on that laid down by Leo XIII in *Rerum Novarum*. On 14 June 1920 he wrote to the Patriarch of Venice: 'The poor and unfortunate know with what special tenderness We care for them, as being closer in likeness to Jesus Christ . . . Therefore let the proletariat lend ear to the Church, even if she should seem to grant them less than her adversaries, for instead of extravagant but illusory advantages she promises them just and lasting good. Let them remember that while she is the mother of all men she embraces themselves with love of predilection, and that if she sometimes defends the rich, it is not as such, but when they are attacked unjustly. At the same time let the rich obey the Church, trusting in her motherly and impartial love'.

During the War regular contacts between the Holy See and the nations of the world had been restricted, but there were more organized pilgrimages during the Holy Year of 1925 than ever before as a result of the restoration and development of foreign travel and increasing prosperity, especially in North America. Benedict himself did a great deal to improve relations with historic centres of Catholicism such as France and Catholics were preponderant in several of the nations that gained their political independence after the War such as Ireland and Poland, Lithuania and Czechoslovakia. Catholics were also numerous in Yugoslavia and Rumania, while Catholic parties exercised an important influence in Germany and Austria, Belgium, Holland and Hungary. Nevertheless increased missionary activity and the growing strength of Catholicism in the United States, dramatically illustrated at the International Eucharistic Congress held in Chicago during 1926, indicated a shift in the comparative strength of Catholicism away from Europe to other parts of the world.

During the conflict French Catholics played their part in fighting for their country and forging a new spirit of national unity. Of the 80,000 priests from all countries who took an active part in the war, no less than 45,000 were French and of these between five and six thousand died, most of them in action. About ten thousand priests served as combatants or military chaplains and another ten thousand served in the auxiliary services as male nurses or stretcher-bearers. Over nine thousand priests received the *croix de guerre*, one and a half thousand received *médailles militaires*, almost nine hundred received the Legion of Honour and over ten thousand were mentioned in dispatches. Priests in the occupied territories maintained the morale of French citizens and defended their interests. Some priests were taken as hostages, deported or even shot. Several of the leading French military leaders such as Foch and Weygand were devout Catholics and at least three generals who received the Marshal's baton went on a pilgrimage of thanksgiving to Lourdes after the War had been won. Priests and religious also played a prominent part in the work of reconstruction which took place after the War.

As a result the force of French anti-clericalism was declining as was the significance of religious issues in the political life of the country. Frenchmen became more concerned about reparations, economic reconstruction and the international situation than the religious questions that had dominated French politics for so long. The Holy See cooperated with the French Government in the appointment of bishops in Alsace-Lorraine and appointed a French Vicar Apostolic to Morocco. The Congregation for Extraordinary Ecclesiastical Affairs even supported the idea of recognizing the *associations cultuelles* condemned by Pius X, though this was only finally achieved during the pontificate of Pius XI. The French Government, for its part, began to recognize what it had lost by breaking off diplomatic relations with the Holy See as more and more countries established links with the Vatican. France lost the privileges previously enjoyed as the protector of Catholics in the East as well as the influence formerly exercised through French missionaries. Consequently in 1920 the French Government was officially represented at the canonization of Joan of Arc and re-established diplomatic relations with the Holy See.

During the negotiations over the restoration of diplomatic relations, the French Government attempted to gain the support of the Holy See for its interpretation of the Treaty of Versailles. The Vatican, however, was only prepared to accept a very general formula or a pledge to do what it could to support and preserve the peace. Benedict's successor was much less reserved in his reaction to contemporary political developments and in the encyclical *Urbi arcano Dei* published in December 1922, the new Pope deplored 'the spirit of bitterness and vengeance' which had been 'increased and almost given official status' by 'an artificial peace established on paper'. In the following year Pius XI urged the evacuation of the Ruhr and the establishment of an impartial tribunal: 'When the debtor gives proof of his sincere desire to arrive at a fair and definite agreement, invoking an impartial judgment on the limits of his capacity to pay, justice and social charity as well as the personal interests of the creditors demand that he should not be forced to pay more than he can without entirely exhausting his resources of productivity. Equally, though it be just that the creditors shall have guarantees in accordance with the amount of their debts, we put it to them to consider whether it be necessary to maintain territorial occupation which imposes severe sacrifices on the occupying nation and occupied territories alike, or whether it would not be better to substitute, though gradually, other more suitable and certainly less odious guarantees'. But in spite of these differences, the anti-clerical legislation associated with Combes was gradually withdrawn and relations between the French Government and the Holy See were largely undisturbed in France itself until the outbreak of the Second World War.

In 1886 and 1918 the French Government had successfully defeated the efforts of both Leo XIII and Benedict XV to circumvent French 'protection' of the Church in China by establishing direct diplomatic relations with the Chinese Government. When Christian missionaries returned to China during the nineteenth century they arrived under the protection of the Western Powers, especially France, and so became identified by the Chinese as agents of western imperialism. Celso Constantini, the Apostolic Delegate to China, later complained: 'The Chinese . . . see the missions as closely linked with the aggressive policies of foreign powers . . . Foreign diplomats, some of them Jews or atheists, handled the affairs of the missions and defended their interests with a rod of iron. There were times when European governments were sending the religious in their own countries to prison and denying them the rights accorded to other citizens, while at the same time showing themselves very solicitous to protect religious working as missionaries in China. If a hand was laid on a missionary anywhere in China, the consul was immediately there behind him, and behind the consul the representative of a foreign power in Peking. If any damage had been caused to mission property, if a missionary had

been killed, they made the Chinese government pay. Chinese judges who had to try a case involving Christians went in dread of missionary intervention. Similarly, although a few missionaries were critical of colonial ex-
of the foreigner's exemption from Chinese jurisdiction, the missions ended by constituting a State within a State'.

Consequently, the fury of the Chinese nationalists during the Boxer Rebellion of 1900 was directed at least in part against the Catholic Church and some twenty to thirty thousand Catholics, including about a hundred priests, lost their lives. By the end of the nineteenth century there were eighty-two vicariates with a Catholic population of about 740,000. There were 417 Chinese priests and just over 900 missionaries, 340 Chinese and 730 foreign nuns. The number of Chinese Catholics continued to grow during the twentieth century and by 1912 there were almost one and a half million Catholics served by some 2250 priests of whom over 800 were Chinese.

It was perhaps inevitable that in the age of imperialism the missionary activities of the Christian churches should have been associated with the development of colonialism, an association that helped as well as hindered the spread of Christianity. The spread of Catholicism or Protestantism was largely determined by the colonial expansion of Catholic or Protestant countries and Protestant missionaries rejoiced when the British took possession of Nyasaland because over the border the Portuguese would only allow Catholic missionaries to work in Mozambique. However, by the end of the nineteenth century, there were already signs that the age of imperialism was coming to an end and the Churches had not yet successfully established a native clergy let alone native hierarchies.

The reluctance of missionaries in the nineteenth century to promote an indigenous clergy was reflected in a memorandum on the Chinese missions which was sent to Rome in 1847: 'On the necessity in the abstract for an indigenous clergy there is fairly general agreement; but when it comes to the point, no one is willing to put the policy into practice, and the reason nearly always given is that the people of this country are so devoid of intelligence and so weak in character that they are incapable of conceiving the grandeur and dignity of the priesthood and of fulfilling its demands'. The situation was much the same in Africa or India and among Protestant as well as Catholic missionaries.

The number of missionaries prepared to act simply as agents of imperialism was fortunately very small but many missionaries not unnaturally took pride in the colonial achievements of their own countries and were prepared to take advantage of a sympathetic colonial administration. Similarly, although a few missionaries were critical of colonial exploitation and tried to dissociate the Church from western imperialism, local populations were inevitably tempted to identify missionary activity with colonial expansion. In 1901 Father Vincent Lebbe told his bishop in Peking: 'We are here in actual fact, in spirit and intention, a foreign body, indeed a body wielding foreign influence. Our Christian communities are semi-colonies'. Over ten years before, another missionary working in Togoland, Franz Michael Zahn, declared: 'I am completely against colonies . . . when a missionary becomes involved in politics and furthers the colonial acquisitions of Germany through his influence, then I maintain whatever else his intention may be, that he has made a big mistake, if he has not committed a crime'. But such prophetic voices were rare.

A further difficulty affecting Catholic missions was created by the policy adopted in the 1820s of 'commissioning' a particular order or congregation to accept total responsibility for a particular territory. As a result, to quote Constantini again: 'The missions, because they are conceived as religious colonies belonging to this or that institute, have created in the missionaries a special mentality, let us call it territorial feudalism. The archives of the Congregation of Propaganda are stuffed with documents on the subject'.

It was Benedict XV who began the radical reorganization of missionary activity, the recruitment of indigenous clergy and the formation of native hierarchies. According to one recent historian, Benedict's missionary policies 'brought about one of the greatest revolutions ever attempted by a Pope'.

On 30 November 1919 Benedict published the encyclical *Maximum illud*, an eloquent and authoritative plea for the creation of an indigenous clergy and the establishment of native hierarchies. He demanded that Catholic missionaries renounce the spirit of nationalism and recognize the value and significance of native cultures. Benedict outlined a new programme which differed radically from previous practice and marked a turning point in the history of the Church that was not always welcomed by those who believed that 'The creation of a native episcopate and the institution of a native clergy are errors of judgment'. The Pope, on the other hand, argued: 'For since the Church of God is Catholic, and cannot be a stranger in any nation or tribe, it is proper that out of every people should be drawn sacred ministers to be teachers of the Divine law and leaders in the way of salvation for their own countrymen to follow. Hence, wherever there exists a sufficient number of indigenous clergy, well instructed and worthy of their holy vocation, it may justly be said that the missionaries have successfully completed their work, and that the Church has been thoroughly well founded. . . . Remember that you have to make citizens

23

not of any country upon earth, but of the heavenly country. And indeed it would be deplorable if any missionaries should be so forgetful of their dignity that they should think rather of their earthly country than of the heavenly, being unduly anxious to widen its influences and to extend its glory above all else. This would indeed be a very plague in the Apostolate, which would destroy in the preacher of the gospel all the vigour of his love of souls, and would weaken his authority among the people. For even barbarians and savages understand well enough what a missionary is for, and what he wants from them, and have the sagacity to perceive if he demands anything besides their spiritual good'.

Benedict also established the Missionary Union of the Clergy and reorganized the Society for the Propagation of the Faith, the Society of the Holy Child and St Peter the Apostle for Native Clergy in order to spread the missionary ideal and provide financial support for the missions.

Pius XI continued and developed the work of Benedict in promoting foreign missions to such an extent that he became known as the 'Pope of the Foreign Missions'. Pius gave his personal support to the Missionary Union of the Clergy and the Association for the Propagation of the Faith. He urged bishops, orders and congregations throughout the world to increase their missionary activities. The Society for the Propagation of the Faith was transferred from France to Rome, a new College of Propaganda was opened and a new Missionary Institute established. Pius XI encouraged the autonomy of missionary churches by consecrating native bishops. In 1923 he appointed the first non-European bishop of the Latin rite in India and instituted a native hierarchy for the Malabar Uniates. The first Japanese bishop was consecrated in 1927 and by 1941 all the bishops in the country were Japanese.

When Pius XI died in 1939, 48 missionary territories were in the care of native bishops: 26 in China, 13 in India, 3 in Japan, 3 in Vietnam, 1 in Ceylon, 1 in Korea and 1 in Ethiopia. The balance of the ecclesiastical hierarchy had been fundamentally changed between the two world wars. By 1939 the combined total of bishops or vicars apostolic in North and South America was slightly less than the number of European bishops who numbered just over a third of the Catholic bishops throughout the world. There were some 1,200 Catholic archbishops and bishops and a further 300 vicars apostolic: 650 were in Europe, 120 in Africa, 180 in Asia, 70 in Australasia, 240 in North America and 180 in South America; there were also 120 prefects apostolic half of whom were in Asia.

In 1922 Pius XI ignored the objections of the French Government and French churchmen and established an apostolic delegation in China with Celso Costantini as first Delegate. Costantini was instructed to seek for suitable episcopal candidates from the ranks of the Chinese clergy, while the new Delegate himself was determined to 'replace as quickly as possible, the protection of missions by foreign diplomats by guarantees under Chinese law'. In October 1926 the Pope consecrated the first six Chinese bishops in St Peter's – the first and only previous Chinese bishop had been consecrated in the seventeenth century – and he personally indicated the dramatic change that had taken place in the Catholic Church when he told them: 'It is well-known – and the history of every age bears witness – that the Church adjusts herself to the laws and constitutions of each nation and country; she respects, and teaches others to respect, the dignity attaching to the lawful heads of civil society; she claims no more for her labourers in the mission field or for her faithful than the right to live in freedom and security under the common law'. In 1929 an agreement between China and the Holy See was on the point of being signed when the French again intervened and diplomatic relations were not finally established between the Vatican and China until 1947.

When a Belgian Jesuit who had supported the formation of a native clergy was ordered to return to Europe – an incident which occasioned some controversy in missionary periodicals – Pius XI developed the teachings of his predecessor in an encyclical *Rerum Ecclesiae* published in 1926. The Pope asked: 'Why should the native clergy be prevented from governing its own people? What are the missions for, except to establish the Church on firm and regular foundations? And how can the Church take root among the pagans by means other than those whereby she did so long ago among ourselves?'

He gave positive encouragement to the formation of a native clergy: 'Suppose that on account of a war or of other political events, one government supplants another in a missionary territory and requests or demands the withdrawal of foreign missionaries of a certain nationality. Or suppose again (although this is less likely to happen) that the inhabitants, having attained a higher degree of civilization and consequently a higher degree of civil development, desire to make themselves independent and wish to drive from their territory both the official rulers, the soldiers and the missionaries of the foreign nation which rules them, and that they cannot do this except by recourse to violence – what disaster would threaten the Church in those regions unless the native clergy, having been spread like a network through the country, could provide completely for the population converted to Christ?' But the Pope was not content to remain on the merely practical level: 'There is another reason why you cannot allow indigenous priests to remain relegated as it were to an inferior rank, and dedicated solely to the humblest forms of ministry. Are they not invested with the same priesthood as yourselves and partakers in the self-same apostolate? And is it not your duty to look on them as on those who must one day govern the communities and Churches you yourselves have founded in toil and sweat? Let there be no distinction, therefore, between European and indigenous missionaries, and let no gulf separate them: rather, let them be united by the bonds of mutual respect and mutual charity'.

On the whole, by the middle of the 1930s, the Roman authorities seemed more willing than before to leave decisions about local customs and adaptations to the local churches. In 1936 Propaganda instructed the Apostolic Delegate to Japan: 'Never seek in any way to persuade these peoples to change their rites, their customs or their manners, provided these do not openly conflict with faith and morals'. Japanese Catholics were to be permitted to take part in patriotic ceremonies and to: 'conduct themselves on those occasions in the manner customary for citizens, declaring this to be their intention if such declaration seems necessary to avoid misinterpretation of their actions'.

The missionary experience, the revolution in communications and the persecution of Christian churches by totalitarian regimes were some of the factors influencing the development of the ecumenical movement which originally began under the leadership of Protestant churchmen. The Catholic authorities were reluctant to become involved in the ecumenical movement. They were more interested in the Eastern than the Protestant Churches and the 'return of' rather than 'reunion with' heretics and schismatics. At the same time a few individual Catholics were aware of the significance of the early development of the ecumenical movement. Although no Catholic representative was present at the inaugural Missionary Conference of the World Council of Churches held at Edinburgh in 1910, the liberal Bishop Bonomelli of Cremona sent a friendly message in which he spoke of the 'noble aspiration on the part of various Churches and denominations for the making of Holy Church one in all the children of the Redemption'.

The Roman Catholic authorities however showed a particular concern for the plight of Orthodox Christians in the East. The events and consequences of the First World War had a dramatic and disastrous effect on the churches in the East. The collapse of the Turkish Empire, the Bolshevik Revolution in Russia and the rise of Arab nationalism seemed to threaten the very future of the Orthodox Churches. The Patriarch of Constantinople was caught between the rival and hostile claims of Greece and Turkey, while at one stage during the persecution of the Church in Russia, some 150 bishops were interned in a concentration camp on the White Sea.

Even the training of Catholic priests to work among the Orthodox in Communist or hostile countries helped to create a sense of sympathy and kinship even if the original motives of those involved were mainly apologetic. In 1925 Patriarch Basil III impressed on Angelo Roncalli among others the necessity of reunion and indicated his own willingness to visit the Pope in order to support the idea of summoning a synod of bishops to study the issues involved. Indeed, Roncalli's own mission as Apostolic Visitor to Bulgaria and Apostolic Delegate to Turkey and Greece was partly responsible for his obvious affection for his 'beloved Orthodox'.

Pius X, unlike his predecessor in some respects, had given his support to policies which were calculated to widen divisions among Christians and to Romanize the eastern Uniate Churches. Benedict XV, on the other hand, was not so hostile to eirenic moves and wanted to safeguard the position of the Uniate Churches by providing them with institutions properly established within the Roman Curia. His creation of the Sacred Congregation of the Eastern Church under Cardinal Marini, who had a great sympathy for Eastern Christianity, was intended to safeguard the interests of eastern Catholics who were finally given an official place within the constitutional framework of Roman Catholicism: 'This present act will make it still more clearly manifest that the Church of Jesus Christ, which is neither Latin nor Greek nor Slav but Catholic, makes no distinction between her sons, and that the latter, whether Greek, Latin, Slav or of other national character, are all of the same degree in the eyes of this apostolic see'. Unfortunately it cannot be said that the later history of the Congregation succeeded in putting this high ideal into practice.

Benedict had issued his prayer for the return of eastern Christians to the Church in April 1916: 'O Lord, who hast united the divers nations in the confession of Thy name, we pray to Thee for the Christian peoples of the East. We, remembering the eminent place which they held in Thy Church, supplicate Thee to inspire them with the desire to take it once more so as to form with us one fold under the guidance of the same Shepherd. Make them, with us, to be imbued with the teachings of their Holy Doctors who are also our Fathers in the faith'.

In the following year he established the Pontifical Institute, which was also open to Orthodox students, for those priests wishing to work in the East and he encouraged efforts to revive Basilian monachism as a further means of restoring unity with eastern Christians. At a consistory in March 1919 Benedict himself repeated that it was necessary to protect and honour the liturgy and the customs of the Eastern Churches and to smooth the way for reunion as well as to provide help for the eastern victims of the Great War. In October 1920 the Pope declared St Ephrem a Doctor of the

Universal Church, not only because of the Saint's loyalty to the See of Peter, but as a sign of Benedict's respect for the customs and liturgy of the Eastern Church and as a manifestation of his desire to restore the unity of the Churches.

Not unnaturally, Benedict showed little sympathy for the activities of Protestant 'missionaries' in Italy and when he was invited to send representatives to the preliminary meetings of the World Conference on Faith and Order to be held in Lausanne during 1927 he courteously declined. Nevertheless the Pope and Gasparri showed a sympathetic if very guarded interest and in May 1919 Benedict cordially received a deputation from the Protestant Episcopal Church of America which called at the Vatican to repeat the invitation. The official communique explained: '. . . the teaching and practice of the Roman Catholic Church regarding the unity of the visible Church of Christ are well known to everybody, and therefore it would not be possible for the Catholic Church to take part in a congress such as the one proposed . . . [However] His Holiness does not mean in any way to disapprove of the conference in question for those who are not united to the See of Peter; on the contrary, he seriously desires, and asks with prayer, that if the conference takes place those who participate in it may, by the Grace of God, see the light and become reunited to the visible Body of the Church, by which they will be received with open arms'. On 4 July, however, the Holy Office republished a decree issued in 1864 which prevented Catholics taking part in organizations promoting Christian unity or representing non-Catholic bodies as constituent parts of the one Church. Furthermore in 1921, when Catholics were invited to the Universal Christian Council for Life and Work to be held at Stockholm in 1925, Cardinal Gasparri expressed the Pope's gratitude for the letter but ignored the invitation.

On the other hand, the Holy See found it possible to be more accommodating when matters of principle were not considered to be at stake. At the end of the nineteenth century Pope Leo XIII had called for an octave of prayer for the 'reconciliation of our separated brethren', and the January octave which developed into the Week of Prayer for Christian Unity was approved by Pius X as well as Benedict XV and Pius XI. In 1916 Benedict ordered that a novena of prayers should be recited throughout the Church for the reunion of Christendom and on the opening of the Malines Conversations in 1921 Cardinal Gasparri told Cardinal Mercier: 'The Holy Father authorizes Your Eminence to tell the Anglicans that he encourages your conversations and prays God with all his heart to bless them'.

At first Pius XI seems to have shared the guarded interest of Benedict XV in the early ecumenical movement. Pius is said to have given unofficial encouragement to those taking part in the Malines Conversations and on several occasions he emphasized the need to '. . . abandon the false notions adopted in the course of centuries as to the non-Catholic Churches, and make a deeper study of the Fathers with a view to discovering a common Faith'. In a reference to the oriental Churches, he declared: 'Do we realize all that is good, all that is precious, in those fragments of ancient Catholic truth? The separated parts of a gold-bearing rock are themselves auriferous also'.

The Pope referred to 'reciprocal prejudices', 'mistakes and mis-understandings'; he paid tribute to the 'holiness' of the Eastern Churches and reproached Catholics for their 'lack of a just appreciation of their duty of fraternal understanding and sympathy'. Yet in the same year, on the eve of the Lausanne meeting in 1927, the Holy Office declared that Catholics must not take part in 'congresses, meetings, lectures, or societies which have the scope of uniting into a religious confederation all who in any sense whatever call themselves Christians'.

The Malines Conversations came to an end in 1926, the same year in which two of the leading Catholic participants, Mercier and Portal, died. The first report of the Conversations was published by Lord Halifax in 1928 but in January of that year Pius XI published his encyclical *Mortalium Animos* which was widely interpreted as an expression of his disapproval of the Malines Conversations as well as a warning to Catholics against participating in the Faith and Order programme. In February the *Osservatore Romano* declared that although the Pope had followed the course of events at Malines, he had 'never taken official note of them, regarding them merely as something that had taken place between private individuals without mandate of any kind'.

According to the Pope, the ecumenical movement, as it then existed, was associated with theological relativism and indifferentism in ecclesiology; it seemed to imply that the Roman Church was not in fact the true Church of God. And so *Mortalium Animos* was a condemnation of the attempt to establish a 'Pan Christianity' without basic agreement in faith: '. . . . congresses, meetings, and addresses are arranged, attended by a large concourse of hearers, where all without distinction, unbelievers of every kind as well as Christians, even those who unhappily have rejected Christ and denied His divine nature or mission, are invited to join in the discussion . . . the Apostolic See can by no means take part in these assemblies, nor is it in any way lawful for Catholics to give to such enterprises their encouragement or support . . . the unity of Christians can come about only by furthering the return to the one true Church of Christ of those who are separated from it'.

Although the Orthodox were bitterly offended by *Mortalium Animos*, where Pius XI referred to them as 'adherents of the errors of Photius', the Pope continued to show a genuine interest in Eastern Christianity in his letters and encyclicals on the Council of Nicaea and the great saints of the Eastern Churches. In one of the first letters of his pontificate, *Equidem Verba*, he had expressed the hope that a monastic institution would dedicate itself to the conversion of Russian refugees arriving in the West. Dom Lambert Beauduin established a monastery where he hoped that Catholics and Orthodox might learn to understand each other but he himself was later forced to retire from the work. The French Dominicans also established a centre for the study of Orthodoxy first at Lille and then in Paris.

The Pope again emphasized the need for Catholics to study the Eastern Churches in his encyclical *Rerum orientalium* published in September 1928 and in the following January he initiated work on a special code of Canon Law for the Eastern Catholics. In 1935 the Syrian Catholic Patriarch, Ignatius Tappouni, was raised to the cardinalate. But these different measures tended to reinforce rather than allay the suspicions of the Orthodox who not only suspected the proselytizing activities of the Romans but were offended by the subordination of the Uniate Churches to Rome and the way in which Roman attitudes seemed to confuse the Orthodox and the Uniates.

However, as the attitudes of the Roman authorities towards the ecumenical movement seemed to harden, the development of Catholic ecumenism came to depend more and more on the work of individuals like Paul Couturier, Yves Congar and Max Josef Metzger. Metzger himself received official permission to attend the Lausanne meeting and unofficial Catholic observers were also present at Oxford and Edinburgh in 1937. Metzger, a Catholic priest who had been impressed by the cooperation between Catholics and Protestants during the Great War, was determined to advance the unity of Christians. He established an institute, which eventually became known as the Society of Christ the King, to promote Christian reconciliation and in 1938 founded the *Una Sancta* movement whose members were to pray for Christian unity. In the following year he wrote to Pius XII asking the Pope to call a General Council to promote Christian unity but by then his pacifism and his work for reunion had attracted the attention of the Nazis. He was arrested several times and eventually executed as a traitor in 1944.

The fate of Metzger illustrates how the major issues with which the Church had to deal were changing after the death of Benedict XV and the election of Pius XI. The Italian Government had fallen on the very day the cardinals entered the Conclave and the Secretary of State, Gasparri, was well aware of the political dangers facing the Church from the appalling instability of Italy and the economic problems resulting from the impoverishment of the Holy See. It is said that Gasparri himself supported the election of Achille Ratti who received only two votes on the first ballot. The Secretary of State then transferred the twenty-four votes which he had received to the Cardinal Archbishop of Milan.

The new Pope entered a seminary in 1867 at the age of ten. After a few months as a parish priest, he became a seminary lecturer at Milan before being appointed prefect of the great Ambrosian library. He became Vatican librarian in 1911, an ecclesiastical diplomat in 1918 and Cardinal Archbishop of Milan in 1921. Pius XI himself has been reported as saying that Gasparri visited him on the evening before he was elected Pope and suggested to him that he should bless the crowds from the outer portico of St Peter's and take the name Pius. In choosing his name, the new Pope announced that he did so in memory of the two popes during whose reigns he had been born and called to Rome; he went on 'Pius is a name of peace, and in the desire to devote my endeavours to the work of pacification throughout the world, to which my predecessor Benedict XV consecrated himself, I choose the name of Pius XI'.

Mussolini listens to the blessing of the new town of Pontinia after the draining of the Pontine marshes

Mussolini and Cardinal Pietro Gasparri sign the Lateran Treaty

Chapter II

Church and State in Fascist Italy

From the very beginning of his reign Pius XI was determined to improve relations with Italy and he immediately broke with the precedents of his three immediate predecessors by giving his blessing from the outer portico of St Peter's: 'I affirm my purpose of safeguarding and defending all the rights of the Church and all the prerogatives of the Holy See. But having said this, I wish my first benediction to go out, as a pledge of that peace for which humanity is yearning, not merely to Rome and to Italy, but to the whole Church and the whole world. I will therefore give the benediction from the outer balcony of St Peter's'. Within a short time the news spread throughout the capital and the entire area between the Tiber and the Basilica was crowded with people. When a newly-elected pope appeared on the outer balcony for the first time since 1846 the crowds cheered and the Italian troops drawn up before the steps of the basilica presented arms. The Pope repeated the same gesture on the following Sunday and gave his blessing to the people assembled in St Peter's Square including units of the Italian army. The election of Pius XI and these public appearances were warmly welcomed by the Italian press including those newspapers which supported Mussolini and the Fascist Party.

In his first encyclical, the new Pope deplored the absence of Italy from the ranks of those nations who were now represented at the Vatican, though he also insisted on the necessity of securing the independent sovereignty of the Holy See: 'The divine origin and nature of this sovereignty require, and the inviolable right arising from the universality of the faithful of Christ spread throughout the world requires, that this sacred sovereignty shall not appear to be subject to any human power, to any law, even such law as might profess to secure the liberty of the Roman Pontiff with certain safeguards and guarantees, but must be an absolutely independent sovereignty and must manifestly appear as such'. In short, if the Pope wanted a solution to the Roman Question, as he did, the solution must be based not only on the Law of Guarantees devised by the Italians but also on a publicly recognized independent sovereignty.

In May 1919, during the peace negotiations in Paris, an American prelate had suggested to the Italian Prime Minister the possibility of arranging direct negotiations between the Italian Government and the

Holy See. V. E. Orlando had agreed in principle and an official of the Secretariat of State was sent to Paris with proposals from Gasparri. But although Orlando was favourable, he was not as enthusiastic as Gasparri in seeking a solution to the Roman Question and his Government fell before any real negotiations had begun. Nevertheless it was becoming increasingly obvious that the Question must eventually be solved and the problems were very considerably eased simply by the passing of time. Relations between Church and State had continued to improve and on the death of Benedict XV the Italian Government adopted an unprecedented form of official mourning.

After the loss of the Papal States and the temporal power of the Pope, Italian Catholics had been forbidden to play an effective or organized part in the political life of the nation by their own ecclesiastical authorities. Furthermore, although the unification of Italy had originally been associated with support for liberal democracy, the 'liberal' anti-clericals in Italy had not fully accepted the spirit of democracy. However Italian Catholics emerged from the Great War strengthened in numbers and influence and convinced of their ability to play a significant part in the progress of Italy. During the War they had proved to be loyal citizens, a fact which helped to moderate the suspicions of Italian 'liberals' and anticlericals. Members of the aristocracy and middle classes, well-known for their devotion to the papacy, proved to be gallant officers and soldiers, while patriotic priests ministered to the spiritual needs of the troops. Even Benito Mussolini paid tribute to the heroism of military chaplains and Benedetto Croce said of the Italian Catholics: 'Without belying their profession of faith, which condemned violence and bloodshed, without failing in their respect for the precepts of the Church, they did not allow their faith or their loyalty to conflict with their duty as Italian citizens'.

In December 1918 Don Luigi Sturzo secured permission from Cardinal Gasparri to establish a new political party independent of the Church, though he was told that the *non expedit* restricting the political activities of Italian Catholics would only be lifted at the time and in the way which the Pope himself might decide. On 18 January 1919 the Partito Popolare Italiano issued its manifesto: 'We support the political and moral programme, heritage of the Christian peoples, previously expounded in the august words of the Supreme Pontiff and today championed by Wilson as a basic element of the future world order; and we reject the imperialisms that create dominant nations and provoke reactions. Accordingly, we call upon the League of Nations to recognize just national aspirations, to hasten the advent of universal disarmament, to abolish secret treaties, to enforce the freedom of the seas, to urge international acceptance of the principles of social legislation, equal pay for women and, in the religious sphere, individual freedom from all sectarian oppression; and to invest itself with full legal authority and with the means to uphold the rights of weak nations in face of the arrogance of the strong. We wish to see the centralized State ... replaced by a truly democratic State, which will recognize the limits of its authority, respecting the individual personality and the natural units and organisms – the family, the various social classes, and the communes – and encouraging private enterprise'.

Sturzo has been described as 'the very antithesis of Mussolini in appearance, character, behaviour and thought ... a radical social reformer, a pacifist, candid, fearless, brilliant, and above all else an honest man'. He had an exalted view of parliamentary democracy and parliament itself as the legal expression of the will of the people; parliament must be above suspicion, must work efficiently and must abide inflexibly by the constitution. Sturzo and his supporters regarded the Popular Party as 'undenominational' in the sense that although members of the Party accepted the claims of Christian morality, it had no claim on the allegiance of Catholics as such, who were free to accept or reject its policies and even to support other political parties. The Party was also completely independent of the Holy See and the ecclesiastical authorities in matters political. For Sturzo the terms Catholic and Party were inevitably opposed: 'Catholicism is a religion, it is universal; a party is political, it is division'.

At first relations between Sturzo and the Popular Party on the one hand and the Pope and the Vatican officials on the other were reasonably harmonious and the new Party received widespread Catholic support especially from Catholic newspapers. Benedict XV did not share his predecessor's dislike of Catholic political parties independent of ecclesiastical control and he was anxious that Catholics should play their part in deciding the future of Italy after the War. But although Benedict was not unsympathetic to the policies of the Popular Party, he adopted a neutral attitude and was far too prudent to allow the Church once again to become involved in politics. The failure of Pius X's political policies in Italy had helped to convince many Catholics including his successor that the Church should no longer be identified with any particular party. Consequently in December 1918 the *Osservatore Romano* was able to deny publicly that the Holy See had given its consent to the formation of an Italian Catholic party.

In November 1919, a few days before the Italian elections, the Pope lifted the *non expedit* and the Popular Party, with the support of rural and middle classes and a little support from the working classes, won over a hundred seats and a fifth of the votes, though only half of the electorate actually went to the polls. But the Popular Party received support from Catholics of very different political, economic and social views, though the danger of a split in the Party never really became imminent until the rise of Fascism. Furthermore although the Party claimed to be non-confessional, as to some extent it undoubtedly was, it could hardly ignore the instructions of the Pope or the ecclesiastical authorities since it clearly depended on the support of the clergy and the faithful. But the Party was divided on 'religious' as well as social, economic and political issues: should it be a Catholic party with Catholic aims and, perhaps in the event most important of all, should it attempt to solve the Roman Question?

At the same time more conservative Catholics distrusted the Party and magazines like *Civiltà Cattolica* regarded it with suspicion and hostility. Vatican officials were always suspicious of Catholic movements and political parties organized and supported by Catholics outside their own control. They preferred to give their support to Catholic Action which was controlled by the ecclesiastical authorities and was directed towards spiritual rather than political or civil reform. *Osservatore Romano* increasingly ignored the Popular Party and supported Catholic Action and although individual Catholics might be members of the Popular Party as well as the Popular Union, the Popular Party and Catholic Action found it impossible to co-operate with each other. Even Benedict XV, who prevented the development of a more open hostility between the two movements, revealed his own reservations in March 1920 when he reminded Catholics that: 'the Popular Union is the principal agent of Catholic Action. If other activities have been able to arise, even recently, in different fields, they are nothing but little streams springing from the regal river'. In January 1922 Catholic newspapers criticized the Popular Party on the grounds that it was no substitute for Catholic Action and an attempt was even made to establish an alternative Catholic conservative party.

As early as August 1920 the Leader of the Government told Cardinal Gasparri that the refusal of the Popular Party to support the Government was in danger of provoking renewed anti-clerical attacks, while the introduction of divorce was forcing the lower middle classes into the ranks of the Socialists. The Church itself was held to be responsible because the Popular Party was led by a priest. At once Catholic Action began to campaign against the introduction of divorce, insisting that Catholics unite with moderate forces against the Socialists and complaining of the intransigence of the Popular Party. Supporters of Catholic Action clearly felt that Catholics must unite in the face of Socialist attacks which had resulted in the deaths of seven Catholics at Sestri, Mantua and Siena where a church was invaded. In 1920 during the Midnight Mass a band of

Socialists singing the Red Flag invaded a small church just outside Bologna. They expelled the congregation and the old and sick priest and danced to the playing of the organ. However, Sturzo and the Popular Party were determined to preserve their political independence and to avoid becoming 'captive' votes for older liberal or conservative parties in spite of the danger of losing some Catholic support.

The most fundamental difference between the Popular Party and the Holy See resulted from the fact that the former did not seem sufficiently interested in finding an immediate solution to the Roman Question. The Party regarded this issue as one to be resolved with time and patience after the establishment of a new Italian social order based on social justice. The Party attacked the Italian Government for failing to defend the dignity of bishops and priests, and their freedom to exercise their religious ministry in the face of violent anti-clericalism. But on *the* Question, the Party expressed the conviction 'that an essential precondition of a settlement of the Roman Question not entailing any violation of our country's territorial integrity is a more enlightened Christian consciousness on the part of the Italian people'. It must have seemed to Vatican officials that a political party, led by a priest and based on Catholic support, was less willing than some of the secular parties to find a solution to the Roman Question.

The new parliament faced formidable problems. Over four million Italians had served in the armed forces during the War and half a million died. After the War many of the demobilized soldiers were unable to find jobs. Although Italy had been on the 'winning' side, the nation was economically weaker, troubled and leaderless. There were conflicts between Socialists and Fascists, frequent strikes which crippled industry and the public services, while politicians were bitterly divided among themselves. Such a situation favoured the rise of the 'strong man' when the last relics of the democratic legacy of the Risorgimento were so dissipated that there was little to be destroyed. Meanwhile as one recent historian has put it: 'Those very conditions of national anxiety, bred from distrust in the parliamentary process, disenchantment with the monarchy, suffering from economic hardship and sheer weariness with the brutality of war were already shaping dreams of greatness in the head of the leader to be'.

It also seemed quite possible that the success of the Bolshevik Revolution in Russia might well be followed by similar upheavals in Hungary, Germany and even Italy itself. The Socialist Party in Italy was unstable and divided. Some of its members and newspapers were publicly supporting developments in Russia and when the Socialists finally split in October 1920, the Italian Communist party was established with the avowed aim of setting up a Soviet Italy. The danger of a Communist Revolution or a

Socialist Government in Italy was undoubtedly one of the reasons why the Holy See was originally prepared to tolerate the Popular Party as it was in its later decision to come to an accommodation with Fascism.

During 1920 there was a widespread reaction throughout Italy against the forces in favour of change and reconstruction. The Popular Party alienated more conservative Catholics while the Socialists alienated most Italians who had any sense of tradition or moderation. Although the Socialists were becoming increasingly divided, the situation was rapidly developing where the Fascists seemed to be the only adequate alternative to the Socialists and in the violent struggles between right and left, Fascism seemed to many to be the lesser of the two evils.

The Popular Party and the Socialists both tended to ignore the claims of the middle classes, the small shopkeepers and workers in service industries, the civil servants and the military forces, the students who found it impossible to find employment after years of study, all of whom were looking for the restoration of the social and economic life of the nation. A succession of helpless governments and violent strikes – two and a half thousand lives were lost in 1920 – destroyed the faith of many Italians in parliamentary democracy and the Fascists gained increasing and apparently respectable support from the middle classes, the army and young people won over by the ideals of false patriotism. Furthermore the Socialists as well as supporters of the Popular Party fell into the temptation of regarding Fascism as a passing phenomenon which could safely be ignored. In time only the Communists and the Fascists seemed to know where they were going and Fascism owed much of its success to its opposition to Communism fighting under the popular slogan, 'Rome or Moscow'.

In the middle of 1920 the Socialists called a General Strike which the Communists interpreted as an act of revolution. However, the workers were disorganized, the mass of the population was weary of disorder and the Fascists were becoming increasingly strong. The Fascists believed that the strike was an attempt to ensure the return of a left-wing Government. Mussolini therefore asked his supporters to continue working and threatened 'to take the place of the State' if the strike was not over in two days, which it was. A commentator in *Osservatore Romano* deplored the fact that as a result of this strike, the Fascists had been able to regain all the support which they had previously lost because of their violent behaviour.

The Popular Party and the Socialists failed to combine in forming the only political alliance that might have been able to resist the rise and ultimate success of Fascism, though there were occasional attempts especially on the local level. The Italian Socialists had been greatly influenced by anti-clericalism and tended to dismiss the Popular Party as a clerical institution. When the Vatican had appealed for help on behalf of the victims of famine in Russia, the Italian Communists warned the Russians that they were threatening the future of the Russian Revolution by accepting help from the Holy See. For their part, Italian Catholics could not easily forget the bitter anti-clericalism and anti-Catholicism of some of the Socialists, particularly in the North of Italy, even when it was becoming increasingly obvious that the Fascists were the main agents of violence and that their efforts were directed at least in part against the Church and ecclesiastical associations. During the pontificate of Pius XI, the Holy See was afraid of the progress of Socialism and strongly opposed any form of political alliance between Catholics in the Popular Party and the Italian Socialists. Although Pius XI was not a conservative in the sense in which his predecessor Pius X had been, he did not sympathize with the Catholic democratic movement to the same extent as Benedict XV or even Leo XIII.

The strength of the Fascists increased during the April and May of 1921. Membership increased from 80,476 to 187,098 and the number of sections from 317 to 1001. Meanwhile the fighting and the killings continued. During the second half of May seventy-one people were killed, including sixteen Fascists and thirty-one Socialists, and 216 people were seriously injured. In July the Fascists destroyed Catholic newspaper offices in Udine, Treviso and Verona. The violence to which Italy had been subjected since the end of the War by extremists from right and left was creating a sense of anger as well as weariness and hopelessness. By the end of the year the Fascists were receiving increasing support from the Carabinieri and those large financial and industrial interests who regarded Fascism as the only effective defence against the establishment of a Socialist state.

The Church authorities and the Catholic press were not slow to criticize Fascist attacks on Catholics and the Church or to ridicule some of Mussolini's more absurd statements. Even as late as August 1922, when violence, woundings and murders were widespread, *Civiltà Cattolica* claimed that Fascism had 'the violent spirit' of Socialism, 'not only imitating it but even surpassing it with its bullying, killings and barbarities'. Catholics could not support Fascism or Socialism since they were both opposed to 'the most elemental principles' of Christianity. On Christmas Day 1920 the *Osservatore Romano* derisively quoted *Il Fascio*: 'The revolver is more beautiful than a woman. The woman talks too much, never arrives at a conclusion and betrays. The automatic speaks very little, but makes itself understood immediately'. But perhaps the editor of *Osservatore Romano* should have given greater attention to the significance of one of Mussolini's remarks during the previous October: 'I think that Catholicism could be used as one of our strongest national forces for the expression of our Italian identity in the world'.

It has been said that Mussolini was not simply inconsistent at different times, he was able to communicate totally inconsistent impressions to different people at the same time. He was also a supreme and unprincipled opportunist. 'It is not the same road that I saw in advance', he once confessed, 'but it is the same traveller.' Originally he was anti-religious and anti-Christian as well as anti-clerical. In 1908 he described priests as 'black microbes who are as fatal to mankind as tuberculosis germs' and on one occasion in 1916 the Archbishop of Milan and other members of the hierarchy banned Mussolini's newspaper. In 1919 Mussolini wrote: 'Detesting as we do all forms of Christianity, that of Jesus as of Marx, we feel an immense sympathy with the modern revival of the pagan worship of strength and courage'. Pope Benedict himself felt obliged to protest against 'the terrible blasphemies uttered against the person of our Divine Redeemer by a man who unjustly proclaims himself to be a representative of the Italian people'.

However shortly afterwards Mussolini began to appreciate that he might not be able to destroy the hold of the Church, that he might need to come to terms with it and that 'the religion of the Italians' might even be useful to him not only at home but even abroad – to secure international prestige and support for his expansionist aims. When Parliament opened in June 1921 Mussolini, one of the new deputies and leader of the Fascist party, firmly declared: 'that the Latin and Imperial tradition of Rome is today represented by Catholicism. If, as Mommsen said twenty-five or thirty years ago, one does not remain in Rome without acquiring a universal outlook, I consider and affirm that the sole universal concept which exists today in Rome is that which radiates from the Vatican'. Mussolini went on to suggest that the State should support the Church and give financial help for Catholic churches, schools and hospitals on the grounds that: 'the development of Catholicism in the world, a further increase in the number of human beings, already four hundred millions, who in all parts of the earth look towards Rome, is a matter of interest and pride for us Italians'. These views were not only markedly different from those irreligious and anti-Catholic opinions he had previously expressed but also very unlike the attitudes adopted by Italian 'liberals' and anti-clericals.

This was also true of Mussolini's suggestions about solving the Roman Question. Francesco Crispi once said that 'the greatest of Italians will be he who succeeds in settling the Roman Question' and Mussolini not only knew who was the greatest of Italians but hoped to win the support of Italian Catholics for his régime and his imperial designs, raise the international prestige of a Fascist Italy and gain sufficient control over the Italian Church by coming to an agreement with the Holy See. He told his supporters that a Fascist regime would give 'full freedom to the Catholic Church in the exercise of its spiritual ministry' and promised to end the differences between Italy and the Holy See. Mussolini's promises on this occasion must again be contrasted not only with the sentiments of Italian anti-clericals but with the apparent reluctance of the Popular Party to solve the Roman Question.

Mussolini adopted the policy of alternately threatening and tempting the Church but he consistently made it clear that he considered Sturzo and the Popular Party among his leading opponents. He described the Party, which could still have helped to block his rise to power, as 'dangerous to the interests of religion and faithless to those of the fatherland'. He also condemned Sturzo: 'There are two popes in Italy: the first, don Sturzo, has the care of the flesh, the second, Pius XI has the care of souls. Isn't it possible that don Sturzo is the antipope and an instrument of Satan? . . . Grave tempests will arise on the horizon of the Church if the PPI continues . . . its materialistic, tyrannical and anti-Christian politics'. Mussolini argued that the Popular Party was 'infected with Socialism' and was therefore 'anti-Catholic and anti-Christian'.

By July 1922 over eight million Italians were unemployed and many of them were becoming convinced by Mussolini's claim that the only hope lay in the establishment of a military dictatorship. Several Italian bishops warned Pius XI, if their warnings were needed, that Italy was on the verge of civil war. At the beginning of October Gasparri reminded the Italian bishops that the Holy See was 'totally extraneous' to the Popular Party and that the clergy should have nothing to do with it. At the end of the month *Osservatore Romano* declared that the Popular Party had no connection with the Vatican and that Catholic Action was the only instrument of the Church in the field of lay activity.

By August 1922 the Fascists controlled the Adriatic, the Tyrrhenian coasts and the valley of the Tiber and Mussolini made his plans for the march on Rome at the end of October. He was asked to form a Government by the King and assumed office on 30 October. Since 1920 the Fascists had threatened the stability of Italian democracy by violence but in the event they came to power without encountering resistance or even protests. By a combination of threats and promises, by violating the law and then pretending to uphold it, Mussolini had won over most Italians or lulled them into a false sense of security and even the *Osservatore Romano* reminded those who were 'solicitous above all for the welfare of the people' of their duty to collaborate with the new Government.

The distinguished Italian historian, A. C. Jemolo, has claimed that the

March on Rome did not receive any support whatever, either material or moral, from any of the Catholic clergy while their bishops remained 'aloof and apprehensive'. He contrasts their conduct at that crucial time with the treachery of the police and the army and with the equivocal or vacillating attitude of the civil service. On the other hand only a few Catholics consistently opposed Fascism; these included survivors of the 'Democratic League', Catholic activists who had been subjected to Fascist violence as well as men of principle. In spite of regional variations, Italian Catholics on the whole gave their support to the new Government.

Priests and laity who had suffered the petty persecutions of local anti-clerical officials welcomed the apparent respect for the Church shown by the Fascists. Conservative Catholics, particularly those who were hostile to Communism and Socialism, anti-clericalism, 'liberalism' and Freemasonry, did not regard Fascism or its extreme nationalism as irreconcilable with their religious beliefs. In fact, Giovanni Semeria, a patriot priest well known for his charitable work, encouraged Catholic support for Fascism. He maintained that the soul of Fascism was shot through with nationalism and patriotism and that although the Party had been guilty of violence, it had also saved the country from Communism and was, on the whole, favourably disposed towards religion. Semeria proclaimed that 'priests in full communion with their Bishop are Fascists, and even belong to Fascist administrations'; 'it is our Catholic duty to christianize Fascism'. Similarly when the Archbishop of Messina took possession of his diocese in March 1923, he declared; 'I feel it my duty to send my greeting also to him who is leading Italy along the right road, to him who is imbuing the Nation with new vigour – I mean, to the Head of the Government'.

Other Catholics were also explicit and direct in their enthusiasm. At the end of June 1923 some of them issued a manifesto – though *Osservatore Romano* made it clear that this was not supported by Catholic Action – proclaiming their 'complete accord' with the Fascist Government as a result of the fact that Fascism, 'openly recognizes and honours those religious and social values which constitute the basis of any sound political system, seeking to establish within the State, to the detriment of outmoded democratic and sectarian ideologies, a régime based on discipline and a hierarchical social order such as may accord with the religious and sociological doctrines proclaimed from time immemorial by the Church'.

Some of the Fascists and their Catholic supporters like Cardinal Schuster frequently claimed that the rise of Mussolini had 'saved the Papacy from the horrors of the Red Weeks and paved the way for the Lateran treaties'. But such a claim ignores the extent to which the Holy See was in the process of establishing a *modus vivendi* with a 'liberal' and secularist Italy and the fact that the Vatican did not particularly welcome the advent of the Fascist Party whose programme called for the confiscation of all ecclesiastical property. Even in 1921 the Fascist press was consciously and explicitly anti-clerical. Catholic priests were 'parasitic excrescences' or 'propagandists of obscurantism'. Some of the worst examples of Fascist violence – as Catholic newspapers at the time reported – were directed against the Church. Fascist attacks on priests in Mantua during the first quarter of 1922 were such that the local bishop felt obliged to appeal to the central Government for protection.

Yet within two weeks of assuming power Mussolini helped to save the Banco di Roma, which was facing financial collapse, in an effort to win the support of the Church and as a means of easing relations between Church and State. He opposed legislation that would have affected ecclesiastical taxes and property, he imposed State examinations on public as well as Catholic schools and restored the catechism in all schools. In his first speech as Prime Minister he asked for God's help and in November 1922 solemnly declared: 'My spirit is profoundly religious; religion is a fundamental force that must be respected and defended . . . Catholicism is a great spiritual and moral power and I trust that the relations between the Italian State and the Vatican from now on will be very friendly.'

In December 1922 the Chigi collection of books and documents, mostly dealing with papal history and bought by the Italian Government in 1918, was presented to the Vatican library. This must have given particular satisfaction to Pius XI who as Vatican Librarian had previously unsuccessfully urged the Holy See to buy the collection. The Vatican responded by removing the interdict from the chapel in the Quirinal Palace where the marriage of a daughter of the Royal Family took place a few days later with a suitable religious ceremony. In February 1923 the Fascist Grand Council declared that Fascism and Freemasonry were incompatible. The *Osservatore Romano* described this as 'an intelligent act, worthy of praise' and the Dean of the College of Cardinals saluted Mussolini as the man already acclaimed by all Italy as the reconstructor of the fate of the nation according to its religious and civil traditions'.

Officials of the Fascist régime ostentatiously treated the ecclesiastical authorities with respect and public functions often included a Mass attended by members of the Government or the Royal Family. A crucifix was re-erected on the Capitol and when a cross was replaced in the Coliseum the Queen of Italy attended the ceremony. Crucifixes were also restored in schools, hospitals and law courts. Religious instruction was reintroduced into primary schools, Catholic institutions of education were put on the same level as those of the State, and anti-clericalism was discouraged among university students. Ernesto Buonaiuti, the 'Modernist' Professor of Religious History, was dismissed from his position in the University of Rome. The Council of Ministers granted three million *lire* for the restoration of churches destroyed during the Great War. Clerics were exempted from military service. Chaplains were appointed to the army and navy, to the Fascist militia and youth organizations. Clerical stipends were increased as were the penalties for offences committed against the Church and the clergy. Papal titles awarded after 1870 were given official recognition and three major holy days were recognised as public holidays. Some confiscated ecclesiastical property was returned and the Penal Code was reformed in favour of the Church.

In view of the history of the Church in Italy since 1870, it is hardly surprising that Catholics should have welcomed Mussolini's initial support for the Church. One Jesuit periodical commented: 'The earlier Liberal State professed to ignore religion; more than that, it actually persecuted it. Fascism, on the contrary, recognises the social importance of religion, and of the Church as a force useful to the government, with some of the same ideals. Its ecclesiastical policy is a recognition and a restitution of the rights of the Catholic conscience and the clergy which have been violated during fifty years of liberal-democratic government'.

Although a periodical like *Civiltà Cattolica* did not ignore Fascist violence particularly when this was directed against the Church, its writers enjoyed the discomfiture of their 'liberal' and Socialist opponents: 'Ample reservations can, and indeed should, be expressed with regard to the methods adopted for the purpose of seizing the reins of government; but one cannot deny the Duce credit for the wise intention of ensuring that the *reconstruction* of the nation's life should be characterized by respect for Catholic feelings and by the assertion of *spiritual values*. This intention is all the more praiseworthy in that it has already been given practical expression through the maintenance of the principle of the indissolubility of marriage, the reintroduction of religious education, and other similar measures'.

Of course, at least initially, secular as well as religious, international as well as national, opinion was largely in favour of the new régime. Mussolini himself was a constitutionally elected Member of Parliament who had been asked to form a Government by the King and under his régime public services seemed to function with reasonable efficiency. His annexation of Fiume and Corfu helped to restore a sense of national pride and the basic economic problems were hidden at least for the time being. When George V visited Italy in May 1923 he decorated Mussolini with the Order of the

Bath, referred to the crisis recently surmounted by the Italian people 'under the wise guidance of a strong ruler' and assured Mussolini of an 'intimate collaboration' between their two countries. During the following month the American Ambassador to Italy offered his praises to Mussolini: 'During the last eight months Italy has reconciled itself in an extraordinary manner with the moral progress of the whole world by raising on high the ideals of human courage, discipline and responsibility.' In February 1923 the *New York Times* quoted the opinion of the Cardinal Archbishop of Boston: 'Italy has undergone a profound moral, economic and social transformation since Mussolini was named Prime Minister. . . . There is order, loyalty, industrial development and cleanliness everywhere'.

Nevertheless, Catholics did not remain uncritical of Fascist activities. In March 1924 the Pope himself expressed his satisfaction at the increase in clerical stipends and the reform of the laws governing charitable institutions. He welcomed the reintroduction of Catholic teaching into schools and the restoration of the crucifix. However he also deplored the violence which was too often directed against religious and Catholic organizations which were not involved in politics and solely concerned with religious activities. In 1928 the *Osservatore Romano* protested against a display of physical training and a military march of young Fascist women. It was as indecorous for girls to 'raise their rifles to heaven' as for boys to be told 'to carry their daggers between the teeth'. 'When female hands are raised to heaven', said the Pope in an allocution, 'they should be in prayer, not holding rifles'. But, at least originally, the Holy See was lulled into a false sense of complacency by Mussolini's apparent willingness to settle the Roman Question, by the peace and unity which he seemed to have brought to Italy, by the concessions granted to the Church, by the restraints imposed on Freemasons and Socialists, and by the recognition the new régime gained from governments abroad. For the time being the harassment of Catholics and ecclesiastical institutions, and the murders of Minzoni and Matteotti were ignored.

On the evening of 23 August 1923 Don Giovanni Minzoni, who had been decorated for gallantry as a military chaplain during the Great War, was battered to death. Minzoni, a Christian Democrat, had effectively moderated the growth of Fascism among the youth of his parish. The Archbishop of Ravenna sent a telegram to Mussolini who immediately replied with an expression of indignation and a promise to punish the criminals. Seven local Fascists, including the two suspected murderers, were arrested but never brought to trial. The Archbishop found himself 'unable' to attend Minzoni's funeral and was represented by a Fascist priest. The *Osservatore* reported the murder without comment except to record that Mussolini had been saddened by it. The Pope himself said nothing and the supporters of Catholic Action were preoccupied with their campaign against verbal blasphemy. Only a week after the murder the seventh Eucharistic Congress opened in Genoa and the organizers received a good deal of help from the Italian Government. But the secular authorities prohibited a service of commemoration on the first anniversary of Minzoni's death on the ground that it was not in the interests of public safety.

Towards the end of 1924 a former Fascist official accused Italo Balbo, head of the national militia, of shielding the murderers and supported this accusation with sworn and documentary evidence. However the seven accused were acquitted after a short parody of a trial in August 1925 and their acquittal was turned into a local Fascist triumph. Balbo later became Minister for Air and celebrated a successful return flight from Chicago at an official banquet in London. Among the official telegrams of congratulation read out on that occasion was one which ran: 'Unable to participate in the flesh, I am present in spirit. DON MINZONI'. In November 1937 His Excellency Marshal Balbo, Governor of Libya, was patron of the twelfth Italian Eucharistic Congress held at Tripoli.

On 30 May 1924 the Socialist deputy Giacomo Matteotti, who had already published an account of Fascist crimes, denounced what he called the treachery, violence and illegality of the Fascist Government. On 10 June he was forced into a car, stabbed to death and buried in the Roman campagna. During the days following his disappearance his mother and widow requested an audience with the Pope which was refused. The body was not discovered until August but his murder was immediately accepted as a fact. A wave of revulsion swept through the country and eventually almost all the opposition parties including the Popular Party withdrew to the Aventine. However the Government was saved because no one with the necessary moral or legal authority was prepared to act. Pius XI did not lack either the courage or the moral authority but he feared the consequences of condemning the Fascist Government. Not only would such a condemnation jeopardize the concessions granted to the Church and the possibility of solving the Roman Question, but it would strengthen the forces of Italian Socialism and even throw the country into chaos. The *Osservatore* expressed the hope that justice would be done and peace would prevail, while reminding its readers that to change the régime would involve 'a fatal leap in the dark'.

The ecclesiastical authorities made the first great concession to Mussolini and Fascism and eventually opened the way to the signing of the Concordat by destroying the Popular Party. But the attitudes of the Pope and his Secretary of State towards the Popular Party were not determined by Fascist threats against the Church. In all probability they would have come to the same decisions even without the rise of Fascism. By the middle of 1923 the Popular Party, the Socialist and Communist Parties were losing political influence as well as their sense of unity. The Popular Party was not sufficiently opposed to Fascism for its left wing supporters and insufficiently in favour of Fascism for its right wing supporters. Vatican officials were suspicious of the Party at the same time that its opponents were dismissing it as an instrument of Vatican politics. The industrialists and land-owners feared the Party because of its support for industrial and agricultural workers but it was despised by the Socialists because of its opposition to class conflict.

Initially the Popular Party had been prepared to cooperate with Mussolini on certain conditions that would have safeguarded the freedom of workers' associations and the laws governing elections. Mussolini, however, who also attempted to win over members of the increasingly divided Popular Party by a combination of threats and promises, threatened Parliament with his Fascist forces until measures were adopted to ensure that there would be a Fascist majority in the next Parliament. At the same time Mussolini revealed to Vatican officials his desire to solve the Roman Question and his determination that the policies of the Popular Party should not be allowed to prevent the reconciliation of Church and State. He also indicated that any cooperation between the Popular Party and the Fascist Government would depend on its total support for the Government, the expulsion of 'Left Wing elements' from the Party and the resignation of Don Sturzo.

Meanwhile in his very first encyclical, the Pope had expressed his desire for a reconciliation between Church and State and had given his support to the forces of Catholic Action. He united Italian Catholic Action in Italy in one body directly subordinated to the hierarchy and controlled by a central committee whose president was appointed by the Pope and directly responsible to him. Pius XI tried to establish Catholic Action as synonymous with the lay apostolate and distinct from party politics. During 1922 and 1923 Pius XI repeatedly stressed that Catholic Action was the one organization through which Italian Catholics might play their part in the civil life of their country and that it should not become involved in the political life of the nation. As a result Catholics and their newspapers increasingly transferred their support from the Popular Party to Catholic Action and in due course worked to establish at least a *modus vivendi* with Fascism.

As increasing numbers of Italian Catholics began to join the Fascist

Party, Catholic newspapers urged Don Sturzo not to do anything to embarrass the ecclesiastical authorities or to endanger Catholic organizations. *Civiltà Cattolica* commented: 'the most impetuous and thoughtless adherents of Fascism – on the fringe of the party at least, if not at its centre – will easily be able to find in the present state of affairs an excuse for reverting to the abominable technique of violence. They will identify with the Popular Party, if only in the excitement of the moment, Catholic circles and associations which neither have, nor should have, any common bond with groups or parties of whatever political orientation, even though these may consist predominantly of Catholic men who profess to be inspired by Christian principles'.

Cardinal Gasparri informed the Italian bishops that the Holy See had no connection with the Popular Party and that, 'his Holiness desires all those who *in any way or to any extent* represent the interest of religion to pay attention to the rule of strictest prudence, avoiding even the very appearance of attitudes towards and approval of political parties'.

In 1924 Mussolini demanded a general election in the hope that changes in the electoral system combined with acts of violence would ensure a Fascist majority. A week before the election an influential Jesuit wrote an article in *Osservatore Romano* praising Mussolini who had had 'the good sense to reject sectarianism and to turn more to religion'. The writer urged his readers to 'salute the noble intentions' of Mussolini and to pray that 'they may endure and be efficacious' and result in the reconciliation of Church and State. The Popular Party won over half a million votes, more than the votes cast for any of the other minority parties, but insignificant compared with the four and a half million votes in favour of Mussolini's Fascist Party. The Government had a majority of 240 over the Opposition, though the 135 members of the opposition parties were still a constant source of irritation to Mussolini, and the Fascists reacted with the violence that was now typical of them. Supporters and offices of Catholic Action and Catholic trade unions as well as the Popular Party were attacked, sacked or burned and in one region alone some forty-three Catholic cooperatives were destroyed. Pius XI was genuinely horrified and he sent half a million *lire* to help the Catholic associations that had been subjected to these acts of terrorism.

In 1925 the Pope again deplored continued acts of Fascist violence as well as another attempt on Mussolini's life: 'even while We, and with Us the Bishops, Priests and all good Catholics, have been offering prayers of thanksgiving and supplication in recognition of the inestimable benefit conferred on the nation by its leader's miraculous preservation, behold! another storm has burst over Italy, a storm of violence and destruction, directed against persons and property, against institutions and the buildings in which their work is performed; a storm which spared neither the sanctity of the temple, nor the venerable dignity of the Bishop, nor the sacred character of the priest. This blind fury seemed to identify with the enemies of order those good and faithful Catholics whose very faith and religion makes them the best friends and guardians of that same order; and, with an evil discrimination sought out the best among the Catholic faithful in order to subject them to harsher treatment – themselves and their choicest works and organizations, which are of religious, cultural, economic and social benefit to all. . . . It seems that once again there is being revealed and enunciated a conception of the State which cannot be the Catholic conception, so long as it makes of the State the end, and of the citizen, of the individual, merely a means, causing all things to be monopolized and swallowed up by the State'.

Unfortunately Pius XI did not also protest against the summary execution of the fifteen-year-old boy held responsible for the attempted assassination. Not only were there serious doubts as to whether he actually fired the gun, but his body showed signs of strangulation and he had been stabbed fourteen times before he was finally shot.

Alcide de Gasperi, like Don Sturzo himself whom he succeeded, moved in favour of some form of political collaboration between the Popular Party and the Socialists. At the time Catholics were collaborating with Socialists in other countries, particularly in Prussia where from 1920 until 1932 a Coalition Government of the Centre and Socialist Parties formed the basis of the German Republic. However, the Catholic newspapers in Italy were generally opposed to the prospect of any collaboration with the Socialists: in spite of the excesses of the Fascists, they had succeeded in removing the threat of Socialist tyranny and supported Catholicism, they had repudiated the Freemasons and restored law and order. On the other hand even moderate Socialists were hostile to Catholicism and Christianity, authority and private property, the sanctity of marriage and the rights of the family. Socialists were also atheists and advocates of a class war.

Civiltà Cattolica described the possibility of a coalition between Catholics and Socialists as 'neither decent, nor opportune, nor lawful'; it would cause anxiety 'to every serious citizen and still more to the ecclesiastical authorities'. Most Italian Catholics seem to have believed that collaboration with the Socialists would be a great mistake; it would involve a total surrender to the forces of atheistic Socialism and delay the restoration of civil liberties and constitutional order. Of course it is by no means clear that the Socialists themselves would have been willing to support the idea of collaborating with Catholics but in the event the Popular Party refused to form a united front with the other opposition parties though some individual representatives later joined those who abstained from parliamentary activities in the futile hope that the King might still intervene to save the Italian constitution.

On 9 September 1924 Pius XI repeated his opposition to any form of collaboration with the Socialists in an address to university students who were well known as a group to be supporters of the Popular Party: 'Instances are also cited of collaboration between Catholics and Socialists in other countries; but here there is confusion, due perhaps to insufficient experience, between two totally different sets of circumstances. Apart from the differences in environment and historical, political, and religious conditions, it is one thing to find oneself face to face with a party which has already reached power, but quite another thing to open the way and provide the possibility for a party to come to power. . . . And it is truly painful to the heart of the Pope to see good children and good Catholics divided and engaged in mutual combat. Why, in the name of Catholic interests, oblige others or hold oneself obliged to adhere to a quarter where "non-confessionalism" is erected into a programme, which might lead to ignoring even the Catholic confession itself?'

The Pope's address effectively ended the Popular Party since he had made it clear that it could no longer act as an independent and autonomous body of Catholics in the political life of Italy. Sturzo's own political activities were also brought to an end when the Secretary of State ordered the Italian bishops to prohibit the political activities of their priests and in particular to prevent them from contributing to periodicals connected with political parties. Sturzo himself had resigned on 10 July 1923. He later told Cardinal Bourne, the Archbishop of Westminster, that he had done this 'at the request of the Holy See'. Sturzo was also informed that it was 'the desire, nay the command of the Holy Father' that he should leave Italy and he only returned in 1946. Yet in spite of everything Sturzo did not lose his sense of faith in the Church; as he told Guiseppe Stragliati in the 1930s: 'If we believe in the Church it is not because of the merits of Pius XI or of any other pope, nor will we leave it because of their unworthiness; we believe in the Church because Jesus Christ himself founded it'.

In February 1925 the Government set up a committee including three canons nominated by three of the major Roman Basilicas to review the entire field of legislation governing the Church and to suggest whatever modifications of the existing laws might be needed. The *Osservatore Romano* made it clear that the three canons were not acting on behalf of the Holy See, though they would hardly have been nominated by their chapters without at least the tacit approval of the Holy Father. The proposals suggested by the committee such as clerical pensions or legal recognition for ecclesiastical institutions were not unnaturally welcomed by Vatican officials, though the basic issue of compensation for the loss of the temporal power was unresolved and early in 1926 the Pope made it clear that he could not: 'concede the right and the power to make laws affecting such matters and persons to others unless they have first entered into proper negotiations and concluded valid agreements with this Holy See and with Us'.

In 1926 the Government played a leading part in the celebrations commemorating the seventh centenary of the death of St Francis of Assisi who was described by Mussolini as 'the most saintly of Italians and the most Italian of saints'. A special train, flying the papal and the Italian flags, was put at the disposal of the papal legate, Merry del Val. This was the first 'papal' train to leave Rome since 1870. The Cardinal was greeted with a twenty-one gun salute and received full military honours at every station along the route. At a reception, Merry del Val described Mussolini as 'the man who has raised Italy's reputation in the world, and is visibly protected by God' and paid tribute to him 'who holds the reins of government in Italy, and who with clear and realistic vision has willed that religion be respected, honoured and practised'. In reply the Italian Minister of Education pledged the devotion of all Italians to 'the august and venerated head of our religion' and asked that 'the divine blessing may descend from the Apostolic See on Italy for its moral, spiritual and social welfare.' On the same evening, the feast of St Francis of Assisi, Mussolini authorized the opening of confidential negotiations with the Holy See to explore the possibility of settling the differences between Church and State in Italy.

The attitudes of the ecclesiastical authorities towards Mussolini and Fascism were inevitably mixed. Pius XI himself probably never really sympathized with Fascism, though he had been Archbishop when Mussolini established the headquarters of his movement at Milan and had allowed the blackshirts to mount a guard in the Cathedral when the requiem was being celebrated for the victims of a bomb explosion. As Pope, Pius XI appeared willing to negotiate with any Italian Government that shared his desire for a settlement though the advent of Mussolini undoubtedly simplified the problem by removing some difficulties and even some of the internal opposition that might have faced a more 'liberal' Italian Government. Certainly one of the reasons why Gasparri decided to negotiate with the Fascists was because he believed that it would be difficult if not impossible to agree to a Concordat with a democratic or parliamentary Government in Italy at that time and so it was important to make an agreement with the Fascists while they remained in power.

On the other hand, as Binchy pointed out, the very support given to the Church by the Fascist Government made it important for the ecclesiastical authorities to solve the Roman Question. Otherwise the Church might become too closely associated, or even identified with, the Fascist régime. The alternative policy of continuing to adopt an attitude of *non possumus* might simply provoke a retaliation that was incomparably worse than anything experienced under former anti-clerical governments. In short, unless the Roman Question was solved, the Church would either become identified with the Fascist régime or in a state of open warfare with it. It was therefore crucial to establish the fact of the international independence of the Holy See and in so far as it was possible to define the distinct jurisdictions and rôles of Church and State in Italy.

The actual negotiations with Mussolini were precipitated by the unfortunate intervention of the French Government which protested that the 'rights of France' would be adversely affected if the Church signed a Concordat with Italy. The first official announcement of the agreement was given to the Diplomatic Corps accredited to the Holy See on the morning of 7 February 1929 after an invitation similar to the one issued on the fateful morning of 20 September 1870. They were informed that: 'As a result of long and laborious conferences and most careful study a Treaty and a Concordat corresponding to the sentiments of the Holy Father have been elaborated; a Treaty which effectually secures to the Holy See that position which it has always claimed and which belongs to it of Divine Right, namely, a situation which secures full liberty and real visible independence to the Government of the Universal Church, and a Concordat which adequately provides for the needs of the Church and religion in Italy'.

Few people were aware that the negotiations were actually taking place; therefore the signing of the Treaty by Mussolini and Gasparri on 11 February surprised the Italian people and Catholics in the rest of the world. Within half an hour the news spread throughout the city of Rome, papal and Italian flags were flown side by side and delighted crowds cheered for the Pope, the King and the Duce. The celebrations continued on the following day, the seventh anniversary of the Pope's coronation, as peoples and newspapers everywhere welcomed the agreements and letters and telegrams of congratulation that poured into the Vatican from individuals and governments in all parts of the world. The first official message sent by the Pope as Sovereign of the Vatican State was a telegram to the King of Italy and at the end of the year the King and Queen of Italy paid a state visit to the Holy See and so ended the bitter divisions and quarrels between Church and State that had followed the unification of Italy. The Lateran Treaty was in fact three documents. The Pope first recognized the Kingdom of Italy and surrendered his territorial claims in return for a sovereign and independent Vatican City State. A second document guaranteed financial compensation for the lost territories and the third document was a Concordat between Church and State. The purpose of the Concordat was simply to define the rights and liberties of the Church within a particular territory and so far as possible to restrict and limit the interference of the secular government in ecclesiastical affairs. The ecclesiastical authorities always insisted on two instruments: a political treaty establishing the sovereign independence of the Holy See and a Concordat regulating the position of the Catholic Church in Italy. Although previous Italian governments might have been prepared to end the political dispute by negotiating a treaty of independence, it would seem that the terms of the Concordat negotiated with the Fascists were far more favourable to the Church than they might have been if an agreement could have been reached with a more secularist or 'liberal' Italian Government. The agreement of 1929 was facilitated by the fact that what had great significance for one of the parties meant very little to the other and the Church won almost without effort many of the battles that it had failed to win during the previous century.

However a basic difference of approach still remained. According to the Pope, 'The Concordat explains and justifies the Treaty'; 'The solution was not easy but We may be grateful to the Lord for having made it clear to Us and to the other side. The solution was to make both settlements advance together step by step. And so, side by side with the Treaty, a Concordat in the proper sense of the word was also studied'.

The Treaty and the Concordat were negotiated, signed and ratified together and Pius XI undoubtedly believed that the fate of one determined the fate of the other and that to repudiate one would render the other invalid. Furthermore the Concordat fixed the respective rights of Church and State and defined the limits of secular interference in ecclesiastical affairs. If the Italian Government exceeded these limits, the Holy See would at least have a legal basis on which to protest. The Fascists on the other hand, refused to accept the Pope's interpretation. They regarded the Concordat as the price of the Treaty. The Treaty was immutable, but the Concordat, dealing with contemporary and future relations, must be subject to later modification.

Pius XI believed that 'Sovereignty, *at least under present conditions*, is only recognized on the basis of a certain amount of territory'. The territories of the Vatican City State fixed by the Treaty of 1929 consisted

Mussolini introduces Anton Pavelich, the Catholic dictator of Croatia, to the Roman crowds

of the Basilica and Square of St Peter's and the adjacent Vatican buildings over which the Holy See was to exercise 'full ownership, exclusive and absolute power, and sovereign jurisdiction'. The territorial base of the Vatican City not only guaranteed the autonomous government and legislative power of the papacy, but permitted it to have its own police force and civil service, postage, coinage and flag, public services, radio and even railway station. Nevertheless the area was small enough to meet the needs of the Pope without embarrassing the Italians. A larger area might also have created problems for the Church because, as Gasparri once remarked, 'We do not want to have to deal with a tram strike'. Papal churches, palaces and buildings outside the Vatican were given the extra-territorial immunities normally enjoyed by foreign embassies and although papal colleges were not given extra-territorial privileges, they were exempted from taxation and guaranteed against expropriation.

The Treaty guaranteed the immunity of representatives to the Holy See, 'even if their States are not in diplomatic relations with Italy', and free access to the Holy See across Italian territory. The Vatican was also given a considerable financial indemnity from the Italian Government of an immediate payment of 750 million *lire* and the permanent interest on Italian Government Stock at a nominal value of a billion *lire*. However, there were restrictions and controls over how the Holy See could use these funds. Furthermore, according to Mussolini himself, the total indemnity amounted to 450 million gold *lire* and, as the preamble to the Convention recognized, was much less than, possibly only half of, what was due to the Holy See under the Law of Guarantees.

The Concordat with the Italian Government satisfied the ecclesiastical authorities on all important points. Catholicism was declared the sole and official religion of the Italian state and nation and although priests were barred from belonging to political parties, all issues involving religion and politics were to be settled according to the laws of the Church. The Concordat guaranteed free communication between the Pope and Catholic bishops throughout the world, freedom to appoint Italian bishops subject only to the political objections of the State, and the payment of bishops and priests by the State. Italian legislation against Religious Orders was abolished and religious congregations were given legal recognition. Catholic Action was promised favourable treatment and the freedom of its non-political activities was guaranteed. Catholic education was made compulsory in all schools and the Government recognized ecclesiastical schools and universities. Holidays of obligation became public holidays.

At the Socialist Party Congress held in 1910, Comrade Benito Mussolini had proposed that those members who contracted a religious marriage or who allowed their children to be baptized should be expelled. When Mussolini came to sign the Concordat, however, he had either changed his views or regarded the issues as insufficiently important to jeopardize the prospect of an agreement. He was also prepared to make every concession to the Church on the subject of marriage partly because the Church's moral code supported the Fascist 'ethic' and partly because the attitude of the Church towards marriage was widely shared by the vast majority of Italians at the time. As a result, much of the Church's teaching on marriage was incorporated into the Concordat and this was signalled out for special praise in *Casti Connubii* (1931), the Pope's encyclical on marriage. As the Pope told Cardinal Gasparri: 'On the subject of matrimony the Concordat secures for the family, the Italian people and country even more than for the Church a benefit so great that for it alone We would have willingly sacrificed life itself'.

The Pope expressed his personal satisfaction with the other provisions of the Concordat when he remarked, 'if not the best that could possibly be made, [it] is certainly among the best that have so far been devised; and it is with profound satisfaction that We express the belief that through it We have given back God to Italy and Italy to God'. And this opinion was shared by Catholics throughout the world. Nevertheless the Pope was not unaware of what he called the 'doubts and criticisms' with which the Lateran Treaty would be received. To come to terms with Italy inevitably restricted the Vatican's freedom to criticise Italian policies and increased the danger that curial officials might tend to become unduly 'Italian' in their outlook.

It was argued at the time, as it has been since, that the Pope 'blessed' Fascism by coming to terms with Mussolini. But such an interpretation of events ignores the fact that in the same year, 1929, the Holy See concluded a Concordat with the predominantly Socialist Government of Prussia. Pius XI was willing to treat with any government or régime of any political colour or ideology in the interests of the Church. He maintained friendly relations with the *Front Populaire* and secularist governments in France. In 1937 his Secretary of State, Cardinal Pacelli, visited France at a time when relations between Italy and France were more than usually strained. The pontificate of Pius XI exemplified the need for the Holy See to pursue its own policies, which sometimes coincided with and sometimes opposed the interests of Fascist Italy, and to show that the Vatican's relations with other states would not be influenced by an exaggerated concern for the opinions of the Italian Government. At a time when Anglo-Italian relations were almost at breaking point, the Pope seemed to go out of his way to pay a long tribute to 'Our dear England' and to express his satisfaction at having been represented at the King's coronation. Finally, Pius XI was one of the first world leaders to denounce the anti-Christian implications of Fascism at a time when other statesmen were still competing for Mussolini's favours.

At the same time, however, it must be admitted that Mussolini seldom indulged in *Realpolitik* to better effect than in his approach towards relations between Church and State. By making significant formal concessions to the Church, the Fascists were able to win the support of many Catholic clergy and laity, secured a voice and even a veto over ecclesiastical appointments, the supervision of ecclesiastical property and some control over the ecclesiastical organization of Italy. In practice the Fascist Government was able to veto episcopal appointments particularly those which affected national minorities and this power was effectively used. The first appointment to an Italian see after the reconciliation between Church and State, that of Cardinal Schuster as Archbishop of Milan, was widely welcomed in the Fascist press and on the very day on which he took possession of his diocese, the Archbishop delivered the first of a long series of speeches in support of the Fascist régime.

Mussolini's speech to the Assembly of the Fascist Party in March 1929, even before the Treaty had been ratified, contained the first suggestions of an inevitable conflict between the Church and a totalitarian State. On the very eve of the election when Catholics, including some significant Vatican officials, publicly and ostentatiously voted in favour of the Fascist Party, the Duce referred to the future of a régime 'which tomorrow will be more totalitarian than yesterday'. At the opening of the new parliament in April both the King and the Duce attempted to reduce the significance of the agreement with the Holy See and to assert the full authority of the State over ecclesiastical affairs and especially over education. It was therefore hardly surprising that on 13 May Mussolini should have delivered his now infamous speech to the Chamber of Deputies. Mussolini bluntly told his audience: 'within the State the Church is not sovereign, nor is it even free ... because it is subordinate, both in its institutions and its members, to the general laws of the State. . . . We have not resurrected the Temporal Power of the Popes, we have buried it'. He also made his notorious statement on the origins of Christianity when he contrasted the petty Jewish sect with the Church of Rome: 'This religion was born in Palestine, it became Catholic in Rome'. The Duce reduced the significance of all the important provisions in the Concordat and in particular declared that 'Education must belong to us'; 'in the sphere of education we remain intractable. Youth shall be ours!' He then warned members of Catholic organizations and Catholic Action: 'The régime is vigilant, nothing escapes it. Let nobody believe that the smallest parochial bulletin of the smallest parish is not known to Mussolini. We will not permit the revival of parties and organizations which we have destroyed for ever. Let everyone remember that the Fascist régime, when it begins a war, fights it to a finish and leaves but a desert behind'. He went on to affirm the 'ethical character' of the State which was 'Catholic but also Fascist, indeed before all else exclusively and essentially Fascist'.

Mussolini's extreme language was possibly an attempt to avoid the criticisms of some of his own supporters as well as a direct warning against the extravagant claims of some Catholics which would also help to explain his favourable references to Cavour and Napoleon. Nevertheless the press, Fascist as well as Catholic, was silenced and embarrassed. Catholic publications were also conscious of the Duce's boast that he had 'confiscated more Catholic journals than in the previous seven years, that was probably the only way to bring them back to the correct intonation'. Pius XI, however, was not the sort of character to suffer such language in silence.

On the following morning the Pope gave an address to a group of Catholic students. He began with the rights of the Church over education and his opposition to the Fascist doctrine of 'educating for conquest': 'We are, We will not say intractable [*intrattabili*] – for intractability is no virtue, it is rather a sign of weakness – but simply intransigent. . . . When it is a question of saving souls or avoiding greater evils, We would find the courage to treat [*trattare*] with the Devil in person. . . . We have spoken to you of intransigence about principles and rights. We have only to add that We have no material means of enforcing Our intransigence. Nor do we regret this, for truth and right have no need of material force: they have their own force, irrefutable, indestructible, and irresistible'.

On 6 June, the eve of the date fixed for the exchange of ratifications, the Vatican published the text of a letter sent from the Pope to Cardinal Gasparri during the previous month. The Pope distinguished the doctrine of Catholicism from that of Fascism, gave detailed criticisms of Mussolini's views as expounded in the Chamber and an analysis of Mussolini's interpretation of the settlement which was rejected. Pius XI deplored the Duce's 'harsh, cruel, drastic words' and especially his 'heretical, and worse than heretical, comments on the very essence of Christianity and Catholicism' which were 'in keeping with the most pernicious and abominable Modernism'. The Pope dismissed Mussolini's later attempt to distinguish between the historical and doctrinal aspects of the question as 'Modernism of the worst and most dangerous kind'. The Pope also took the opportunity of defining the Vatican's interpretation of the

Concordat and insisted on the indissolubility of Treaty and Concordat. He declared in conclusion that if Fascist Italy was indeed a Catholic State, then, 'the Fascist State, in the domain of ideas and doctrine as in that of practical action, will admit nothing which is not in accordance with Catholic doctrine and practice; otherwise it would not and could not be a Catholic State'. In spite of this controversy, Mussolini, who had received a copy of the letter a week before it was published, drove to the Vatican on the following day to exchange ratifications with Cardinal Gasparri.

Relations between Church and State in Italy from the signing of the Lateran Treaty until the spring of 1940 were marked by efforts to cooperate and compromise and occasional bitter conflicts. The laws incorporated into the Concordat were frequently given the widest possible interpretation in favour of the Church, especially in the case of marriage. Legal decisions extended the rights of ecclesiastical organizations and freedom from taxation, while the ecclesiastical authorities were given grants for the building of churches. But although these concessions reflected the Government's desire to co-operate with the Church, they were only possible because the Government also regarded them as insignificant. In return Catholics accepted the Fascist régime and adopted Fascist practices like the Roman salute. Houses of the Fasci, the shrines of those who had died for the Fascist cause, were blessed by bishops who also addressed Fascist conferences. In fact it was difficult to find an episcopal sermon or pastoral letter after 1929 that did not contain favourable references to the Duce.

Catholic newspapers, like the secular press, were strictly controlled and forced to pay their daily tributes to the régime as well as avoiding making any criticisms. Within six months of the signing of the Lateran Treaty, three of the oldest Catholic daily papers had to suspend publication because of the increasing demands of the Press Office and the unfair competition of the Fascist press. At the beginning of the War, only two Catholic newspapers remained in general circulation and these, like local journals and parish magazines, were strictly controlled. As a result many of the Catholic supporters of Fascism had only a vague knowledge of its official creed and how widespread were its despicable practices, while the Fascists themselves, who were always willing to sacrifice ideology for accommodation, exaggerated or highlighted points of agreement between Catholicism and Fascism.

There is also a remarkable contrast in the number and the force of Catholic denunciations of Fascism on the one hand and Communism on the other at this time. The attitude of Catholics to Fascism undoubtedly seems to have been more reserved and more qualified than their attitude towards Communism. This would appear to have been the result not simply of a lack of moral courage but of a recognition or reflection of the genuine opinions of too many Italian Catholics. Catholics showed a greater tolerance of Fascism because of the concessions which the State had made to the Church, because of a mutual interest in country, family and property, and as a defence against such common enemies as Communism, 'liberalism' and Freemasonry.

However, neither side really trusted the other. Few genuine Catholics held positions of any importance in the Party or the régime while Fascist officials simply decorated ecclesiastical ceremonies with their presence. Almost all genuinely committed Fascists sympathized with the Italian tradition of anti-clericalism and those members of the diocesan councils who wore small shields of the Fascist Party in their lapels were usually only camp-followers. Few Italian Catholics actually experienced the clashes between their bishops and the Fascist officials, and although Fascist priests might not be censured or punished, they did not often enjoy the confidence of their own ecclesiastical authorities. Certainly Cardinal Schuster celebrated Mass at the funeral of a Fascist official murdered by partisans, but there were numerous other occasions when bishops personally offered the consolations of religion to those who were condemned as political prisoners. Bishop Bortignon of Belluno personally embraced fifty partisans on the scaffold on which they were about to be hanged and he condemned their executioners. The number of priests arrested and imprisoned by the régime cannot be estimated because Church and State both preferred to remain silent on the issue. But Fascist denunciations of the 'survivors of Popolarismo' would seem to suggest the existence of a number of clerical supporters of Christian Democracy.

Furthermore, the mere suggestions of unorthodox opinions expressed in Fascist journals were immediately repudiated by the Pope himself or authoritative Catholic sources. In 1932 all the writings of Giovanni Gentile, the 'philosopher of Fascism' during its formative years, were put on the Index. Several contemporary observers interpreted this move as an indirect condemnation of those aspects of Fascist doctrine for which he was responsible. Although the Pope himself might have been temperamentally inclined to sympathize with authoritarian governments, his experience of Fascist Italy and Nazi Germany probably helped him to realize that modern dictatorial regimes were even more dangerous to the Church than the 'liberal' governments of the past. During the final years of the reign of Pius XI, the policies of the Holy See so paralleled those of the western democracies that Cardinal Verdier, Archbishop of Paris, was able to claim that the Church and the great democracies were united in opposing the spread of totalitarianism.

Certainly the most important factor governing relations between Church and State in Italy was the fact that Fascism was totalitarian. The totalitarian claims first formulated by the Fascists but carried to even more sinister lengths by the Nazis and the Communists inevitably opposed the claims of Christianity. Mussolini's Fascism was a curious combination of extreme right-wing nationalism and Socialism, idealism and positivism but he always made it clear that Fascism was not simply a political régime but a doctrine and a faith. 'Fascism', according to Mussolini, 'is totalitarian, and the Fascist State – a synthesis and a unit inclusive of all values – interprets, directs, and potentiates the whole life of a people'. He explicitly stated that the individual only existed within the State and was subordinated to its necessities: 'Nothing outside or above the State, nothing against the State, everything within the State, everything for the State'.

The 'ethical State' of Fascism recognized only its own morality and Mussolini claimed to represent 'the moral and spiritual force of the State'. As he put it on another occasion: 'The State, as conceived and realized by Fascism, is a spiritual and ethical unit for the organization of the nation, an organization which in its origin and growth is a manifestation of the spirit . . . Transcending the individual's brief spell of life, the State stands for the immanent conscience of the nation'. It is therefore hardly surprising that the 'Prayer of the European Fascist' should have read: 'O Jesus, my Lord . . . give unto us the European Catholic unity. Join us all together in that which Thou Thyself hast called Thy Church, the Church of Peter. . . . Let all men of good will close their ranks around the LEADER whom Thou has given to us, so as to form a shield of pure consciences radiant in the sacred flame of European Fascism. . . . Let Fascism be Thy instrument O Lord; we, the rising generation, long to hurl our darts on every side'.

The Pope consistently opposed totalitarianism from the moment that Mussolini first began to expound the notion of the ethical State. In 1926 Pius deplored the emergence of 'a theory of the State which is directly repugnant to Catholic doctrine, namely that the State is its own final end, that the citizen only exists for the State'. At the very beginning of his controversy with Mussolini in 1929, the Pope declared, 'The State does not exist to absorb, swallow or annihilate the individual and the family; that would be absurd and unnatural.' Two years later in a public letter significantly addressed to Cardinal Schuster, the Pope declared that the State was entitled to a 'subjective totalitarianism' 'in the sense that the totality of the citizens shall be obedient to and dependent on the State for all things which are within the competence of the State, having regard to its special end'. However an 'objective totalitarianism' which subordinated the citizen's whole life, 'individual, domestic, spiritual and supernatural', to the State 'is a manifest absurdity in the theoretical order and would be a

61

monstrosity were its realization to be attempted in practice'.

If it was relatively easy for Church and State to come to an agreement on many issues, it was impossible for a totalitarian régime and the Christian Church to agree on the subject of education, the very issue on which Mussolini had described himself as intractable. The Fascists proved willing both to use and to attack the Church in their efforts to dominate the youth of Italy and began by destroying those Catholic youth organizations, particularly the Catholic Boy Scouts, that were regarded as rivals to their own Balilla. The Catholic Boy Scouts had almost 100,000 members with branches in over 1000 districts and not unnaturally appeared a more attractive alternative to the Fascist militaristic youth organizations. As early as 1925 the Holy Office had condemned the Balilla 'catechism' as 'a blasphemous parody of the Christian catechism'.

The Fascists pretended that the scouts were associated with the Popular Party and refused to recognize that they were affiliated to Catholic Action. Government legislation was passed in favour of the Balilla, while a press campaign bitterly attacked the scouts and other 'foreign' organizations such as the YMCA. Bitter clashes occurred, usually occasioned by the Fascists, between the Balilla and the scouts and the Pope himself expressed his fears: 'A vague menace confirmed by the suspicions, interference and attacks of many persons, seems to brood over Our associations and their activities, especially over those of the youth of Catholic Action which are dear to Us as the apple of Our eye. It is to be feared that the sound education of Our Catholic youth is in peril'.

The Government attempted to make the Catholic organizations superfluous by appointing chaplains to give religious instruction to members of the Balilla. At the same time, smaller branches of the scouts were ordered to close. As a result of Government support, membership of the Balilla increased, while members of Catholic organizations were subjected to physical attacks. In due course the Pope seems to have been prepared to accept the dissolution of the Catholic scouts in an effort to save the other Catholic youth clubs and guilds associated with Catholic Action. In 1929 he himself remarked: 'when the fate of Our dear Catholic scouts was being decided, We had to make sacrifices in order to avoid still greater evils, but We have placed on record all the grief We felt at being compelled to do so'. The first official action in the later campaign against Catholic Action was an attempt to dissolve its youth associations and although these eventually survived, every Italian child was compelled to join the national militaristic organization *Gioventù Italiana del Littorio* which was incorporated into the Fascist Party.

In 1929 the Pope published his encyclical, *Divini illius Magistri*, on the

Christian education of youth in which he denounced the attempts of the State to monopolize the training of the young and uncompromisingly reasserted the primary claims of the family and the Church. This encyclical was issued shortly after the Lateran agreements and its uncompromising tone echoed the controversy between the Pope and the Duce which had followed the political settlement. The Pope argued that primacy in education belonged to the family by natural right and to the Church by divine ordinance. Although the State had an important part to play in the work of education, this was not a primary role and was subordinate to the rights of the family and the Church. The State should cooperate with and not try to supplant the family and the Church.

According to the Fascists, on the other hand, the State was prepared to provide time for religious education and to allow the ecclesiastical authorities a voice in the programme and the nomination of those who taught religion. However in effect it was the State that taught religion and integrated it with other disciplines. Although the Church was able to achieve many of its formal aims in primary schools, religious instruction was under threat in secondary schools. Furthermore, in both cases the religious education of children was severely jeopardized by the obvious contrast between the beliefs and virtues of Christianity and the nationalistic and militaristic claims of Fascism. The position of priests giving religious instruction in secondary schools often became quite impossible with the spread of Fascism and even anti-clericalism among Italian teachers.

The Church in Italy had long experience in dealing with 'secularist' education. Before the Concordat, those children who went to religious schools were penalized both academically and financially because the system of public examinations was unfairly weighted against them. Moves were already being made to remove these grievances when the Fascists came to power and were able to claim the credit for removing them. But however unorthodox or anti-religious secular education might have been, it was not totalitarian. Furthermore a totalitarian regime was not content to remove grievances without exacting a price. And on the eve of the outbreak of the Second World War, the future of religious education in Italy was clearly threatened as the Italian Fascists increasingly tended to imitate the methods and measures of the Nazis.

In 1938 the Minister of Education introduced a decree establishing a new public corporation with responsibility for secondary education. The corporation was instructed to introduce 'fundamental unity – didactic, educational and political – into the private institutes of secondary education'. Somewhat surprisingly, the Catholic press ignored this instruction, the *Osservatore* for nearly three months and *Civiltà Cattolica* for over nine months. The corporation did in fact promise to respect the special character of ecclesiastical schools but the *Osservatore* expressed the fear that this vague guarantee would not be sufficient to safeguard their educational freedom. *Civiltà Cattolica* actually welcomed the establishment of the corporation while expressing the hope that it would restrict its activities to non-religious private schools. A few days after the death of the Pope, the Fascists published a *Carta della Scuola* which defined Fascist education as 'a popular culture inspired by the eternal values of the Italian race and civilization' and the only reference to religion guaranteed that Italian children would be brought up 'along the paths of the religion of their fathers and of the destinies of Italy'.

The Lateran Treaty had been in force for less than two years when conflict broke out between Church and State over Fascist attacks on Catholic Action as well as Catholic youth organizations. Pius XI often expressed the hope that he would be remembered primarily as 'the Pope of Catholic Action' and although he himself did not actually begin this movement of 'the apostolate of the laity', he extended and enhanced its activities beyond all recognition. In 1923 the Pope had reorganized Catholic Action into three main groups: the Federation of Catholic Men and Union of Catholic Women, the Youth organizations and the University Students who were the principal victims during the conflicts of 1931. Members of Catholic Action could engage in party politics but the organization itself remained outside and above politics. Pius XI mistakenly believed that the forces of Catholic Action would provide a better defence of Christian principles than Catholic political parties, at least in Italy. Nevertheless conflict with the Fascists was almost inevitable because as the Pope himself declared: 'when religious or moral interests are at stake, Catholic Action can and must intervene directly, and by the full exercise of its strength lead an organized campaign in favour of the paramount interests of the Church and of the souls entrusted to her care'.

The ultimate conflict between the Holy See and the Fascist Government in the summer of 1931 was simply the culmination of many years hostility and was deliberately organized and directed by the Fascist authorities. Catholic Action was not only independent of totalitarian control but its increasing popularity, in spite of official disapproval, was not something the régime was prepared to ignore. The Fascists accused Catholic Action of being a political agency and a relic of the Popular Party. Fascist newspapers launched a press campaign as a prelude to physical attacks on individuals and offices while the periodicals of those Catholic editors who dared to protest were suppressed. Papal or episcopal protests produced official assurances of regret but little action from Fascist authorities.

The violence was directed primarily against Catholic Action, rather than priests or churches, though there were some examples of anti-clericalism and anti-Catholicism. In fact Fascist violence against the Church at this time was more frequent and more intense than any of the anti-clerical violence to which Catholics in Italy had been subjected since 1870. Furthermore only the *Osservatore Romano* was able to report the attacks on the Church and the protests of the Pope and copies of this newspaper were frequently confiscated by the authorities when they reached the territory and jurisdiction of Italy. Formerly the Catholic press had been able to condemn anti-clerical attacks on the Church, but now Catholics were beginning to learn that the 'friendship' of a totalitarian régime could be more constricting than the hostility of secularists.

However the Pope was still able to appeal to the consciences of Italians through his public audiences. He used this means with consummate skill and was widely and sympathetically reported in the foreign press. He immediately protested at a public audience when the Police dissolved the Catholic University Federation with their usual acts of violence and contempt for persons and property; 'they can demand Our life', he said, 'but not Our silence'. Pius retaliated by suspending the mission of the Cardinal Legate to the celebrations of the seventh centenary of the death of St Anthony at Padua and the open-air processions on the feast of Corpus Christi.

On 26 April 1931 the Pope sent a memorandum to Cardinal Schuster demanding the protection which had been guaranteed in the Concordat and went on: 'Fascism declares itself to be Catholic. Well, there is one way and one way only to be Catholic – Catholics in fact and not merely in name, true Catholics and not sham Catholics, not Catholics who by their words and actions afflict the hearts of their spiritual Mother and Father, sadden their brethren and lead them astray by their bad example – it is necessary to fulfil one condition only, one that is, however, indispensable and unalterable: it is necessary, in short, to obey the Church and her Head, and to be in sympathy with the Church and her Head'.

At the end of May the Pope publicly deplored the 'tempest of intrusions, appropriations, sequestrations and depredations' unleashed against Catholic Action. Moreover these incidents had been 'preceded, with the connivance of the civil authorities, first by a Press campaign compounded of falsehoods, insults and calumnies, then by a campaign, conducted in squares and streets, of insults and improprieties, of acts of violence and oppression, not seldom involving bloodshed and very often committed by large numbers of malefactors against small, always unarmed groups of Our sons, and even of Our daughters'.

On 29 June 1931 the Pope prayed at the tomb of the apostles on the feast of Saints Peter and Paul before signing his encyclical *Non abbiamo bisogno* which significantly was written in Italian and was first distributed abroad. Copies of this encyclical were flown to Paris and appeared in the foreign newspapers before being published in the *Osservatore* on 5 July. On that day the *Osservatore* went on sale several hours before the usual time in order that it might be sold before it was confiscated by the secular authorities.

Although the Pope did not directly condemn either the Fascist Party or the régime, he warned Catholics against Fascist ideology and condemned the Fascist understanding of education as 'pagan worship of the State'. He also condemned the Fascist oath as unlawful and recommended those Italian Catholics who were forced to join the PNF, *per necessità familiale*, to add a mental reservation such as 'Saving the laws of God and of the Church'. The encyclical began with a protest against: 'the irreverences, oftentimes of an impious and blasphemous character, and the acts of violence and vandalism committed against places, things, and persons throughout the country and in Our very episcopal city'. The Pope defended Catholic Action from the charge of being political in character and decribed as the most glaring instance of ingratitude 'that shown towards the Holy See by a party and a régime which, in the judgement of the entire world, derived from their amicable relations with the Holy See, both at home and abroad, an accession of prestige and credit which some in Italy and elsewhere considered inordinate, just as they regarded the favour and trust evinced on Our side as unduly generous'.

Pius XI went on to refer to 'a real and a true persecution': 'We find Ourselves confronted by a mass of authentic affirmations and no less authentic facts which reveal beyond the slightest possibility of doubt the resolve (already in great measure actually put into effect) to monopolize completely the young, from their tenderest years up to manhood and womanhood, for the exclusive advantage of a party and of a régime based on an ideology which clearly resolves itself into a true, a real pagan worship of the State – the 'Statolatry' which is no less in contrast with the natural rights of the family than it is in contradiction with the supernatural rights of the Church. . . . We must say, and do hereby say, that he is a Catholic only in name and by baptism (in contradiction to the obligations of that name and to the baptismal promises) who adopts and develops a programme with doctrines and maxims so opposed to the rights of the Church of Jesus Christ and of souls, and who also misrepresents, combats, and persecutes Catholic Action which, as is universally known, the Church and its Head regard as very dear and precious'.

The Fascist press retaliated by bitterly denouncing the Pope and the régime was annoyed and irritated by the international support and sympathy the Pope received and not only from Catholics. The Secretary General of the Party declared that membership of the Party was not compatible with that of Catholic Action and it is said that within twenty-four hours some 50,000 men and women felt obliged to resign from Catholic Action. Many of these resignations were inevitable because, as the Pope himself had explicitly recognized, membership of the Fascist Party was often a prerequisite for earning a living. However both sides were anxious to avoid an open break. The Pope was still grateful for the Lateran Treaty and did not want to drive the Duce to even greater extremes. Mussolini had not allowed himself to become personally involved in the controversy and did not like to contemplate breaking with the Church. He merely wanted to keep the Church 'in its place' and seems to have been both surprised and angered by the strength of the Pope's resistance. Furthermore, Mussolini feared that his prestige might be reduced throughout the world and especially in America if he came into open conflict with the Holy See.

Suddenly the Fascists altered course. The press ceased to denounce the Church and Fascist demonstrators disappeared from the streets as the two sides negotiated a compromise. Differences between Church and State were apparently resolved following a meeting between the Duce and Cardinal Pacelli. At the end of August the Government revoked its ban on Catholic youth organizations and at the beginning of September the ecclesiastical authorities agreed to restrict and control the activities, especially the political activities, of Catholic Action. It was decided that those individuals who had played an active role in the political opposition to Fascism should be excluded from positions of authority in Catholic Action, whose members were also restricted from taking part in some trade-union activities. The ecclesiastical authorities were also forced to modify the structure of Catholic Action in Italy to make it more acceptable to the Government. A new constitution was adopted as a result of which the movement was decentralized and placed under the direct control of the diocesan bishops. For the time being peace was restored between Church and State. In February 1932 Mussolini was received by the Pope and decorated with the Papal Order of the Golden Spur. The King of Italy received the Supreme Order of Christ, while Cardinal Gasparri received Italy's highest decoration, the Order of the Annunziata.

Subsequently Catholic Action tried to coexist with the Fascist régime. Some Catholics were alienated by the growing alliance between Hitler and Mussolini, the murder of Dollfuss and the destruction of the Austrian Republic, and the passing of the Italian racial laws. But other Catholics supported 'the high colonizing mission of Italy' and military rearmament.

Most Italian Catholics believed that the army of General Franco in the Spanish Civil War was fighting a crusade against Communism and enthusiastically supported Italian volunteers fighting in Spain. At the beginning of 1939 the Archbishop of Gorizia wrote: 'Good Italians (and today we are entitled to believe that in the Fascist climate all Italians are worthy of their name) know that in Red Spain all the worst elements of the sinister democratic régimes have united to make a final effort against the granite mass of Christian civilization'.

Meanwhile the Fascists attempted to use the Vatican in pursuit of their expansionist aims in Malta and the Middle East and in disputes over the Holy Places. Italian missionaries were given free passage to the Middle East and the Italian Government spent huge sums of money in establishing schools and hospitals in Palestine. However, the Abyssinian War provided the most dramatic illustration of the determination of the Fascists to exploit the Concordat in the interests of Italian nationalism. Even without the Lateran Treaty, the Vatican would probably have remained neutral during the second Abyssinian War as it had during the first war which had been waged by Crispi, one of the most bitter enemies of the Holy See. However the Pope was effectively 'silenced' in the face of Mussolini's blatant imperialist aggression by one of the provisions of the Concordat: 'With regard to the sovereignty which is its due in the international sphere, the Holy See declares that it desires to remain extraneous to all temporal disputes and to international congresses held to deal with such things, unless the contending parties make an appeal in unison to its pacifying mission'. Nevertheless many foreign critics, Catholic and non-Catholic alike, both at the time and subsequently, inevitably wondered whether the Holy See had not become too dependent on the Fascist régime and whether the Lateran Treaty had effectively reduced the spiritual and moral independence of the Church.

Mussolini invaded Abyssinia in October 1935 and in the following month the League of Nations applied economic sanctions against Italy. Three months before the actual invasion the Pope had made a rather ambiguous statement of 'neutrality': 'One thing however appears certain to Us – namely that if the need for expansion is a fact, we must also take into consideration the right of defence, which also has its limits, and a moderation which must be observed if the defence is to remain guiltless'.

Mussolini immediately sent one of his ministers to protest against this sentence which was omitted by those Fascist newspapers which reported the Pope's speech. What was printed gave the impression that the Pope unreservedly supported the Italian claims. The *Osservatore Romano* also adopted an ambiguous position. Although the newspaper briefly stated that Catholics could not accept the thesis that the need for living-space justified a war of conquest, it also seemed increasingly inclined to accept the propaganda of the Italian Government.

During the War the Pope's sense of patriotism occasionally resulted in the use of some unhappy phrases in his reference to the conflict but he did try to maintain the formal neutrality of the Holy See if not that rigid impartiality associated with Leo XIII or Benedict XV. Contemporary reports that the Vatican had joined with the rest of Italy in celebrating the outbreak of war or subsequent Italian victories were later shown to be false or based on misunderstandings. The Pope's position was also deliberately misinterpreted by the Fascists as well as their opponents and he himself recognized 'that Our words may be misunderstood, or even openly twisted and deformed'. However, as in the case of the Spanish Civil War, the interests of the Vatican did coincide with those of the Fascist régime, while an Italian defeat might well have been followed by the formation of a secularist or even a Communist Government in Italy. Consequently the Pope was content to make general appeals for a peace based on truth, justice and charity: 'The Pope, as father of all, is praying for peace, is doing everything possible to secure and conserve peace. That is his peculiar and essential duty. And he further wishes that the hopes, desires and needs of a great and good nation, which is also his own nation, may be recognized but in justice and in peace'.

Meanwhile Catholic as well as Fascist newspapers identified the claims of nationalism with the interests of the faith as bishops and priests blessed the departing troops. The *Osservatore Romano* is said to have reported the War as 'as objectively as if it were the Sino-Japanese conflict' but the same cannot be said of other Catholic periodicals. During the first Abyssinian War, *Civiltà Cattolica* had denounced the Italian aggression. During the second War the same journal tried to identify the interests of 'Religion and Fatherland' and *Civiltà Cattolica* was much more cautious than the rest of the Catholic press. The Holy See made a subtle distinction, lost on the majority of people, between the blessing of soldiers as individuals and as military personnel but the Bishop of Cremona had no such scruples: 'The blessing of God be upon these soldiers who, on African soil, will conquer new and fertile lands for the Italian genius, thereby bringing to them Roman and Christian culture. May Italy stand once again as the Christian mentor to the whole world'. Many of the Italian bishops went much further in their nationalist sentiments and support for Mussolini than the Pope himself might have wished and this could be illustrated by the fact that the *Osservatore Romano* did not report their speeches.

The Bishop of Siena publicly praised 'Italy, our great Duce, and the soldiers who are about to win a victory for truth and righteousness'. The Bishop of San Miniato claimed that 'for the victory of Italy the Italian clergy are ready to melt down the gold of the churches and the bronze of the bells'. Cardinal Schuster, Pius XI's successor as Archbishop of Milan and a close associate of the Pope, commemorated the March on Rome which he described as 'an essentially religious festival' and called on his people to cooperate: 'in this national and Catholic work, more particularly at the present moment when, on the plains of Ethiopia, the Italian standard carries forward in triumph the Cross of Christ, smashes the chains of slavery, and opens the way for the missionaries of the gospel'.

On a later occasion Schuster expressed his belief that the March on Rome had 'prepared souls for the redemption of Ethiopia from the bondage of slavery and heresy and for the Christian renewal of the ancient Empire of Rome'. The imposition of sanctions brought Church and State even closer together. Schuster, echoing the Pope's comments at the time of the Concordat, referred to Mussolini as 'he who has given Italy to God and God to Italy'.

After the defeat of the Abyssinians, the Archbishop of Rhodes was sent to Addis Ababa as Apostolic Visitor and celebrated a Pontifical Mass during which he 'saluted all the heroic soldiers of the Italian army which the world admires, but at which Heaven has no need to marvel since it is their ally'. A French Catholic bishop as well as Protestant missionaries were expelled from the country and the Head of the Coptic Church, who had refused to submit to the Italians, was beheaded. The ecclesiastical authorities took advantage of the Italian conquests and tried to bring the Church of Ethiopia into full communion with Rome. The Holy See also publicly accepted the new political situation and recognized the King of Italy as Emperor of Ethiopia. Later Mussolini himself even expressed his satisfaction with the attitude of the Vatican during the Abyssinian War.

The territorial gains which Italy had already made after the First World War involved incorporating some three-quarters of a million subjects who were alien in speech and race if not in religion. Actually the new German and Slav subjects were almost all better practising Catholics than the native Italians, though the fact of a common religion did not modify the resentment of Germans and Slavs nor did it protect them from Fascist persecution. Monasteries and traditional centres of pilgrimage were taken out of the control of German priests and handed over to Italian religious. Individual priests were persecuted for such 'anti-Italian conduct' as teaching the catechism in German. German and Slav children were to be taught in Italian and were not allowed to learn their mother tongue at school. 'Secret' schools, like the clubs and newspapers of Germans and

Slavs, were suppressed, German leaders were exiled, German property confiscated, and colonists were introduced from southern Italy. When the Archbishop of Zagreb, on behalf of the Yugoslavian hierarchy, appealed for prayers for their persecuted kinsmen in Italy, Italian priests joined Fascist officials in protesting while the *Osservatore Romano* maintained a diplomatic silence.

The Pope found himself in a difficult position. In 1928 he himself replied to the criticisms of Austrian Catholics that he had not acted strongly enough in supporting German-speaking Catholics. 'Tell your Catholic flock', he told Cardinal Pfiffl, Archbishop of Vienna, 'that the Pope has done what he could, but that he is not free'. In spite of the protests of the Holy See, the State insisted that religious instruction should be given in Italian and 'well-disposed' Italian priests should be sent to minister to the Slovene population. Meanwhile the minorities often suffered from un- suitable episcopal appointments once these were controlled by the provisions of the Concordat. Almost every episcopal appointment after 1929 proved detrimental to the interests of the minorities. It is even possible to see how, during the negotiations leading to the Concordat, the Holy See had failed in its attempts to safeguard the linguistic and religious rights of the minorities. In practice, the Concordat effectively gave the State a free hand in pursuing its policy of Italianization with the tolerance, if not the actual support, of the local bishops.

The original 'draft' of the papal representative would have done a great deal to safeguard the rights of the minorities: 'Religious instruction in the elementary schools of the new provinces shall be given in the mother tongue. In those districts where the numbers of priests of Slav or German speech who possess Italian citizenship are not sufficient for the religious needs of the population, the State shall suffer the Ordinary to summon from abroad, subject to the *nihil obstat* of the Italian political authorities, suitable priests of either speech who have not Italian citizenship'. The final version was an inadequate substitute: 'No ecclesiastics who are not Italian citizens shall be appointed to benefices in Italy. Further, both bishops and parish priests must be able to speak Italian. Where necessary, coadjutors shall be assigned to them who understand and speak, in addition to Italian, the language in local use, for the purpose of supplying the faithful with the ministrations of religion in their own tongue, as the rules of the Church require'.

Bishop Antonio Santin of Fiume was accused of threatening to suspend dissident Slav priests who refused to give religious instruction in Italian. A decree of the Congregation of Rites issued in 1906 had allowed some of the Croat communities to follow their traditional custom of using Old Slavonic for parts of the Mass. The local clergy had extended this decree and substituted Croatian for Old Slavonic but in 1934 Bishop Santin, armed with another decree from the Congregation, began a campaign against 'linguistic abuses' and suspended several Croatian priests who refused to obey. On the other hand Archbishop Francis Borgia Sedej of Gorizia ordered his clergy to ensure that Catholics received religious instruction in their own native language. The Fascists then launched a violent campaign against Sedej who eventually resigned and was succeeded by Carlo Margotti who won the approval of the régime and actually reformed his seminary along the lines demanded by the secular authorities.

German-speaking Catholics in the diocese of Brixen were supported by their Bishop but Bishop Endrici of Trent and the Italian members of his chapter publicly supported Fascist policies. The Bishop offended many German Catholics by blessing a monument to Cesare Battisti, the Italian nationalist and anti-clerical supporter of Freemasonry, at a great public ceremony attended by distinguished representatives of the Fascist régime. Bishop Karlin of Trieste resigned almost immediately after the Italian annexation and he was succeeded by a former Chaplain-General and Army Bishop, Bartolomasi, who put pastoral concerns before nationalist interests. During the elections of 1921 Fascist thugs insulted and molested Slav priests and the Bishop protested against 'the threats and intimidation by force of arms, the savage torture and the physical injuries and ill-usage inflicted on parish priests and curates'. Pope Benedict also protested against the outrages inflicted on priests 'the only accusation against whom can be that they belong to the same nation and speech as the faithful entrusted to their charge by the lawful authority of the Church, and that they love them and watch over them'. Bartolomasi's successor, Luigi Fogar, consistently and continually defended the religious rights of minorities. He was boycotted and publicly insulted by the Fascists who also invaded churches where the Slovene language was being used. In due course the Holy See 'promoted' Fogar to the Archbishopric of Patras and Bishop Santin was transferred from Fiume to Trieste.

German-speaking Catholics retaliated by means of a legal boycott which had originally been devised to protect the civil rights of non-Catholics and non-believers. German-speaking parents, whose children would have received religious instruction in Italian, simply applied to have them excluded so that hardly any German-speaking children presented themselves for religious instruction. The policy of Italianization tempted German Catholics to show some sympathy towards Hitler and the Nazi Party until official German policy became 'disinterested' in the fate of these particular people of German stock. By an agreement made in July 1939 the

Tirolese were completely sacrificed in the interests of the Rome–Berlin Axis and even forced to leave their lands. Similarly the treaty of friendship and collaboration between Italy and Yugoslavia signed in March 1937 did nothing to improve the situation of Croats and Slovenes in Italy. Exiled priests were not allowed to return, hymns and sermons in Slovene or Croatian were still prohibited and the civil authorities continued to refuse to register Cyril or Methodius as Christian names.

The freedom of the so-called permitted religions under Fascism was strictly controlled by special regulations and courage among members of the permitted sects was as rare as it was among Catholics. Practically all the religious newspapers welcomed the advent and the legislation of the Fascists, while the Union of Jewish Communities struck a special gold medal which was presented to Mussolini. Italian Jews originally enjoyed a constitutional position under the Fascist régime which was widely praised by several distinguished Jewish writers as a model of Fascist tolerance and enlightenment and during the Abyssinian War the attitude of Italian Jews was described by a leading opponent of Fascism as 'even more servile and abject' than that of Italian Catholics.

Mussolini changed his attitude towards the Jews largely in 'imitation of Germany', as the Pope taunted him, and as a result of the formation of the Rome–Berlin Axis. Hitler's visit to Italy in May 1938 marked the beginning of the new alliance and a close collaboration between the two dictators in their domestic as well as their foreign policies. It was discovered that the Jews did not belong to the Italian race, which was Aryan in origin and civilization. The sacrifice of some 40,000 Jews seemed but a small price to pay for collaboration between Fascism and Nazism.

Tension between Church and State reached a new height during Hitler's visit to Rome. When Pius XI was asked whether he would be willing to receive Hitler in audience, the Pope had stipulated that their discussions should include the persecution of Catholics in Germany. In the event, Pope Pius left for Castel Gandolfo three days before the Führer's arrival and two months before he usually left Rome. Papal museums and galleries were closed to the public and the *Osservatore Romano* studiously ignored Hitler's visit. At a public audience on the morning after Hitler's arrival the Pope deplored the fact that, among his many sorrows: 'it is not found either out of place or out of season to hoist in Rome, on this the feast of the Holy Cross, the symbol of another cross which is not that of Christ'. And only a short time before his death the Pope warned Italian Catholics not to trust Germany.

Although few of the Italian bishops were willing to give public support to the anti-Semitic policies of the Fascists, many of them were prepared to ignore the issue and in 1939 one of them even issued a Lenten Pastoral on the virtue of prudence. A few of them, however, did protest including some supporters of the régime like the Patriarch of Venice, the Archbishops of Milan and Bologna, who were outspoken in their condemnation of racialism. Cardinal Schuster attacked the 'heresy born in Germany and now insinuating itself almost everywhere' which, 'not only attacks the supernatural foundations of the Catholic Church, but by materializing in human blood the spiritual concepts of individual, nation and fatherland, refuses to humanity all spiritual values, and thus constitutes an international danger not less serious than Bolshevism'. The Cardinal concluded by declaring that there was no room for racial divisions within the Christian Church on the grounds that 'Christ cannot be divided into fragments'. Cardinal Nasalli Rocca of Bologna emphasized the brotherhood of all men in Christ and denounced 'exotic ideologies inspired by an exaggerated and exasperated nationalism'. Other Italian Catholics followed their lead. Leaflets were distributed claiming that 'Catholics must be philo-Semites', parochial and diocesan bulletins urged the faithful to be charitable to Jews and during 1938 there is evidence that many Jews were 'converted' and their certificates of baptism antedated in order that they might take advantage of a loophole in the anti-Semitic legislation.

However although official and responsible organs of opinion in the Church did not encourage racialism or anti-Semitism, too many Catholics, clergy as well as laity, were influenced by anti-Semitism, a fact that they became increasingly willing to reveal with the rise of Fascism and Nazism. In January 1939 a Franciscan friar, Agostino Gemelli, publicly referred to Jews as the 'deicide people' who 'because of their blood and religion, cannot form part of this magnificent country'. Gemelli, a brilliant experimental psychologist, was largely responsible for the establishment of the Catholic University of the Sacred Heart at Milan of which he was the first Rector. He was one of the outstanding Catholic figures in the intellectual life of Italy and became an uncritical supporter of Fascism. In his lectures and writings, Gemelli tried to identify Catholicism with *Italianità*. Students at the University were asked to give the Fascist salute. A branch of the Fascist university organization flourished there in spite of the fact that Fascist students had played a prominent part in attacks on Catholic students in 1931. It has even been said that many of the publications produced by the University Press might well have been issued by one of the Fascist organizations.

In the Pope's Christmas Allocution delivered only a few weeks before his death, Pius had referred to the 'grave anxieties and bitter sorrows' marring the joy with which he wished to celebrate the tenth anniversary of the signing of the Lateran Treaty. His protests against Fascist attacks on Catholic Action, the 'inhuman and therefore anti-Christian' policies of racialism, Fascist attempts to modify the terms of the Concordat, were obviously influencing the Pope's attitudes at this time. It was therefore widely expected that the address to be given to the Italian hierarchy on the anniversary would consist of a denunciation of the Fascists and their policies. Although Pius XI beseeched his doctors to keep him alive, he died before he could deliver his address and it was only published later by John XXIII. The address was a powerful appeal for peacè, a strong protest against the Italian Government and a stern warning against Fascism, the Duce and 'the insane presumption of the man who believes and declares that he is omniscient, when it is transparently clear that he knows not what is the Church, the pope, a bishop, that he knows not the bond of faith and charity that unites us in the love and service of Jesus, our King and Lord'.

Pope Pius XI

Chapter III

Pius XI and the Rise of the Dictators

Pius XI had been Archbishop of Milan when the Fascists were consolidating their strength and Mussolini had been in control of Italy for about two months when the Pope issued his first encyclical *Ubi Arcano Dei* in December 1922. This encyclical was a general survey of the results of the First World War and of the urgent need for reconciliation among the nations, a call to end class warfare and internal strife, and a reminder of Christian duties. The Pope called for a peace based on justice but a peace tempered with charity and he consistently urged peace on the nations, strongly condemning exaggerated patriotism and extreme nationalism.

In several important respects, Pius XI continued to work for peace along lines laid down by Benedict XV. Disregarding the usual precedents, the new Pope at least initially reappointed Cardinal Gasparri as Secretary of State which was an indication of his intention to continue and to forward the same policies as his predecessor. In an effort to deal with the economic breakdown caused in part by the terms of the peace treaties, the Great Powers called a conference at Genoa in 1922 to which for the first time both Germany and Russia were invited to participate on equal terms. On the eve of this conference the Pope sent a public letter to the Archbishop of Genoa urging the need for reciprocal concessions and for disarmament: 'If, according to the fine motto of the Red Cross, *Inter Arma Caritas*, Christian charity should rule even during the clash of arms, this should be still more true when once arms are laid down and peace treaties signed, all the more so because international hatreds, the sad legacy of the war, work to the injury even of the victors and prepare a future fraught with fear for all. It must never be forgotten that the best guarantee of peace is not a forest of bayonets but mutual confidence and friendship'.

The Pope sent a second letter a few weeks later emphasizing that 'true peace consists primarily in reconciliation of spirit and not merely in a cessation of hostilities'.

A German newspaper once described Pius XI as 'the most German pope in history' because of his support for the legitimate aspirations of Germany in the period after the First World War. The Pope believed that Germany was incapable of paying the immense financial indemnities imposed by the Allies and expressed the opinion that Poland was attempting to absorb too many Germans as well as his disapproval of the French occupation of the Ruhr. The Pope also worked for reconciliation between France and Germany. At the New Year receptions in 1927 the Nuncios in both Paris and Berlin made almost identical speeches when delivering the greetings of the diplomatic corps to the French and German Presidents. The Nuncio in Paris, Maglione, had been Pope Benedict's Nuncio in Switzerland during the First World War. Pacelli had been Nuncio in Berlin since his promotion from the legation at Munich where he had served under Benedict XV. The two Cardinals expressed the particular gratification of the Holy See at Briand's support for the admission of Germany to the League of Nations. *Le Temps* commented: 'The words of Mgr Maglione, therefore, contain an approval, without any sort of reservation, of the policy of reconciliation, which M. Briand has inaugurated at Locarno, and which he has pursued at Geneva'.

Pius XI warmly congratulated the authors of the reconciliation at Locarno and publicly approved of the attempt to 'outlaw' war in the Briand–Kellogg Pact of 1928. In an effort to strengthen the League of Nations and to preserve peace and security should the League fail, the Powers signed a series of separate and supplementary agreements. In 1921 France formed an alliance with Poland and then with Czechoslovakia, Yugoslavia and Rumania. As a result of the 'spirit of Locarno' in 1925 Germany guaranteed the frontiers of France and Belgium, and promised to alter her frontiers with Poland and Czechoslovakia only after mutual agreement or arbitration. Britain guaranteed the frontiers between France and Germany and between Germany and Belgium. The United States and France took the initiative in formulating the Briand–Kellogg Pact. The signatories renounced war as an instrument of national policy and the Pact was in fact signed by some sixty nations, most of the nations in the world.

The Pope also encouraged the French Government to come to an understanding with Italy, tried to restrain Turkey's attack on Greece, and supported China against Japanese aggression when the League of Nations refused to give military support to China and proved unable to guarantee international security. He again appealed for peace at the time of the Munich crisis and one of his last audiences just before he died was a long meeting with Chamberlain and Halifax when they visited Rome in an effort to promote friendship between Britain and Italy. After the Munich settlement the *Osservatore Romano* declared that the Prime Minister of England had been revealed as a statesman of the first rank and that the world would now know to whom it owed its salvation. Privately, however, Pius XI described Munich as a somersault rather than a capitulation and he reminded Chamberlain that any 'peace' was a mockery which ignored the persecution taking place in Germany.

However, the Pope's work for peace was threatened not only by the rise of political totalitarianism but by the economic situation at the time which was giving rise to, what he called, an economic nationalism that was also dividing the nations. *Quadragesimo Anno* was published in May 1931 forty years after the publication of Leo XIII's encyclical *Rerum Novarum*. *Quadragesimo Anno* first listed the beneficial results of *Rerum Novarum* and underlined the principles of Catholic social action. Pius XI then expanded and developed the social teaching of Leo XIII and tried to bring it up to date. Criticisms of socialism were accompanied with warnings against the excesses of capitalism and for the first time a Pope recommended the redistribution of national production, profit sharing and co-partnership of workers in industry. Pius XI proved more willing than his predecessor to contemplate the fundamental changes in the social and economic order, to dissociate himself from economic liberalism and to denounce contemporary abuses, particularly the unfair distribution of wealth and the exploitation of labour, the increasing concentration of power and the economic domination of the few: 'This accumulation of power, the characteristic note of the modern economic order, is a natural result of unlimited free competition, which permits the survival of those only who are the strongest – which often means those who fight most relentlessly, who pay less heed to the dictates of conscience'. Concentration of power led to internal conflicts as well as conflicts between nations, to 'economic nationalism or even economic imperialism'.

As the economic situation throughout the world became increasingly dangerous the Pope earnestly appealed to Catholics to be generous in supporting those who were suffering from unemployment and deprivation. In October 1931 he returned again to the economic depression in an encyclical *Nova impedit* in which he deplored the rising unemployment and increasing human misery. He called for the relief of suffering, particularly the sufferings of children, and expressed his fears at the race to rearm. In May of the following year, as the economic depression worsened, the Pope published *Caritate Christi compulsi* condemning the causes of the depression: human envy and greed, economic, political and national imperialism, irreligious propaganda and militant atheism, and the divorce of morals and religion. He appealed for charity at a time when the enemies of nations and of society were exploiting in their own interests the sufferings caused by economic distress: '. . . if selfishness abuses this love of country and exaggerates this sentiment of nationalism, and insinuates itself into the relations between one people and another, there is no excess which will not seem to be justified. What would be condemned by everyone in private relations is now regarded as lawful and praiseworthy if it is done in the name of exaggerated nationalism. In place of the great law of charity and human brotherhood, which embraces and unites in one family all nations and peoples with one Father who is in heaven, there enters hatred, driving all to destruction. In public affairs those sacred principles which guide all social intercourse are trampled upon; the solid functions of right and honesty, on which the State should rest, are undermined; polluted and destroyed are the sources of those ancient traditions which were based on faith in God and fidelity to His law, and which secured the true progress of nations'.

Pius XI hoped to win support for his social and economic policies as well as to contribute towards the sanctification of family life, the education of the young and the religious instruction of the masses through Catholic Action. One of the most striking features of the development of Catholicism during the pontificates of Pius XI and Pius XII was an increasing recognition of the role of the laity in the missionary and pastoral life of the Church. Originally the laity worked in close collaboration with and were even controlled by the clergy and the bishops. But as time went on it was increasingly recognized that the role of the laity in the Church was unique and complementary rather than subordinate to that of the clergy.

Throughout his pontificate Pius XI encouraged the work of Catholic Action which he defined as 'the organized participation of the laity in the hierarchical apostolate of the Church, transcending party politics, for the establishment of Christ's reign throughout the world'. It was 'nothing less than the apostolate of the faithful, who, under the guidance of the bishops, place themselves at the service of the Church and help her to carry out her pastoral ministry to the full'. Early in his pontificate, the Pope decided to give his full support and encouragement to the development of Catholic Action as part of a general programme of reconstruction after the World War and as a means of organizing Catholics in defence of their religious and ecclesiastical interests. Catholic Action was to embrace all forms of activity – social, pastoral, educational, not political – and always worked under clerical and episcopal control. In his encyclicals the Pope spoke enthusiastically of these new apostolic initiatives. But Pius XI was not simply content to encourage Catholic Action; he tried to integrate these lay movements within the constitutional administration of the Church.

Pius XI also gave his personal support to the work of Joseph Cardijn, the Belgian priest who founded the Young Christian Workers. The Pope described this particular organization as 'a perfect example' of Catholic Action or a form of 'specialized Catholic Action'. Two of the first members of the YCW died in the concentration camp at Dachau during the Second

World War. Incidentally the Pope seems to have had a special sympathy for the working classes. When Bishop Achille Liénart of Lille gave a donation to a strike fund, he was bitterly attacked by right-wing newspapers as 'The Red Bishop' and delated to Rome as a Marxist. Pius XI responded by making Liénart a Cardinal.

In due course the impact of Catholic Action was felt in every area of social and economic activity, in education, communications and religious observance, while the development of Catholic Action also gave a great impetus to the Liturgical Movement and the intelligent participation of the laity in the public worship of the Church. In countries like Italy or Spain Catholic Action tended to be highly centralized and national, and closely dependent on the ecclesiastical authorities. In France and Belgium greater emphasis was laid on social or professional groups. In the Netherlands Catholic Action was applied to a loosely federated assortment of organizations. In Germany and the English-speaking world the term Catholic Action was rarely used but many lay organizations developed such as the Bonifatiusverein or the Legion of Mary.

Although Catholic Action deliberately avoided party politics and political issues, it was inevitable that it should have come into conflict with totalitarian régimes. Pius XI himself denounced the extension of State control over personal and religious rights in several of his encyclicals such as *Divini Illius Magistri* on Christian education and *Casti Connubii* on family life in which he also denounced the exploitation of sex, abortion and divorce, sterilization and contraception. The Pope made himself familiar with the mass media and the art of communication. He devoted more time to public audiences than any of his predecessors and celebrated no less than three jubilee years. He protested against attacks on the Church and Catholic Action over the Vatican Radio – which he himself had established – and in publications which were sometimes sent by air to be published in other Catholic countries. He issued 136 official documents including thirty encyclicals during his pontificate. The first, issued within a month of his accession, extended to fifteen days the period before the election of a Pope and the last was to urge the restoration of family life and the establishment of the social apostolate by Catholics in the Philippines.

In spite of the economic dislocation which followed the First World War, Benedict XV and Pius XI were very successful in rebuilding many of the pastoral and social organizations of the Church which would later be destroyed by the totalitarian forces of left and right in Germany and Austria, Italy and Spain, Mexico and Russia. Pius XI himself established 128 residential sees, 116 apostolic vicariates, 113 apostolic prefectures, 24 abbeys and prelatures. He canonized some 33 saints and beatified another

500. He strengthened various Vatican departments and established new pontifical commissions, institutes, colleges and schools. The development of Catholic Action had been very marked in Slovakia, Hungary and Poland, while Austria was described by a contemporary commentator as 'the most completely Catholic in its constitution and its public life'. As the pattern of events unfolded, Pius XI was undoubtedly justified in feeling that much of his work as Pope was under threat from Spain in the West to Russia in the East as well as in Latin America with the suppression of Catholic organizations, the confiscation of ecclesiastical property and the closing of monasteries, schoois and colleges by totalitarian régimes.

In an effort to define relations between Church and State in the modern world and to safeguard the rights of the Church so that it might be able to oppose effectively those forces hostile to Christianity, Pius XI continued Benedict XV's policy of making agreements or signing concordats with different secular régimes. One of the most surprising agreements was that made with Czechoslovakia where the Government of the new republic was considered to be extremely secularist and even hostile to the Church but concordats were also signed with Austria, Italy and Germany, Bavaria, Baden and Prussia, Poland and Yugoslavia, Latvia and Lithuania. The terms of these concordats varied according to the different religious and political situations and the relations already existing between Church and State. But in all cases an attempt was made to define the legal status of the Church and to secure freedom of worship, to safeguard papal rights over the appointment of bishops and their freedom to communicate with Rome, to obtain the legal recognition of religious orders and ecclesiastical property, and the freedom of Catholic education and Catholic Action. The Church was occasionally forced to make concessions especially in the case of marriage laws and the political activities of Catholics but if Pius XI could secure what he regarded as essential, he was quite prepared to compromise over the political activities and loyalties of priests. These agreements again illustrate how the authority of the Holy See was increasingly recognized by more and more secular governments.

Benedict XV and Pius XI clearly differed from Pius X in their attitudes towards the Church in France. The two later popes consistently pursued Leo XIII's policy of *ralliement* and, in spite of the opposition of some of the French bishops, many of whom had been appointed by Pius X and supported his policies, Pius XI solemnly approved of the *associations cultuelles* in his encyclical, *Maximam Gravissimamque*, published in June 1924. During elections held in the same year the Pope prevented the publication of a pastoral letter urging French Catholics to vote for opponents of secularism and in 1925 he dissociated himself and the Church from a violent document issued by the French hierarchy in opposition to the so-called secular laws.

The influence of writers like Joseph de Maistre, the significance of events like the Dreyfus Affair, Catholic suspicions of 'the monstrous Judeo–Masonic régime', the failure of Leo XIII's *ralliement* followed by the disestablishment of the French Church and the refusal of Pius X to accept the *associations cultuelles*, had all contributed to the formation of the political and theological attitudes of many French Catholics. These conservative and intransigent Catholics found themselves uniting with members of *Action Française* – the name of a political movement as well as its newspaper – against their common enemies, Liberals and Republicans, Freemasons and Jews, Protestants and Modernists. Charles Maurras, for his part, defended the interests of the Pope and the Church against anti-clerical politicians, he opposed the conscription of priests and seminarians during the Great War, he fought for the freedom of Catholic education and for the restoration of diplomatic relations with the Vatican. Maurras succeeded in identifying his own programme and aims with those of the Church at least in the minds of those Catholics who supported him. These tended to be aristocratic monarchists and conservative nationalists, university students and seminarians, and a number of prominent 'integrists' and opponents of 'Modernism' who had survived the reign of Benedict XV. But these Catholics ignored the fact that Maurras regarded Catholicism as 'Christianity divested of its poisonous content by its Roman-heathen form' and that his supporters put nationalism above everything else, even above those religious and moral principles that must govern any Christian order.

The policies of *Action Française* were not only opposed to the claims of Christianity but to the policies being advocated by the Holy See. Maurras condemned democratic republicanism on the grounds that it had, by its foreign policy, left France at the mercy of Germany and allowed the French Government to fall into the hands of Freemasons and Protestants, 'foreigners' and Jews.

Action Française was totally committed to the demand for reprisals and completely opposed to a restoration of the European order on the basis of reconciliation. Pius XI, who had already alienated French opinion by his criticisms of the treaties of Versailles, became increasingly annoyed by the bellicose nationalism of *Action Française* and its demands for a strict interpretation and application of those treaties. In short *Action Française* was not only endangering the position of the Church in France by opposing any attempt to secure a *ralliement* but was also threatening the moves made by the Holy See in favour of reconciliation and peace throughout the world.

Action Française was resisted by more liberal Catholics and Christian Democrats. In 1910 Laberthonnière published a book which showed that the views of *Action Française* were scarcely compatible with Christianity and Catholicism. In the same year Bishop Péchenard of Soissons congratulated another priest who had publicly criticized Maurras: '. . . how grateful I am to you for your courageous exposure of that laboratory of abominable doctrines: atheism, materialism, contempt of our holy religion, outrage of Jesus Christ, insult to all the Christian virtues, glorification of all concupiscence, of sensuality, of ambition, pride, the worship of force, the oppression of all that is weak. And to say that they contemplate building a political system on these negations and these ruins, and wish to force us to bow down before such monstrosities! How blind and misled are those Catholics – and priests above all – who do not hesitate to collaborate with these apostles of doctrinal negation and of oppression!'

At the end of 1912 the same bishop spoke 'very strongly on the matter' to Merry del Val and other Cardinals during his *ad limina* visit to Rome. In the following year Archbishop Mignot of Albi referred to: '. . . the scandalous theories of . . . atheist Catholics. . . . We cannot condemn too severely . . . the return of paganism. . . . It is surprising that competent theologians, alert to the least error of doctrine, or, at any rate, what they consider as such, should not perceive these cleverly dissimulated blasphemies, and that they should give – by their silence at least – the benefit of the personal sympathy, frequently deserved as it is, that they feel for the writers'.

Maurras' writings had in fact been delated to the Roman authorities as early as 1910 or 1911 and at least six bishops took action including one who sent a memorandum to Rome seeking the condemnation of *Action Française*. However Pius X felt some sympathy for the political attitudes of Maurras whom he described as a 'defender of the Church and the Holy See' and the Pope was also grateful for his help in the campaign against 'Modernism'. When several of Maurras' works were put on the Index in 1914 the Pope decided that they were *damnabilis*, *non damnandus* and that the decree should not be published. On the accession of Benedict XV, Archbishop Mignot warned the new Secretary of State against 'the danger to morals and faith of an association whose theorists are agnostic and anti-Christian'. Benedict re-examined the question in 1915 but, since he was already regarded by the French as too sympathetic to the Germans, he decided that 'with the war still on, political passions would prevent any such act by the Holy See from being fairly judged'. In the words of the decree of the Holy Office which was finally published at the beginning of 1927: 'The Sovereign Pontiff (Benedict XV of happy memory) questioned the Father Secretary concerning the books of Charles Maurras, and the periodical the *Action Française*. The Father Secretary reported in detail to His Holiness all that the Sacred Congregation had done in the matter, and how His predecessor Pius X, of saintly memory, had ratified and approved the proscription decreed by the Most Eminent Fathers, but had deferred to another and more propitious time the publication of the decree. Having heard this, His Holiness declared that the time had not yet come, for, as the War still continued, political passions would prevent the formation of a just judgment upon the action of the Holy See'.

The actual decision to censure the movement was taken during 1925 and 1926 but first the Pope had to overcome several difficulties. In the first place to make a distinction between *damnabilis* and *damnandus* and to withhold a condemnation on political or pragmatic grounds could well imply that any future condemnation was also simply a matter of policy. In the opinion of at least one recent historian the action of Pius X not only made it more difficult for the Church to dissociate itself from *Action Française* but also explains why the condemnation took place in stages and why the final formulation was based on events which happened during the actual process.

Furthermore, after the Modernist crisis, French bishops and superiors tended to reflect the intransigence of Pius X and Merry del Val who had been largely responsible for appointing many of them. The Consistorial Congregation, which dealt with French episcopal nominations, was at the time strongly influenced by integrist Cardinals and especially its Secretary, Cardinal de Lai, who was an outspoken defender of *Action Française*. In 1925 Pius XI transferred the nomination of bishops to the Congregation of Extraordinary Affairs which meant in effect the Secretariat of State. In the following year Maglione was sent to Paris with the task of renewing the French episcopate and recommending candidates who were free from conservative political ties, committed to social reform and determined to put into effect the policies of Pius XI.

Finally the difficulties of the Pope were increased by the strength and extent of support that *Action Française* enjoyed among French Catholics and particularly among the youth of France. It was estimated that about a quarter of the students in the French Seminary in Rome were members of *Action Française* and even higher proportions in some of the diocesan seminaries. However when it was reported that the influence of Maurras was extending into Belgium and Cardinal Mercier warned the Pope that Belgian youths were supporting *Action Française*, Pius XI decided to act. Incidentally, it is revealing that when the Pope came to re-examine the question it is said that he found the papers missing. It is also reported that when he decided to sign the decree originally presented to Pius X in 1914, the document was apparently 'mislaid' in the archives of the Holy Office. Pius XI simply announced that unless it was found, all the superiors in the Supreme Congregation would be sacked. The document was immediately produced.

Encouraged by the Vatican, Cardinal Paulin Pierre Andrieu of Bordeaux, who had formerly sympathized with and even supported the movement, began to criticize *Action Française* strongly and in detail. On 27 August 1926 he published a letter in answer 'to a question asked by a group of young Catholics on the subject of the *Action Française*': 'They [the directors of the *Action Française*] repudiate all the dogmas which it [the Church] teaches. It teaches the existence of God, which they deny because they are Atheists. It teaches the divinity of Jesus Christ, which they deny, for they are anti-Christian. It teaches that it was founded by Christ, God and man, and they deny its divine institution, for they are anti-Catholic, notwithstanding the sometimes most eloquent praises which they give to the Church, for reasons which are not perhaps altogether disinterested . . . Being Catholics for their own ends and not by conviction, the directors of the *Action Française* make use of the Church, or at least hope to make use of it, but they do not serve it, since they repudiate the divine teaching, which it is its mission to spread. . . . the directors of the *Action Française*, and in particular their chief, the one whom they call their Master, have had to take refuge in amorality. They have wiped out the distinction between good and evil. . . . Atheism, agnosticism, antichristianism, anticatholicism, amoralism of the individual and of society, the necessity for the maintenance of order in spite of these subversive negations, the restoration of paganism with all its injustices and all its violence; that, my dear friends, is what the directors of the *Action Française* teach to their disciples'. The document itself was dated 'on the feast of St Louis, King of France, who called himself the sergeant of Christ, and who always fulfilled so well the duties inherent in that glorious title'.

In September 1926 the Pope expressed his approval of and agreement with the line which the Cardinal had taken in a personal letter to Andrieu in which he made it quite clear that Catholics could not follow the leaders of *Action Française* in matters of faith and morals: 'Your Eminence enumerates and condemns rightly (in publications which are not only of remote date) evidence of a new system of religion, of morals and of society; for instance concerning the nature of God, of the Incarnation, of the Church, and in general of Catholic dogma and morality, particularly in their necessary relations to politics, which is logically subordinate to moral law. In these evidences there are substantial traces of a revival of paganism, to which naturalism is akin; which these writers have, in Our belief, unconsciously absorbed, like so many of their contemporaries, in the public teaching of those modern and laic schools that poison our young people, which they themselves often attack with so much vigour'.

Shortly before the signing of the formal and public condemnation of Maurras, the Pope gave an address to the Consistory of Cardinals on 20 December in which he declared: '. . . in no case is it permitted to Catholics to be connected with the activities and, in any way, with the school of those who place the interests of parties above religion, and seek to make the latter subservient to the former. Nor is it permissible to expose one's self or others, and especially the young, to influences or teaching which constitute a danger to the integrity of faith and morals for the young and to their Catholic education . . . it is not permissible for Catholics to support, or favour, or read newspapers directed by men whose writings, in departing from our dogmas and our moral teaching, cannot escape reprobation, and . . . offer to their readers, especially to adolescents and to young people, many occasions of spiritual disaster'.

Consequently the Pope decided: 'that it had become opportune to publish and promulgate the decree of Pope Pius X, and has decided to promulgate it effectively with the date prescribed by his predecessor. . . . His Holiness has confirmed the condemnation decreed by his predecessor, and has extended it to include the said daily newspaper [*Action Française*], while it remains such as it is at present'.

It was this last prohibition – 'in the form in which it is published today' – and not the condemnation of Pius X that was later removed by Pius XII in 1939. The Holy Office therefore published Pius X's decree and put seven of Maurras' books as well as his newspaper on the Index. At the beginning of March in the following year all priests who absolved readers or supporters of *Action Française* were deprived of their faculties to hear confessions, seminarians who read or supported the newspaper were dismissed, the Catholic laity who were guilty of these offences were to be regarded as public sinners and all the French bishops were required to sign a letter approving of the condemnation.

Andrieu's letter and the papal condemnation inevitably occasioned bitter controversies and divisions among French Catholics. In the first place the condemnation seemed so sudden and unexpected, especially in view of the praises previously lavished on the movement by so many ecclesiastical authorities. Catholic supporters of *Action Française* also felt that they had been misunderstood and were being unjustly treated. The Cardinal was in fact undoubtedly justified in condemning the paganism and positivism of Maurras. But he had incorporated passages taken from an earlier Belgian attack on Maurras and his letter included some half-truths and inaccuracies that could not be substantiated. Furthermore the Pope himself seemed to have endorsed one of the Cardinal's accusations that he would later have to withdraw.

The supporters of *Action Française* included members of the French hierarchy. More than half of the French archbishops made no secret of their sympathies for the organization while two French Cardinals who gave only a qualified support to the position of the Pope found their submissions rejected as unsatisfactory by *Osservatore Romano*. In October and November six archbishops and bishops agreed to appoint chaplains in their diocese to groups of supporters of *Action Française* and even congratulated these groups for having asked for them. The Catholic press in France only slowly and reluctantly followed the lead of the Pope and priests who continued to sympathize with *Action Française* had to be removed from influential positions as professors, teachers and chaplains. The Holy See was forced to ask for the resignation of Bishop Marty of Montauban and Père Le Floch, superior of the French Seminary in Rome, who was connected with the mysterious disappearance of the file on Maurras. Cardinal Louis Billot, one of the leading theologians of the day and the Cardinal who had placed the tiara on the Pope's head during his coronation, sent a note of sympathy to the editors of *Action Française*. When this note was published, the Pope demanded Billot's resignation.

One of the leading lay supporters of *Action Française*, Admiral Schwerer, firmly declared: 'The *Action Française* is not a religious organization. It is a political association whose object is to save France, to rescue her from an abject system which is disgracing and destroying her. To achieve that end, it has united believers and unbelievers. But the unbelievers among us are those who respect and defend the Church . . . I claim to be a good Catholic, but I am also a good Frenchman. In serving the *Action Française* I am serving France; to cease serving the *Action Française* would, in my eyes, be to desert my country. No one in the world has the power or the right to put my religious faith in conflict with my patriotic faith. In serving the *Action Française*, I believed that I was serving my religion as well, inasmuch as I was fighting against men who are at once enemies of France and of religion . . . as a son of France, I have no right to desert the *Action Française*, which is alone capable of saving my mother'.

The editorial directors of *Action Française* replied to the Pope's address to the Cardinals with a long provocative article entitled '*Non Possumus*': '. . . the reigning Pope is not immune from human error in matters of politics, and if the Church has the promise of eternal life, Churchmen, as all history shows, can be badly informed, can let themselves be overcome by dishonest influences, and commit themselves to injurious enterprises. . . . In the situation in which France now stands, the act of killing the *Action Française* is not purely, nor even principally, a religious act; it is primarily a political act, an act which would bring grave injury to France, it would injure her mortally. To favour that act would be to betray her. We will not be traitors. . . . We cannot cease to be good Catholics in refusing, but were we to obey we would cease to be good Frenchmen. . . . We will not betray our country. *Non possumus* . . . when called upon to choose between the most important of conventions and the most urgent of duties, they cannot hesitate. *Non possumus*'.

After the condemnation, *Action Française* became one of the most anti-clerical and anti-papal newspapers in France. The Pope himself was described as 'the liar' and bitter attacks were made on the 'ignoble work' of the *Diffamatore Romano*. The Papal Nuncio in France was also subjected to offensive personal attacks and was even accused of being a German spy. The newspaper carried reports of scandalous episodes in the history of the Church such as the execution of Joan of Arc or the activities of the Borgias, the condemnation of Galileo or the massacres of St Bartholomew's Day. *Action Française* maintained that it had been condemned solely for political reasons. The international policies of the Holy See were dominated by the influence of Germany and the Vatican was supporting German interests in Alsace and Belgium, Austria and Poland. Maglione's address to the President of the Republic was used as evidence that the Vatican was totally opposed to the best interests of France. Maurras, who consistently condemned 'that imbecile means towards peace which is disarmament', bitterly condemned Briand and the Nuncio, and accused the Vatican of attempting to dominate Europe by reviving the Holy Roman Empire. The *Osservatore Romano* was nicknamed *Osservatore Tedesco* and the devout Marc Sangnier, who publicly supported Briand's policy, was physically assaulted by young supporters of *Action Française*.

But *Action Française* was not in fact condemned simply for political reasons, though the condemnation had very important political as well as religious consequences. The struggle against *Action Française* was part of the Pope's campaign against theological integrism as well as political extremism. The condemnation enabled the Pope to overcome the resistance of the French hierarchy and helped to promote a second *ralliement* which ultimately would prove to be effective, if more limited in scope than that of Leo XIII. Had *Action Française* not been condemned, the decline of integrism and the emergence of new social and political movements such as

Die Frankreich-Reise des Kardinals

PACELLI

Giftküche
der Volksfront

GREUEL-
LÜGEN

ANTI-
NAZI

Honig

HUMANITÉ

Christenverfol-
gung in Deutschland

KOMMUNE

Zeichnung:

Schön ist sie ja nicht. Aber sie kann gut kochen!

Cardinal Pacelli with Mgr Kaas, Leader of the German Centre Party until 1933

Das Schwarze Korps of 22.7.1937 suggests collusion between French Communism and the Church in the person of Cardinal Pacelli the Young Christian Workers which were to prove so important for the Church in the future might still have taken place but would have developed much more slowly. As a group of priests working in Paris told the Pope in July 1927: 'It may be that among us certain priests have individual preferences for one form or another of political government. But we have always placed the interests of parties far below those of religion, and we were profoundly pained and distressed that we could not persuade the best of our flock among the working classes that the doctrines and the political methods of the leaders of the *Action Française* were not ours. We cannot hope that in this country of ours, where politics have created so many successive barriers between the working classes and the clergy, the bandages that have been tied round the eyes of our workers by the enemies of religion will fall completely away. But the relief which Your Holiness has brought fills us with a glad hope for the future, and gives us new courage to fight among the vast working-class population against false social doctrines and ignorance of religion'.

In July 1939 the Holy Office rescinded the ban on the newspaper, *Action Française*, after the death of Pius XI but as a result of measures initiated by him. The Holy See published a letter in which the editors expressed their 'very sincere sorrow' and in which they admitted that they had been 'insulting and even unjust' in the controversies associated with the condemnation. The Catholics involved repudiated anything in their writings that was false and completely rejected all theories and precepts contrary to the teachings of the Church. In short and in the words of a recent historian, by the condemnation of *Action Française*, the Church had: 'proved itself to be the only established and conservative power capable of breaking with its neo-conservative friends on its own initiative, and of freeing itself from the dangerous parasitic plants which had grown up in its shade and from its own roots'.

Several historians have argued that Pius XI's three years in Poland coloured his whole outlook on the problems and the future of the Church and had a decisive influence on his later pontificate. It was at this time that the future Pope first encountered a modern dictator in the person of Marshal Pilsudski, the romantic, idealistic and Socialist leader of Poland. Ratti had been sent to Warsaw to help in the reconstruction of the Polish Church and to reunite the separate episcopates which had been divided during the earlier partition of Poland. He was also concerned to secure information about the 125,000 Polish and Lithuanian Catholics who had been deported by the Russians to Siberia.

Shortly after Ratti's arrival, Poland regained its independence and Pilsudski was elected head of the new State and supreme commander of the armed forces. The State was recognized by the Holy See at the end of March 1919 and Ratti was appointed to be the first Papal Nuncio in Poland for over 150 years. He now became responsible for establishing friendly relations with the new Government and working out the details of a Concordat. In the event Ratti proved to be wise and prudent in dealing with a Government which was far less Catholic than its people. He moderated the religious claims of the Polish bishops and built up a personal friendship with Pilsudski which lasted until the death of the Marshal. The Government recognized the unconditional primacy of Catholicism and engaged in negotiations for a Concordat exclusively with the Roman authorities which were already far advanced by the time that Ratti returned to Italy.

Pilsudski hoped to unite Lithuanians and Ukrainians, White Ruthenes and Poles in a confederation against Russia. Ratti himself seems to have given his support to this scheme which would have reduced the local authority of the Orthodox Patriarch as well as the political influence of Moscow. However in the summer of 1920 the Red Armies invaded Poland and brought an end to the hopes of the Marshal and the Nuncio. When the diplomatic corps left Warsaw only the American Ambassador and the Papal Nuncio remained at their posts. Many Poles paid tribute to the courage and confidence of Ratti during the Bolshevik siege of Warsaw and when the Russians were finally driven away the Nuncio was overwhelmed with tokens of affection and gratitude.

However, far more significant was the fact that Ratti had seen with his own eyes the Russian armies which might yet sweep into Europe. He could not be unconscious of the fact that the armistice between the two nations had left three and a half million Latin Catholics at the mercy of the Russians. As Nuncio he was responsible for large parts of eastern Europe and for gaining a specialized knowledge of Russian affairs. He would inevitably have been told of the bishops and thousands of priests who had been executed by the Communists and of the 'Anti-God Museums' established in Russia. It was therefore hardly surprising that the new Pope should have become dramatically aware of the threat that the Soviet system posed to the nations of Western Europe as well as to the future of the Catholic Church.

But perhaps those writers who have accused Pius XI of being unduly influenced by his experiences in Poland and of exaggerating the threat of Bolshevism have in effect over-simplified the position. It might be more true to say that, at least originally, Achille Ratti regarded the forces of democracy as too weak and too indifferent to the issues involved to be able to defend Christian civilization against the threat of Communism. Consequently he mistakenly turned to another form of authoritarian government in the hope of finding a more effective means of resistance and in spite of his awareness of the dangers of totalitarian régimes. It was only later in his pontificate that he began to appreciate that all forms of totalitarianism – Communism, Nazism or Fascism – always endangered those Christian values which might in the event be better protected by the parliamentary democracies. The Pope was to learn by bitter experience that totalitarian Governments claiming to control the religious as well as the secular lives of their peoples were far more dangerous to Christianity and to Catholicism than the most 'liberal', 'secular' or 'indifferent' democracies. Furthermore if the Church under Pius XI was concerned to resist the growing influence of Communism, it also attempted to resist the new fanatical nationalism which was spreading throughout the countries of Europe, but particularly in Germany and Italy. It was surely no mere coincidence that Pius XI's encyclicals *Mit brennender Sorge, Divini Redemptoris* and *Nos es muy* should have appeared almost simultaneously, within the same calendar month and almost within days of each other.

The condemnation of atheistic Communism in *Divini Redemptoris* has often been contrasted with the attack on Nazism in *Mit brennender Sorge* on the grounds that the first encyclical was an absolute condemnation and the latter a diplomatic protest. It is of course true that in one case the Holy See was protesting against the repeated breaking of an agreement by a régime with which it was in diplomatic contact and that in the other the Pope was protesting against an ideological system. But such criticisms fail to do justice to the force of *Mit brennender Sorge* and seriously underestimate the significance of the attacks on totalitarianism in *Divini Redemptoris*. The condemnation of Communism, which added little or nothing to the existing teaching of the Church, should surely be seen in the light of Pius XI's growing hostility to totalitarian régimes whilst the juxtaposition of the two encyclicals merely emphasizes the growing similarity between the two régimes and the common threat which they posed to Christianity and the Church. Furthermore the condemnation of Communism had been preceded by the anti-religious campaign in Russia, the persecution of the Church by Marxists in Mexico, the spread of Communism in the Far East, the infiltration of Communists into positions of political influence in Europe and the outbreak of civil war in Spain which in turn threatened the whole of Europe and where ten bishops and thousands of priests had already been killed. These events, coupled with the fact that the philosophy of Communism was more carefully thought out than that of Nazism, would seem to provide sufficient explanation of any differences between the two encyclicals.

The term 'totalitarian' is said to have been coined by Mussolini to describe the total absorption of all authority by the civil power. Totalitarianism was associated with the militaristic and aggressive claims of nationalism in the twentieth century to such an extent that Thorstein Veblen declared, 'Born in iniquity and conceived in sin, the spirit of nationalism has never ceased to bend human institutions to the service of dissension and distress'. Pius XI opposed totalitarian régimes on doctrinal as well as political grounds. He himself declared, 'Man, as a person, has rights which he holds from God and which must remain inviolate. Society is made for man, not man for society'. The encyclical, *Quas primas*, instituting the feast of Christ the King in 1925, should obviously be seen as part of his campaign against totalitarianism: 'States, princes and governments are rulers in their own domains, and Christ, whose kingdom is not of this world, has no wish that His Church should interfere therein; but she must remind them of the spiritual and moral principles to which their labours should conform, and declare repeatedly that they too are bound to promote the kingdom of God'.

In the following year the Pope repeated that: 'The current notion of a State is in formal contradiction with Catholic doctrine. A State which is its own end, a citizen wholly at the disposition of the State, a State to which everything must be related and which must absorb everything – no, that is not Catholic'. Consequently in his encyclical on Communism ten years later, it is hardly surprising that he should have said: 'The community as well as the citizen is of divine origin, and each is adapted to the other; therefore neither citizen nor society can repudiate each other's obligations nor deny or reduce each other's rights. In their fundamentals these mutual relations of citizen and community have been established and regulated by God Himself; and therefore the arrogant claim of the Communists to substitute for the divine law, based upon the principles of truth and charity, a political programme inspired by hate and devised by the wit of man, is beyond all doubt a most unjust and iniquitous usurpation'.

The number of Roman Catholics in Russia was not very great but the Roman Catholic Church suffered the same persecution as the Orthodox Churches. Between 1918 and 1923 the Bolsheviks indulged in a crude and largely unsuccessful attempt to destroy religion. Thousands of priests, monks and nuns, lay men and women were sentenced to death or to starvation in Siberia. In 1923 a Catholic bishop, priests and laymen were arrested for engaging in 'counter-revolutionary activity'. The Bishop was reprieved but his Vicar-General was tortured before being executed on Good Friday. There then followed a more general persecution of bishops, priests and laity who were sent to prisons or to concentration camps. Meanwhile the

'Union of Militant Godless' indulged in crude and offensive anti-religious propaganda and ecclesiastical property was confiscated or destroyed.

During the period of Lenin's New Economic Policy the Soviet Government avoided open persecution which might alienate foreign Governments and attempted to create a Church of its own, but this only lasted for about five years. Priests were not likely to be arrested but found it difficult to obtain board and lodging because they were not entitled to a ration card since they were not members of a trade union. Churches were not destroyed or turned into cinemas but simply closed on the grounds that there were not sufficient faithful to justify keeping them open. The more 'scientific' attack on religion began about 1928.

When it became clear that it was impossible to come to an agreement with the Soviet Government and that persecution in Russia was continuing, the Pope issued an open letter in 1930. He protested against 'the horrible and sacrilegious outrages being perpetrated against the Catholic Church in Russia', and against the murders of priests, the moral blackmail to which workers were subjected, the indoctrination and moral corruption of children. The Russians retaliated by accusing the Pope of plotting a Holy War with Alexander Kerensky and Wall Street bankers. The Pope's attack had an immediate effect throughout the Catholic world and on many of those countries that had not yet established diplomatic relations with the Soviet Union. However, his words were largely ignored by those Governments that had already sent representatives to Russia.

At the same time as the Revolution broke out in Russia, Catholics in Mexico were being subjected to the persecution of a Marxist or Communist régime that had been able to take advantage of the unstable political conditions, the social divisions and the secularist and anti-clerical forces which already existed in that country. Even before the Communists came to power, priests and religious had been imprisoned, tortured and expelled, nuns had been raped and consecrated hosts had been fed to animals. When the Communists came to power in 1917 they passed a constitution which subordinated Church to State and confiscated all ecclesiastical property. Religious orders were suppressed, foreign priests, including the Papal Nuncio, were expelled, and religious shrines and episcopal palaces were destroyed. After 1924 a deliberate attempt was made to eradicate Catholicism. Clergy and laity were expelled or executed, religious were excluded from schools and hospitals, and priests like Father Miguel Pro, who was eventually shot together with his brother, were forced to minister to their people in secret.

Catholic resistance eventually resulted in the open revolution of some 40,000 Cristeros who fought under the battle cry, '*Viva Cristo Rey!*' The extent of the fighting and the bloodshed is revealed in the number of casualties between January and May 1928: two generals, 324 officers and 2892 troops were killed fighting for the Government compared with forty-eight leaders and 6148 Cristeros. The fighting was also vicious. One young priest was nailed to a cross, soaked in petrol and burned alive. Another priest was bound hand and foot and then thrown on to a dung heap where he remained for three days before being killed. The Cristeros, for their part, murdered 'progressive' school-mistresses and were reported on several occasions to have killed the women and children who were travelling on the trains which they had attacked. However, the Government forces eventually triumphed. In 1935 all schools were ordered to teach the Principles of Socialism and those which did not were to be closed. Teachers were forbidden to profess any religious convictions and in selecting teachers preference was given to those candidates who were atheists.

When the Pope issued his encyclical on the persecution of the Church in Mexico, he asked various foreign countries to protest officially to the Mexican Government. But the European Powers did nothing largely because such action might have put their financial and commercial assets in Mexico at risk. Eventually the physical persecution ceased at least in part because of American pressure on the Mexican Government. But by then most of the ecclesiastical lands had been confiscated and the hold of the Church over the Mexican people had been broken. And in spite of efforts to establish a *modus vivendi*, it was only on the eve of the Second World War with the coming to power of a new generation of Mexican politicians that the Holy See was able to send an Apostolic Delegate and prepare for the reconstruction of the Mexican Church.

Consequently in *Divini Redemptoris*, Pius XI had every justification for claiming that: 'Wherever the Communists have gained power and control – We think with fatherly affection especially of the people of Russia and Mexico – they openly proclaim and pursue the policy of using every means to destroy utterly the foundations of the Christian religion and civilization, and to obliterate the memory of it entirely from the minds of men, especially of the young. Bishops and priests have been exiled, condemned to forced labour in the mines, shot, or otherwise cruelly put to death; while laity suspected of defending the cause of religion have been harassed, persecuted, brought to trial, and imprisoned. Even in countries, such as Our beloved Spain ... wherever possible, every church, every religious house, every trace of the Christian religion, even though connected with most precious monuments of civilization, has been beaten to the ground'.

In spite of the claims of contemporaries and Republican propaganda, neither the Church nor Pius XI can justly be accused of provoking a quarrel with left wing forces in Spain. By 1930 the military régime of Primo de Rivera, which had been supported by the Church, came to an end. This régime had been corrupt and was increasingly rejected by the rising middle classes. With the resignation of Rivera, the Monarchists were defenceless, King Alphonso XIII abdicated and in April 1931 a republic was proclaimed under the leadership of Niceto Alcala Zamora. The new Socialist Government abrogated the Concordat and separated Church and State, confiscated ecclesiastical property and expelled the Jesuits, secularized education and introduced divorce, abolished clerical privileges and prohibited religious processions; 'with these measures', declared the Prime Minister, 'Spain ceases to be Catholic'.

The adoption of anti-clerical provisions and total disestablishment in the Spanish Constitution of 1931 has been described by a recent historian of the Spanish Civil War as 'political folly'. Spanish Catholics had 'to oppose the very Constitution of the Republic if they wished to criticize its educational or religious policy'. Nevertheless the end of the Monarchy and the proclamation of the Republic were not originally opposed by Spanish Catholics. The Republic did not immediately enforce its anti-clerical measures and several bishops urged their people to accept the Republic as the lawful Government. Bishops and Catholic activists welcomed the new régime and the *Te Deum* was even sung in thanksgiving. The initial reaction of the Holy See was also restrained. The Papal Nuncio was instructed to establish good relations with the Republicans even before they came to power and this he had done. He was able to have several friendly conversations with representatives of the Government which at least originally showed its respect for the Church. When Cardinal Segura, the Archbishop of Toledo and Primate of Spain, an intransigent Monarchist, condemned the new Republic and was sent into exile, the Vatican authorities were clearly embarrassed. In due course he resigned as Primate and joined the Roman Curia.

The Socialist Government, however, proved incapable of controlling its more extreme and anarchist allies who plundered and destroyed churches, monasteries and convents all over Spain. In 1933 the Pope demanded religious freedom and protested against the violence to which the Church was being subjected in an encyclical, *Dilectissima Nobis*, but again did not attack the Spanish Republic. As political opinion began to polarize and left wing elements began to attack the Church and the clergy, Spanish Catholics rallied to the defence of their religion. The moderation of the Holy See encouraged the emergence of a new Catholic Republican Party led by Jose Maria Gil Robles. The Socialists lost their majority in elections held during 1933 and the new Catholic Party was the largest of the right wing parties which gained control. Negotiations were started with a view to signing a new Concordat and compensation was paid to those clergy who had lost their benefices as a result of the anti-clerical legislation passed in 1931.

The General Election in 1936 was expected to return the right wing parties to power but although these gained several hundred thousand more votes than their left wing opponents, there was a sizeable left wing majority in the Spanish Cortes. The Popular Front included Communists and Anarchists as well as Republicans and Socialists. A political amnesty released thousands more Anarchists as well as common criminals and within days there were further outbursts of violent anti-clericalism. The attacks on churches and religious houses, accompanied with murders and arson, began all over again. Priests and religious were physically attacked and five nuns were lynched. The murder of Calvo Sotelo, a monarchist deputy who had protested in the Cortes against the toleration extended to murderers and arsonists, precipitated the Civil War. A number of regiments in Spanish Morocco mutinied and General Francisco Franco flew there to raise the standard of the Falange. Once the rebellion spread to the Spanish mainland, garrisons throughout Spain rose in sympathy.

Shortly after the outbreak of the Civil War, the Pope received a number of Spanish refugees including bishops, priests and nuns as well as representatives of the laity. He bitterly condemned the persecution of the Church in Spain and gave his blessing: '. . . to all those who have assumed the difficult and dangerous task of defending and restoring the rights and honour of God and of religion, which is to say the rights and dignity of conscience, the prime condition and the most solid basis for all human and civil welfare'.

At the same time he warned the refugees against indulging in selfish interests or party feelings and went on to describe as 'Our children' those who had murdered priests, destroyed churches and proscribed religion: 'We cannot doubt for a single instant what We have to do: to love them, to love them with a special love born of pity and compassion; to love them and, since We cannot do more, to pray for them; to pray that they may come back to the father who awaits them and for whom their return would be an occasion of the truest joy'.

Nevertheless, although there could be little doubt where the Pope's personal sympathies lay, Pius XI adopted a cautious line diplomatically. In spite of the murders of priests and religious, the confiscation of ecclesiastical property and the expulsion of the Jesuits, the official attitude of the Vatican remained conciliatory. On three occasions during the Civil War, Franco unsuccessfully tried to gain the recognition of the Vatican for his régime. However, the Holy See did not immediately join the German or Italian Governments when these recognized the Nationalist Government but continued to maintain a formal, though very tenuous, contact with the administration in Madrid. The Holy See formally recognized the 'Burgos authorities' as the official Spanish Government at the end of August 1937, though a full Nuncio was not sent until the end of 1938.

The Pope could not be unconscious of the fact that with the coming of the Civil War, the Falange had begun to demonstrate a religious fervour that had not been obvious before in either their ideology or their policies. The attitudes of Falangists were unpleasantly reminiscent of those of the Nazis or the Fascists and the motives of all three groups were clearly something less than religious. The Holy See did not associate itself with the authoritarian aims of Franco or with the power politics of his German and Italian supporters. Pius XI did not welcome Franco's close relations with Mussolini and Hitler and he continuously insisted that his sole interest in the struggle was to free the Spanish Church from persecution. Furthermore he refused to condemn the Basques and even complained at the execution of some Basque priests by the Nationalists. But the Pope could hardly remain impassive in the face of the actual conduct of the war.

As left-wing attacks on the Church increased, the sympathies of the Vatican inevitably moved in favour of the Nationalists. Churches and religious buildings were savagely and deliberately destroyed and those which did survive were used as cinemas, store-houses or market-halls, arms dumps or gun emplacements. The number of people killed included twelve bishops, 5255 priests, 2492 monks, 283 nuns and 249 novices. One priest was forced to go through a form of marriage with his housekeeper before both of them were shot. A bishop was led out to his execution naked in front of nuns. The skulls of nuns were used as footballs. A priest was stripped and scourged, crowned with thorns and then shot. Of course the Nationalists were also guilty of murdering their opponents and their victims are said to have numbered about 40,000.

In Spain itself, the Nationalists needed the support of the Church. Wherever they gained power, they restored the freedom of the Church while the Falange insisted that Spanish institutions must be permeated with the spirit of Catholicism. Of course, some priests and monks supported the Republicans and many others criticized the murders committed by the Nationalists even while their fellow religious were being murdered by the Republicans. On the whole, however, as the War progressed Church leaders increasingly described it as a crusade and the Spanish Church, which considered itself threatened by the forces of international Communism as well as by Freemasons and Jews, remained closely allied with the Nationalist régime both during and after the War. Catholic opinion throughout the world tended to be divided. Many French Catholics like Jacques Maritain or François Mauriac were opposed to the forces of Franco as they had opposed the Italian invasion of Abyssinia. On the other hand, almost all the German and Italian Catholics favoured the Nationalists and they also enjoyed the support of the *Osservatore Romano*.

After the War the so-called 'clerical laws of 1938' restored ecclesiastical rights over education and the privileged position of the Church within the Spanish State, while the rights of other Christian Churches were strictly controlled. Franco issued his famous Charter patterned on Leo XIII's *Rerum Novarum* which became the basis of Falangist social and economic policy. But although Franco was able to use the Church in Spain as a result of his financial subsidies and his influence over episcopal elections, the extent of his control over the Church should not be exaggerated. The Vatican did not hesitate to condemn certain features of Falangist rule such as the education of youth on totalitarian lines. When Archbishop Segura returned as Archbishop of Seville he denounced the Falange as irreligious and deplored the influence of the Nazis. He refused to allow a plaque commemorating the founder of the Falange to be placed in his cathedral or the names of those who had fallen during the Civil War to be inscribed on the walls of parish churches. The Primate of Spain, Cardinal Goma of Toledo, was critical, like the Pope, of exaggerated nationalism and in 1942 another Spanish bishop attacked 'the creation of a new ruling class in Spain today which introduces racial laws which are manifestly and unequivocally anti-Christian'.

The first occasion on which the Vatican found itself in direct opposition to the interests of the Nazis was in the case of Czechoslovakia where relations between Church and State were complicated by nationalist as well as religious divisions, especially in view of the fact that almost all the three million Sudeten-Germans were Catholics. As early as 1931 the Papal Nuncio, acting on instructions from Rome, opposed one of the candidates for the bishopric of Leitmeritzer on the grounds that 'the Sudeten-Germans are proposing this candidate less on religious grounds than from a political and nationalist consideration'. The Papal Nuncio, with the full support of the Roman authorities, firmly criticized the Sudeten Catholics, suspended several of their priests and even accepted the resignation of the pro-Sudeten Archbishop of Prague. The German press accused the Pope of interfering in Czech internal affairs, of collaborating with the Russians and even meeting with Stalin himself in an effort to bring about the restoration of the Hapsburgs and the destruction of Czechoslovakia.

After the First World War the Catholic Church had made striking progress in Germany as Catholics rose to prominence in the world of culture and science, social work and especially in politics. The Centre Party, which had been established to defend Catholic interests in the nineteenth century, became the most important political party and played a leading part in the development of a Conservative Republicanism in Germany. During the Weimar Republic no Government could survive without the active support or at least the neutrality of the Centre Party. Catholics occupied about half of the positions in Weimar Cabinets and many of the officials in the *Reichskanzlei* were also Catholics. Three Catholics became Chancellors and a Catholic Priest, H. Brauns, was Minister of Labour in twelve successive Governments between 1920 and 1928.

National Socialism inevitably came into conflict with the Christian Churches from the very beginning; a fact that was on the whole recognized by the German Bishops. Nazism was not only totalitarian but racist and some of its earliest publications were essentially pagan and anti-Christian. In 1920 Bishop Clemens August Graf von Galen of Münster declared that the Nazi programme included ideas 'which no Catholic could accept without denying his faith upon cardinal points of belief' and the German bishops warned their people against Nazism on five occasions between 1920 and 1927. In 1929 the Bishop of Mainz declared that 'a Catholic cannot be a member of the National Socialist Party'. He instructed his clergy to refuse the sacraments to members of the Nazi Party and refused to allow Nazi Storm-troops to attend Church services in formation, in their uniforms or carrying their banners. Although Cardinal Pacelli insisted that the Bishop of Mainz was acting on his own initiative, the Bishops of Berlin and Westphalia also condemned the Nazis in pastoral letters just before the Party seized power. At the beginning of 1930 Cardinal Bertram of Breslau expressed his opposition to the National Socialist movement and infuriated its supporters by refusing a religious funeral for Peter Gemeinder, a devout Catholic and National Socialist Deputy. In February 1931 the Bavarian bishops again condemned National Socialism and even described it as heretical.

Hitler regarded the Catholic Church as a great institution that had served its purpose and outlived its usefulness. He intended to bring it to an end as painlessly and quietly as possible, using only those penal laws that were absolutely necessary. He believed that the institution would simply disappear if he once succeeded in withdrawing young people from its influence and restricted its various activities. However in the meantime, apart from the revealing sentiments expressed in *Mein Kampf*, Hitler was prepared to contain his hostility to the Church and the Centre Party until after he had come to power. In May 1931 he sent Hermann Göring to Rome for an audience with the Pope and the *Osservatore Romano* caused some wry amusement in Germany when it praised Göring for the firm measures he had taken against corruption and immorality. Nevertheless and in spite of Nazi propaganda to the contrary, Göring did not succeed in meeting with the Pope or even with the Secretary of State. He had to be content with meeting an Under-Secretary. The Pope himself was obviously waiting to see if the Nazis actually came to power before committing himself too openly.

When Hitler finally did come to power in January 1933 the Catholic Bishops had already repeatedly forbidden the faithful to support the Party and had condemned its pagan ideology on several occasions. As a result it would seem that before 1933 Protestants were more susceptible to Nazi propaganda than Roman Catholics, though some Catholics undoubtedly gave their support to the National Socialists. On the whole the Nazis were not immediately successful in winning Catholic voters from the Centre Party and, according to a recent historian, in the elections of 1930 and 1932: 'There is no doubt that the Catholic districts resisted the lure of National Socialism far better than the Protestant ones'. When the Nazis won over 100 seats in the elections of 1930, the Catholic Bishops responded by ordering their people to examine their consciences. In the elections held during July 1932, with the exception of Berlin, the ten voting districts most hostile to the Nazis were predominantly Catholic.

Immediately after Hitler became Chancellor, he delivered a speech on 1 February which was designed to remove the suspicions of Catholics. Hitler referred to Christianity as the 'basis of our collective morals' and to the family as the 'kernel of our people'. The State, he promised, would defend 'these religious foundations on which the strength of our nation is based'. The Chancellor repeated these same sentiments some three weeks later, though he also included a veiled threat against the Centre Party, and he wrote a personal letter of reassurance to Cardinal Bertram. Nevertheless, at least initially, the Bishops continued to support the Centre Party, which refused to recognize the full authority of the new Chancellor, and during the elections to ratify Hitler's *fait accompli*, the Bishops continued to recommend that German Catholics should vote for the Centre Party. Yet within a matter of weeks and before the end of March the Bishops adopted a more favourable attitude towards the régime. The Bishops' Conference at Fulda cautiously withdrew the earlier censures forbidding Catholics to join the Nazi Party, while the Centre Party and the Bavarian People's Party were allowed to vote in favour of Hitler and so give him the two-thirds majority which he needed to assume full authority.

Several reasons have been offered to explain this change in attitude such as nationalist sentiment, conservative sympathies, fears of Communism, concern about the economic situation and even the simple fact that more and more Germans, including an increasing number of Catholics, had begun to support the National Socialists. But it would also seem that the German Bishops had been subjected to pressure from the Roman authorities who do seem to have been reassured by Hitler's promises that the Church would be free, that he would resist Bolshevism and that he was committed to peace. During the first half of March Cardinal Faulhaber, the Archbishop of Munich, had been in Rome where, in his own words: 'I found, despite everything, a greater tolerance with regard to the new Government. It is today, moreover, not only in possession of power . . . but it has reached that position by legal methods: indeed it could be said that no revolutionary party has ever come to power in so regular a way. Let us meditate on the words of the Holy Father, who, in a consistory, without mentioning his name, indicated before the whole world in Adolf Hitler the statesman who first, after the Pope himself, has raised his voice against Bolshevism'.

The German Bishops again referred to this papal eulogy of Hitler in their memorandum to the Führer during August 1935: 'In the face of this proclamation of the Pope's confidence, millions of men abroad, both Catholics and non-Catholics, have overcome their initial mistrust and accorded credit to your Government'. But if the Bishops had withdrawn their ban on Catholics joining the Nazi Party, they had not withdrawn their earlier condemnations of the movement and it was in this ambiguous context that the Concordat was signed.

At the end of March 1933 the Leader of the Centre Party, Monsignor Kaas, was received by Hitler on his return from Rome and at the beginning of April Kaas returned to Rome with von Papen, the German Vice-Chancellor and former Deputy of the Centre Party, who had been ordered by Hitler to investigate the possibility of arranging a Concordat with the Holy See. Cardinal Pacelli, who had been recalled from Berlin in 1931 to succeed Cardinal Gasparri, was now Secretary of State. As Nuncio in Germany, Pacelli had been largely responsible for negotiating Concordats with Bavaria, Baden and Prussia which had made concessions to the Church over episcopal appointments and education, had safeguarded ecclesiastical property and secured increased financial support for the Church. Negotiations for a Concordat between the whole of Germany and the Holy See had actually begun under the Weimar Republic and much of the groundwork had been fully prepared. These earlier Concordats with

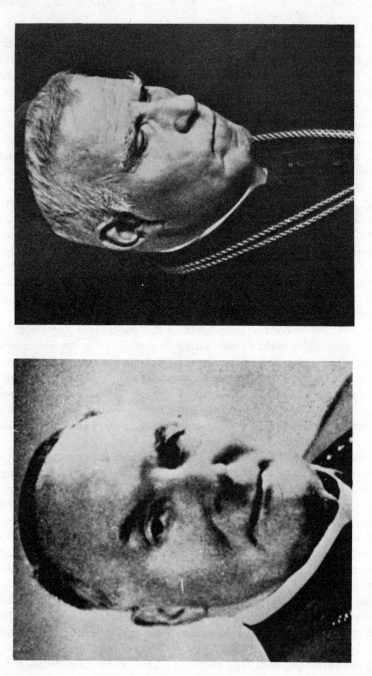

Cardinal von Galen

Cardinal Faulhaber

the individual States were incorporated into the new Concordat with the Third Reich which was signed on 20 July 1933.

By signing the Concordat, Hitler had secured some degree of recognition by the Holy See, gained international prestige at a time when the major Powers were suspicious and reserved, and effectively ended the political resistance of Catholics in Germany. The Chancellor had wanted a Concordat as a means of achieving respectability both at home and abroad and in order to secure control of the Centre Party. Although the influence and prestige of the Centre Party had declined because of the unemployment and poverty associated with the Weimar Republic, there were still enough Deputies to block Hitler's legislation. The Führer was therefore prepared to make concessions to the Church in return for the sacrifice of the Centre Party and the Roman authorities at the time were not particularly interested in the survival of the Centre Party.

The Vatican had few illusions about the Concordat but the authorities probably hoped to establish at least a legal basis on which it might be possible to defend the liberty of the Church in Germany. On paper, the concessions offered by the Nazis seemed more favourable to the Church than those which Governments of the Weimar Republic had been prepared to grant. On the other hand Hitler also threatened to close confessional schools and to abolish confessional youth movements while the Roman authorities feared that the Nazis might even attempt to establish a German National Church. The *Osservatore Romano* claimed that the Concordat was with the German Government and was not a recognition of the Nazi régime, and the Secretary of State told the British Chargé d'Affaires that he had to choose within a week between accepting the concessions made by Hitler or the virtual elimination of the Catholic Church in Germany. The Holy See was certainly told that Nazi extremists would be allowed a free hand until the Church withdrew its claim to special privileges but that these claims could be regulated by a Concordat. Furthermore, if the Vatican was prepared to recognize the totalitarian authority of the State, Hitler promised that he would defend it against the attacks of extremists.

Pacelli himself pointed out that: 'A religious war is easy to start but very difficult to sustain and the Catholics of the country affected are entitled to know that the supreme government of the Church has done everything in its power to spare them the ordeal'. In 1945 he explained at length the situation as he then saw it: 'The German episcopate considered that neither the Concordats up to then negotiated with individual German States, nor the Weimar Constitution, gave adequate guarantees or assurance to the faithful of respect for their convictions, rights or liberty of action. In such conditions the guarantees could not be secured except through a settlement having the solemn form of a concordat with the central government of the Reich. I would add that since it was the German government which made the proposal, the responsibility for all the regrettable consequences would have fallen on the Holy See if it had refused the proposed Concordat. Although the Church had few illusions about National Socialism, it must be recognized that the Concordat in the years that followed brought some advantages, or at least prevented worse evils. In fact, in spite of all the violations to which it was subjected, it gave German Catholics a juridical basis for their defence, a stronghold behind which to shield themselves in their opposition to the ever-growing campaign of religious persecution'.

On paper at least the Concordat between the Holy See and the Third Reich was one of the most satisfactory that had ever been signed from the point of view of the ecclesiastical authorities. The State seemed to recognize all the rights and prerogatives of the Church and to guarantee its complete freedom. The Nazis promised to permit confessional schools and to safeguard the independence of Catholic Youth associations 'in so far as their activities are exclusively religious, cultural and educational'. Similarly the Nazis also guaranteed the uninhibited freedom of action for all Catholic religious and cultural as well as educational organizations, associations and federations. Catholics secured explicit pledges safeguarding freedom of communication with Rome, canonical regulations governing religious orders and ecclesiastical property, and even religious instruction in State schools which was to be given by teachers approved by the bishops. The freedom of ecclesiastical appointments was also guaranteed, though some were restricted to German citizens who had received part of their education in Germany. In return, the ecclesiastical authorities accepted that clergy and religious should no longer engage in party politics, while the Bavarian People's Party and the Centre Party under the leadership of Monsignor Kaas agreed to dissolve themselves as evidence of the willingness of Catholics to cooperate with the new régime.

When Cardinal Pacelli expressed his satisfaction with the Concordat, he also added: '*provided the German Government remained true to its undertaking*'. But in spite of the favourable provisions of the Concordat, the laws needed to implement it were never passed and its provisions were consistently ignored. Some early difficulties arose over the interpretation of the Concordat, the regulations governing its application and the equivocal wording of some of the most significant clauses. It now appears that there were secret clauses dealing with a common front against Russia and the duties of priests conscripted into the German army. At this time conscription in Germany was still forbidden by the Treaty of Versailles! Pacelli had also attempted to insert a clause safeguarding the position of baptized Jews as German Catholics in spite of the objections of the German Government that this question was racial not religious. However, after some hard bargaining, the German negotiators gave a *verbal* promise to Pacelli that baptized Jews would be regarded as Christians and would not be victimized. Further difficulties were caused by the fact that the Concordat was used in the Nazi press as part of its election propaganda. The Papal Nuncio was pictured shaking Hitler's hand and saying: 'Chancellor, I have long attempted to understand you. Today, I am glad to say I do'. What the Nuncio actually said was: 'I have wanted to make your acquaintance for a long time, and today at last I do'.

Furthermore, only five days after the Concordat was signed, the Nazis promulgated a law for the sterilization of certain individuals, a law which the Pope publicly declared was contrary to Christian morals. Within a few months the Vatican was protesting that the provisions of the Concordat were being repeatedly and frequently violated. The Association of German Youth was dissolved, members of Catholic Action and a Catholic Congress were physically assaulted, Catholic offices were invaded and the *Katholikentag*, at which von Papen himself was to speak on the Concordat, had to be cancelled. Catholic Deputies were arrested and Catholic civil servants dismissed, priests and religious were threatened or imprisoned, pastoral letters were confiscated and two letters from the Nuncio to Rome were opened. Catholic organizations and periodicals were suppressed, Catholic property was confiscated and Catholic meetings were banned. Religious education was restricted and Catholic schools were destroyed.

Hitler had begun to remove his political opponents within weeks of coming to power. At the beginning of June 1933 the Archbishop of Munich, Cardinal Michael von Faulhaber, had described Hitler as 'a great spirit' who 'sees what a halo his government will have in the eyes of the world if the Pope makes a treaty with him'. However, within a month, after threats against himself and the arrest of some of his clergy, the Cardinal commented that Catholics would not understand the Holy Father making a treaty with a Government at a time 'when a whole row of Catholic officials are sitting in prison or have been illegally ejected'. In June 1934 Erich Klausener, President of Catholic Action in Berlin, was shot, one of the victims of the 'Night of the Long Knives'. Adalbert Probst, President of the Sporting Association of German Catholics, was summoned to Berlin and a few days later his ashes were returned to his widow. Friedrich Beck of Munich University was killed 'accidentally' and Fritz Gerlich, editor of the largest Catholic newspaper in Germany, was found dead in prison.

For a time the Nazis moderated their hostility to the Church until after the plebiscite in the Saar where the population was overwhelmingly Catholic. But once the Saar basin had been reunited with the German Reich in March 1935, and as the Nazis became more confident of their domination of Germany, the campaign against the Church was resumed in earnest. Several bishops were subjected to physical violence and the episcopal palaces at Würzburg, Rottenburg and Mainz were sacked. Hundreds of priests and religious were arrested and many others driven into exile, accused of immorality or of violating currency regulations. The Nazis indulged in physical attacks on Catholic meetings and Catholic buildings and stink-bombs were thrown into Munich Cathedral during the Corpus Christi procession. Anti-Christian, Anti-Catholic and anti-clerical cartoons, caricatures and scurrilous anecdotes appeared in the Nazi press. A Catholic priest and Protestant pastor were shown surrounded by bags of gold proclaiming '*Ein feste Burg ist unser Gold!*' Pacelli was pictured embracing a gross French Communist Jewess and salacious stories about Alexander Borgia were attributed to Pius XI.

Although the Nazis were committed to tolerating the existence of Catholic schools, party workers or party officials could write to or call on those parents who sent their children to Catholic schools to ask for an 'explanation'. Meanwhile attempts to form 'Catholic Parents' Associations' to defend parents who were being victimized were effectively prohibited by the secular authorities. One protest from the Holy See listed over a hundred incidents which indicated, in Pacelli's own words: 'that a planned attack is in progress against the Catholic schools'. The Government, however, was largely successful in its policy. Between 1933 and 1937 the percentage of parents in Munich who sent their children to Catholic schools fell from sixty-five per cent to a mere three per cent. Convent teachers were declared redundant and some six hundred teaching nuns were told to find civilian employment. The German Bishops issued a Pastoral Letter of protest while Cardinal Bertram of Breslau and Cardinal Schulte of Cologne warned the parents of children attending State schools that they were answerable before God for the faith of their children.

As pressure was put on Catholic teachers to break with Confessional Associations, all youth organizations, except the Hitler Youth, were forbidden to take part in organized sport, to wear uniforms or to march in formation. This legislation was followed by violent clashes between the Catholic Boy Scouts and the Hitler Youth. In 1935 seventeen hundred members of the Catholic Youth smuggled their uniforms across the border in order to appear in them at an audience with the Pope. On their return to Germany they were publicly insulted by Customs officials who imposed duties on their souvenirs and devotional objects and then confiscated their 'uniforms' which were so designed as to include shirts, trousers, underwear, knapsacks, water-bottles, musical instruments, cooking utensils, wallets, cameras, binoculars, banners, pennants and clasp-knives. In his next audience with a group of German pilgrims, Pius XI commented: 'We sincerely hope that you devout pilgrims to Rome will be better received when you return than were those pious and worthy youths who came last time to receive the blessing of the Holy Father. We pronounce before the whole Catholic and civilized world their praise and honour. Alas, we cannot say the same of those Germans who shamed them when they returned to their native land'.

As Nazi pressures on the Church quickly degenerated into simple persecution, German Christians also had to resist the views and policies advocated by the Nazis. Alfred Rosenberg's attempts to free Christianity from its Jewish background or to establish a German Christianity were clearly opposed to Christian belief and tradition, while the persecution of the Jews and compulsory sterilization were also contrary to the teachings of the Church. German Bishops individually and collectively repeatedly protested against violations of the Concordat and those Nazi policies which were opposed to Christian teachings. The Archbishop of Munich denounced the persecution of the Jews, the theories of German Christians and the activities of the Nazis in pastorals and sermons. In 1937 Faulhaber condemned the confiscation of pastoral letters, the dismissal of nuns and Catholic teachers from schools, the banning of the Corpus Christi procession, the personal attacks on the Pope and other churchmen, and the attempt to make political capital out of the currency trials. The SS forcibly entered his Cathedral to plant bugging devices in the pulpit and beat up those priests who tried to prevent them. Bishop von Galen denounced the writings of Rosenberg and the activities of the Gestapo. He also declared that: 'an obedience which imprisons the soul, which violates conscience, the inmost sanctuary of freedom, is slavery – the most degrading form of slavery. It is worse than murder, for it crushes the very person of man; it attempts to destroy his resemblance to God'.

Some German priests were even more outspoken than their bishops. One parish priest denounced the SS from his pulpit: 'Let those stinking SS bastards come at me, two thousand of them if you like, and I'll bash in all their skulls so that their brains squirt out. It'll make enough soup for a week'. Referring to the Concordat, the same priest remarked: 'If I'd been Pacelli having to sign the Concordat with this bunch, I'd have given His Holiness one up the arse for making me do it'. Another priest spoke to school-children about three Nazi Brown Shirts who had been injured in a street brawl. He commented: 'A pity they weren't killed! Then there'd be three less. The Brown Shirt is supposed to be a Shirt of Honour, isn't it? Yes, brown's the word. Like something else that's brown – and stinks!' A speech by Göring was denounced in one pulpit as 'a heap of shit', while another parish priest denounced Göring and Röhm as homosexuals and then referred to Hitler's 'love' of the latter. When the German authorities eventually complained to Pacelli, the Secretary of State was forced to admit that some of the German clergy might be at fault for using such language.

In 1934 Albert Hartl was the subject of a report which complained that very few of the Catholic clergy were committed Nazis. In the previous year Hartl had given evidence against the rector of a seminary who had accused the Nazis of starting the fire at the Reichstag and who was sentenced to nine months in prison. As a result of giving this testimony, Hartl was bitterly criticized by his fellow priests and was forced to resign and cease acting as a priest. In due course he became a member of the SS with a burning hatred of the Church and the Jesuits. He was Eichmann's nominal superior in 1941 and worked for Himmler in organizing an espionage service directed against the Church.

The Holy See also strongly protested against violations of the Concordat, and the Vatican Radio and the *Osservatore Romano* denounced the doctrines and the violence of the Nazis, several of whose leading exponents were condemned by the Holy Office. It has been estimated that between 25 September 1933 and 26 June 1936 the Holy See sent more than fifty notes protesting against violations of the Concordat. Furthermore Pacelli's notes of protest between 1933 and 1939 were not simply concerned with Catholic interests but have been described as reading 'like miniature treatises on natural law'. In January 1936 following the New Year reception of foreign diplomats at the Vatican, the Pope himself made a strong private protest to the German representative. The Pope also instructed the Nuncio in Berlin to make an official complaint about breaches of the Concordat but the Nuncio found it impossible to contact anyone in authority and the German Government simply declined to answer his complaints. At the Opening of the World Exhibition of the Catholic Press in 1936, the Pope described both Nazism and Communism as the 'enemies of all truth and of all justice'. In his Christmas Address of the same year, he accused 'the self-styled champions of civilization against Bolshevism' of using 'the very means employed by their adversaries'.

When the German Minister of Justice requested a papal audience in 1936, his request was refused. The Secretary of State told the German Ambassador that: 'His Holiness . . . refused the audience not on personal grounds, but because the Minister was a prominent member of a government which makes no attempt to protect a foreign sovereign from public insults, and permits the lie to be published in the German press that the representative of Christ on earth has allied himself with Bolshevism, the anti-Christ, against National Socialism. The Pope also feels particularly wounded by the repeated assertion that he is of Jewish origin. He has nothing against the Jews, but a great deal against false statements of fact'.

Pacelli himself seems to have adopted a policy of moderating the anger of the Pope and conciliating German officials. However his own consciousness of the gravity of the situation was revealed in a letter to Cardinal Schulte of Cologne in which he referred to the Nazis as 'false prophets with the pride of Lucifer', 'bearers of a new Faith and a new Gospel'. The Secretary of State also spoke of 'impious hands laid upon the Church' and of 'the perfidious attempt to establish a mendacious antimony between faithfulness to the Church and faithfulness to the Fatherland'.

In August 1936 the German Bishops asked for a papal encyclical on the problems of the Church in Germany. In November Hitler threatened to put more pressure on the German Church if it did not collaborate more zealously with the régime. In December the Secretary of State arranged to meet with leading representatives of the German hierarchy and this meeting took place in the following January. The German Bishops involved included Bertram, Faulhaber, Schulte, von Galen and von Preysing. The Secretary of State asked Faulhaber to prepare the draft and to draw up the main lines of an encyclical condemning the Nazi persecution of the Church which he did the same night under the title *Mit grosser Sorge* ('With Great Concern'). Pacelli himself added an historical introduction on the background to the Concordat and made one or two modifications including the substitution of *brennender* (fervent) for *grosser* (great). Pius XI added the final touches. This encyclical, addressed to the Church in Germany, was distributed secretly by an army of motor-cyclists and read from every Catholic pulpit in the country on Palm Sunday before a single copy had been seen by any member of the National Socialist Party. The Bishops themselves read it in their own Cathedrals.

It has been said that the encyclical was a protest against Catholic grievances rather than a condemnation of National Socialism and was more concerned with the rights of the Church than the evils of Nazism. It is true that the encyclical was 'diplomatic' rather than 'polemic', which was inevitable since the signing of the Concordat and in view of the fact that the German Bishops were still hoping to establish a *modus vivendi* and anxious to avoid a final break with the régime. On the other hand, *Mit brennender Sorge* was one of the most vigorous condemnations of a national régime ever published by the Holy See. The Pope made it clear that he had only agreed to the Concordat in spite of many serious misgivings, and he developed the same thesis which had aroused so much fury in Munich when Cardinal Faulhaber denounced the prostitution of Christianity in his sermons on Judaism and Christianity. The encyclical not only condemned the persecution of the Church in Germany but the neo-paganism of Nazi theories and even by implication the Führer himself; he was a mad prophet possessed of repulsive arrogance who would place any mortal however great on the same level as Christ. Incidentally, the fact that St Boniface, the English apostle of Germany, was condemned by the Nazis for 'crimes' against the Aryan race, had not gone unnoticed in Catholic circles: 'With deep anxiety and with ever growing dismay We have for a considerable time watched the Church treading the Way of the Cross and the gradually increasing oppression of the men and women who have remained devoted to her in thought and in act in that country and among that people to whom St Boniface once brought the light of the Gospel of Christ and of the Kingdom of God. . . . Whoever according to an alleged primitive German pre-Christian conception substitutes a gloomy and impersonal fate for a personal God . . . cannot claim to be numbered among believers in God. Whoever transposes Race or People, the State or Constitution, the executive of other fundamental elements of human society . . . from the scale of earthly values and makes them the ultimate norm of all things, even of religious values, and deifies them with an idolatrous cult, perverts and falsifies the divinely created and appointed order of things. Such a man is far from true belief in God and from a conception of life in conformity to it. . . . Only superficial minds can fall into the error of speaking of a national God, of a national religion, and of making a mad attempt to imprison within the frontiers of a single people, within the pedigree of one single race, God, the Creator of the world, the King, and lawgiver of the peoples. . . . The culmination of revelation in the Gospel of Jesus Christ is definitive and obligatory for all time; it admits no additions at the hands of men, and acknowledges no substitute whatever, and no replacement by the arbitrary "revelations" that certain contemporary prophets try to extract from the so-called myth of blood and race. . . . The Church founded by the Redeemer is one for all peoples and for all nations; and under its dome . . . there is a place and home for all peoples and all tongues. . . . When the tempter or oppressor approaches with the traitorous suggestion that he should leave the Church, then he can only answer, even at the price of the heaviest earthly sacrifices, in the words of our Saviour: "Begone, Satan: for it is written: The Lord thy God shalt thou adore, and Him only shalt thou serve". . . . By a thousand tongues today there is preached in your ears a gospel which has not been revealed by the heavenly Father: a thousand pens write in the service of a sham Christianity which is not the Christianity of Christ. The printing-press and the radio flood you daily with productions the contents of which are hostile to faith and to Church, and unscrupulously and irreverently attack what, for you, must be sacred and holy'.

Mit brennender Sorge was favourably received abroad and had an immediate effect on public opinion, especially in the United States. The German Government retaliated by reducing the significance of the condemnation and was forced to attempt to answer the Pope's criticisms and to explain away the difficulties facing the Church in Germany. At the same time the German authorities took steps to prevent further publication of the encyclical. It was ignored by the newspapers and all copies discovered were confiscated. The presses which had printed it were closed and those Catholic publications which had published it were suspended for three months. Individuals convicted of distributing the encyclical were arrested and financial subsidies, which were to be given to the Church according to the terms of the Concordat, were reduced.

The Nazis also reacted to *Mit brennender Sorge* by threatening to cancel the Concordat but in the event decided not to do so, while their persecution of the Church was even moderated in some respects. Hitler indulged in a propaganda campaign against the Church as well as the notorious 'morality' trials of priests and religious but he did not want to make any martyrs at that time. Apart from military considerations the Nazis were probably influenced by the fact that as a result of the 'Anschluss' or incorporation of Austria and the occupation of Czech and Polish territories, the percentage of Catholics in the Third Reich now equalled if it did not exceed that of Protestants.

In 1922 Ignaz Seipel, a Catholic priest and leader of the Christian Socialists which represented a largely conservative coalition, became Chancellor of Austria. He was succeeded by Engelbert Dollfuss, another advocate of the Church's social teaching, who was murdered by the Austrian Nazis in 1934 and was succeeded in turn by Kurt von Schuschnigg, who made the fatal appeal for a plebiscite in favour of Austrian independence in 1938. The Austrian Constitution, outlined by Seipel and developed by Dollfuss, came very close to Pius XI's notion of a Catholic corporate State. A Concordat with the Vatican, signed in May 1933 and actually incorporated into the new Constitution, was, from the point of view of the Holy See, one of the most satisfactory made with any country in the period between the wars. The State guaranteed that the Church would enjoy complete freedom of action and promised to increase its financial support of the Church. Not unnaturally the Concordat was bitterly attacked by Austrian Socialists and Fascists whereas the Pope referred to Dollfuss as: '. . . the illustrious man who rules Austria so well, so resolutely and in such a Christian manner. . . . Our Beloved Austria, now has the government it deserves. We beseech the Almighty to accompany His blessing with the fulness of His grace and always to support such a Christian, giant-hearted man as the Chancellor, to protect him from all evils and dangers so that he may long strive and delve fruitfully for Our Beloved Catholic Austrian people'.

After the murder of Dollfuss in 1934, a special Requiem Mass was celebrated in Rome at which the absolution was given by the Secretary of State. The Holy See clearly manifested its suspicions of the Nazis by nominating as Austrian Bishops ecclesiastics who were well-known to be opposed to the *Anschluss* with Germany, and the Holy See was particularly pleased when Mussolini, at least initially, showed that he was firmly opposed to the possibility of an *Anschluss*. When the *Anschluss* finally took place an Under-Secretary at the Vatican complained to the British Minister that it was 'a disaster caused by German vainglory, Italian folly and Anglo-French weakness', and the *Osservatore Romano* published an article in defence of Austrian independence. In fact some historians have argued that the real change in the Vatican's attitude towards Germany came during the summer of 1938 when the German Government refused to answer a note from Pacelli about the continued validity of the Austrian Concordat, a refusal which was a direct consequence of the Pope's hostility to Hitler on his visit to Rome.

At the time of the *Anschluss*, Cardinal Innitzer, Archbishop of Vienna and Primate of Austria, was received by Hitler immediately after the celebrations marking the event and expressed his satisfaction with the promises he had received from the Nazis with regard to the Church. A week before the plebiscite, the Austrian Bishops issued a public statement which was read in all the churches praising the achievements of National Socialism in Germany. Innitzer was immediately summoned to Rome but he found excuses for delay. The *Osservatore Romano* revealed that the declaration of the Austrian Bishops had been issued on their own authority without the knowledge, agreement or approval of the Holy See. Innitzer then left for Rome where the Pope refused to receive him until he had signed a statement which appeared in the *Osservatore Romano* to the effect that the declaration of the Austrian Bishops must not be interpreted in any way that was incompatible with the laws of God or the rights and freedom of the Church and that it did not oblige the faithful in conscience. Furthermore Innitzer pledged that the Austrian Bishops would in future insist on securing the previous approval of the Holy See before agreeing to any modification of the situation of the Church in Austria and would at all costs protect the religious education of the young.

At the same time that Innitzer was giving active support to the *Anschluss*, however, Bishop John Baptist Sproll of Rottenburg was driven from his diocese because he refused to vote in its favour. To vote in favour of the *Anschluss* inevitably involved endorsing, at least tacitly, a list of candidates to the Reichstag which included well-known opponents of Christianity such as Rosenberg. For some time Bishop Sproll's sermons, denouncing breaches of the Concordat and the errors of blood and race, had been giving concern to the Nazi authorities and his refusal to vote for the *Anschluss* was simply the final straw.

In due course, Austrian Catholics were subjected to the same pressures and persecution as their German co-religionists. In October 1938 members of the Hitler Youth forcibly entered Innitzer's palace and indulged in that orgy of looting and destruction which was later to be featured in the novel *The Cardinal* and in the film of the same title. In the same year the new ruler of Austria expressed the hope that he would be able to give to Hitler as a birthday present an Austria free from monasteries and convents. Catholic colleges and religious houses were confiscated, Catholic organizations dissolved and Catholic newspapers suppressed.

Throughout 1938 Pius XI continued to criticize totalitarian régimes, and particularly those in Russia and Germany. Only two months before his death he reminded the College of Cardinals that 'in Germany today a full religious persecution is in progress' and in one of his last public audiences he compared Hitler with the Emperor Nero and Julian the Apostate who attempted to 'saddle the Christians with responsibility for the persecution he had unleashed against them'. The Pope also publicly and consistently denounced the evils of racialism as well as 'exaggerated nationalism' which he once described as the 'curse of our time': 'If there is anything worse than the various theories of racialism and nationalism, it is the spirit that dictates them. There is something peculiarly loathsome about this spirit of separatism and exaggerated nationalism which, precisely because it is un-Christian and irreligious, ends by being inhuman'.

As early as 1928 the Holy Office had solemnly declared that the Church: ' . . . just as it reproves all rancours and conflicts between peoples, particularly condemns hatred of the people once chosen by God, the hatred that commonly goes by the name of anti-Semitism'.

Pius XI instructed the Congregation of Seminaries and Universities to oppose the basic errors of 'the superior race' and of 'the State as the end of man'. He ordered that these errors should be scientifically refuted so that the clergy would be well prepared to oppose them on rational as well as religious grounds. In May 1938 the Congregation of Seminaries and Universities instructed Catholic professors to refute in speech and writing those 'pernicious' doctrines of racialism which 'under the false disguise of science, are spread for the perversion of minds and the extirpation of true religion'. Of course, Jews in the past had been harshly treated even in the Papal States, but in September 1938 the *Osservatore Romano* claimed that former Papal Governments had been acting in: '. . . the defence of religion according to the needs of different epochs, not in the name of the racialist principle as understood and applied today, but of a purely religious principle which fought against every danger to the faith and the civilization based upon it, against Judaism exactly as against Mohammedanism, Protestantism and sectarianism'.

Perhaps Pope Pius XI's most memorable protest against racialism and anti-semitism was made on 20 September when he told a group of pilgrims: 'Mark well that in the Catholic Mass, Abraham is our Patriarch and forefather. Anti-Semitism is incompatible with the lofty thought which that fact expresses. It is a movement with which we Christians can have nothing to do. No, no, I say to you it is impossible for a Christian to take part in anti-Semitism. It is inadmissible. Through Christ and in Christ we are the spiritual progeny of Abraham. Spiritually, we are all Semites'.

A Nazi periodical savagely attacked the Pope:

> Go bury the delusive hope
> About His Holiness the Pope.
> For all he knows concerning Race
> Would get a schoolboy in disgrace.
> Old, muddle-headed, doddering, ill,
> His knowledge is precisely nil.
> And, gone in years, he can but keep
> His motley flock of piebald sheep;
> Since he regards both Blacks and Whites
> As children all with equal rights,
> As Christians all (whate'er their hues),
> They're 'spiritually' nought but Jews.
> The Vatican (e'en blockheads know)
> With verdigris is covered so,
> And wants, no doubt, the faithful band
> Of Christians who around it stand –

As far as 'ghostly welfare' goes —
To lead 'em by the (hooked) nose.
A pretty picture all men know —
The firm of 'Juda-Rome and Co'.
An 'Old Man' e'er can tell the tale
And, sure, his pity will not fail.
The banner is at last unfurled:
'Chief Rabbi of the Christian world'.

But 'Chief Rabbi of the Christian World' was not an epitaph of which Pius XI would have been ashamed; he might also have been rather amused by Mussolini's comment on hearing of his death: *'Finalmente se n'è andato'*, the Duce is said to have remarked *'Quel vecchio ostinato è morto'* — that obstinate old man is dead.

Mgr Tiso, ruler of Slovakia, the Nazi puppet state, visits Hitler's headquarters in 1941

Chapter IV

The Holy See and the Second World War

In February 1939 Eugenio Pacelli seemed the inevitable successor of Pius XI who had not only given several indications that he regarded his Secretary of State as a most suitable candidate for the papacy but would seem conspicuously to have promoted his candidature. At the Conclave, Pacelli was obviously the best known of the cardinals both officially and personally while none of the others could equal his ecclesiastical career. As Secretary of State since 1930, Pacelli had been closely involved with the Pope in all important decisions and had met leading ecclesiastics from all parts of the world. On several occasions he had travelled as the Pope's personal representative. In fact Pacelli was the first Secretary of State to travel abroad since Cardinal Consalvi who had signed the Concordat with Napoleon. In 1934 he attended the International Eucharistic Congress at Buenos Aires and then went on to Brazil. Two years later he travelled extensively in the United States. He attended another Eucharistic Congress in Budapest and made two particularly successful visits to France where the former Nuncio to Germany protested against developments taking place in that country. On all these occasions Pacelli demonstrated his sensitivity and intelligence, his grasp of detail and command of languages, his high sense of duty and responsibility, his reserve and dignity, charm and kindness, his prudence and warmness, and, perhaps most important of all, his genuine asceticism and religious devotion.

By 1939 Pacelli had also had long experience in dealing with men and extensive diplomatic experience. He had been Papal Nuncio for thirteen years and had been one of Pope Benedict's leading agents during the abortive peace negotiations in 1917. Pacelli played an active part in promoting the Locarno Agreement and had negotiated the Concordat with Hitler. He had been closely involved in the preparation of *Divini Redemptoris* and *Mit brennender Sorge, Non Abbiamo Bisogno* and *Nos Es Muy*. In fact Pacelli was a man of deep traditional piety and diplomatic experience, rather than of pastoral or administrative experience. During his early years in the Curia, he used to hear confessions in a parish church and teach the catechism to underprivileged children, but he had little experience of the pastoral and administrative responsibilities of a diocese. However, there is little doubt that in the minds of his fellow cardinals, his obvious qualities and particularly his personal virtues, outweighed any possible deficiencies. In spite of any hostility to or reaction against Pius XI's 'candidate' and the Roman tradition against electing Secretaries of State, Pacelli was elected after the shortest conclave since 1623. He was elected on the first day, 2 March 1939, after only three ballots, and apparently by some forty-eight votes out of sixty-three. The Cardinals had elected the first Secretary of State since 1775 and the first native of Rome since 1721.

The election of a new pope in March 1939 was a matter of some concern to both the democratic and the totalitarian governments of Europe and in view of some of the claims made in later years, it is revealing to recall how contemporaries regarded the election at the time. Pius XII has sometimes been accused of being 'pro-German' because of the time he spent in Germany and because of his undoubted affection for the German people and the confidence he continued to place in several individual German priests and religious. But Pius XII disliked the Nazis intensely. As the number of protest notes now available clearly show, Pacelli had been consistently denouncing breaches of the Concordat over the last few years. He obviously believed that Nazism was second only to Communism as a threat to the very survival of Catholicism and Christianity. When the Germans denounced the Treaty of Locarno he expressed the opinion that the signature of the present German Government was not worth the paper on which it was written. When the Germans re-occupied the Rhineland, he told the French Ambassador that his country would have done a great service to the world if it had reacted effectively. It is therefore hardly surprising that in 1939 the Italian and German Governments were clearly hostile to the election of Pacelli, who was so closely associated with Pius XI's condemnations of the religious and racial policies being pursued in Italy and Germany; Nazi newspapers reflected this hostility. Meanwhile the press in Britain, France and America referred to Pacelli in friendly and favourable terms.

From the beginning Pius XII made it clear that he would continue the work of reconciliation promoted by the two previous popes under whom he had served. He took the name of his immediate predecessor, was crowned in the Lateran Basilica where no Pope had been crowned since the beginning of the conflict with the Kingdom of Italy and his first message to the world ended with an appeal for peace. The new Pope had also pledged himself to work for unity and peace throughout the world in the declaration *Dum gravissimum* which was broadcast over the Vatican Radio the day after he was elected. His appointment of Cardinal Maglione as Secretary of State indicated the desire of the new Pope that the former Nuncios in Munich and Berne, in Berlin and Paris, should continue to work closely together. Maglione had been another of Benedict's agents in the peace negotiations of 1917 and had been sent to Switzerland where he was directly involved in Benedict's negotiations for the exchange of wounded prisoners of war and interned civilians, and with the administration of the relief work of the Holy See.

Pius XII's attitude towards the Second World War has often been contrasted as well as compared with that of Benedict XV between 1914 and 1918. Both popes had a conscientious horror of war. Both men devoted themselves first to preventing war, then to containing it and finally to ending it. During the War Benedict XV and Pius XII both had to decide how far they could go in denouncing violations of natural or international law and in reminding Catholics of their Christian obligations. Perhaps the chief explanation of their differences lay in the fact that Pius XII was a professional diplomat who was always prepared to negotiate while there was any prospect of a reasonable compromise and quite prepared to 'wait in the wings' if there was any chance that he might be called upon to play a mediating role. As a result of the solution of the Roman Question and the increased prestige of the papacy since 1914, Pius XII was in some ways in a better position to intervene in the affairs of this world than Benedict XV had been. In 1939 the Pope was able to act quite independently of the Italian Government, at least in theory, while the increased number of nunciatures and delegations established throughout the world gave him more points of contact and channels of information than his predecessors had ever enjoyed.

Within three days of his coronation Pius XII had a meeting with the German cardinals in which he recalled one of the first moves made by Leo XIII who had sent a friendly message to the Emperor Wilhelm I of Germany which had paved the way for the eventual solution of Bismarck's *Kulturkampf*. Pius XII now decided to send a personal message announcing his accession to Hitler and the Pope asked the German cardinals about the forms to be adopted; in the event it was decided not to address Hitler as a 'son'! The question was also raised whether the Holy See should break off diplomatic relations with Germany should Hitler refuse to alter his attitudes or his policies. However, it was decided that the presence of the Nuncio was essential in order to maintain contact between the Pope and the German bishops and that the Nazis would demand further major concessions from the Church before restoring diplomatic relations should these ever be broken. However, the Pope's gesture and the cardinals' advice proved to be unnecessary. Hitler did not even take the trouble to reply to the Pope's letter. Furthermore Germany was the only major Power that did not send a special representative to the Pope's coronation.

During the six months between the Pope's election in March and the outbreak of war in September, Pius XII made every effort to preserve the peace of Europe. In April the President of the United States took steps to inform the Apostolic Delegate, A. G. Cicognani, that he had sent a cable to Hitler and Mussolini urging a peaceful settlement of the crisis and asked for 'the Holy Father's support of the appeal for a peace conference'. The Pope proposed that a conference attended by Britain, France, Germany, Italy and Poland should be held in order to discuss how to avoid war but the response was not encouraging. The Pope urged the Nuncio in Berlin to impress on Ribbentrop the dangers of a conflict between Germany and the United States but the Nuncio simply received a lecture on the strength of Germany. The Secretary of State asked the French Ambassador and the Papal Nuncio to encourage Poland to adopt a more conciliatory attitude and at the same time papal representatives tried to persuade Mussolini to restrain Hitler, but again without achieving any effect. As Sumner Welles, the American Under-Secretary of State, reported in May 1939: '. . . the latest information the United States Government has is to the effect that France and Poland, while highly appreciative of the good offices of the Holy Father in behalf of peace, are fearful that a conference at this time would lead to their being required to make concessions: that the attitude of Germany toward the Holy Father's efforts is antagonistic: that England is non-committal and that Italy's reaction is unknown. Mr Welles declared that regardless of the outcome of attempts to bring about a conference of nations, the efforts of the Holy Father have been of the utmost value, not only by reason of his enormous influence, but also because of the fact that his efforts were made at a moment when international tension was so grave'.

As the situation deteriorated and German threats to Poland grew more menacing, the French Ambassador urged the Pope to abandon his diplomatic reserve and to declare that Germany was entirely responsible for the present dangerous conditions. Pius XII, however, preferred to broadcast on 24 August his final and famous appeal for peace in which he used the phrase, apparently coined by Mgr Montini: 'Nothing is lost with peace: everything may be lost with war' . . . 'It is by force of reason and not by force of arms that justice makes progress. Empires which are not founded on justice are not blessed by God. Statesmanship emancipated from morality betrays those very ones who would have it so. The danger is imminent, but there is yet time. Nothing is lost with peace; all may be with war. Let men return to mutual understandings. Let them begin negotiations anew. Let them confer with goodwill and with respect for reciprocal rights, and they will find that to sincere and conscientious negotiations an honourable solution is never precluded'.

At the end of the same month, the Pope made another futile attempt to organize an international conference of the principal Powers. Such a proposal, as experience at Munich had already shown, would inevitably have involved further sacrifices by the Poles who preferred to rely on the guarantees given by Britain and France. At the same time, it should be pointed out that the Holy See only made this proposal when the pact between Russia and Germany had effectively vitiated these British and French guarantees. Finally and acting on suggestions from Mussolini but in a last desperate attempt to avoid war, the Pope somewhat insensitively tried to persuade the Poles to accede to German demands, and this final if unfortunate intervention effectively ended his efforts to preserve the peace.

In October 1939 the new Pope issued his first encyclical *Summi Pontificatus* at the same time as Russia and Germany were dividing Poland and as Russia was dominating the Baltic States of Estonia, Latvia and Lithuania and preparing for the invasion of Finland. This encyclical reflected the Pope's understanding of history and his belief that the salvation of Europe depended on a renewed recognition of the truths of Christianity and the claims of Catholicism. There had been a long period of infidelity from the time of the Reformation to the Secularism and Liberalism, the Capitalism and Socialism of the nineteenth century which in turn had led to the rise of Bolshevism, Nazism and Fascism. Pius XII made it perfectly clear that: 'We left no stone unturned, no avenue unexplored, to prevent, in any way which our apostolic office or other means at our disposal made possible, a recourse to arms. The door must not be shut upon all chances of deciding the question on terms honourable to both sides. We were persuaded that if one party to the conflict made use of force the other would take up arms in turn. We felt it to be due, both to our apostolic duty and to the dictates of Christian charity, to preserve if we could humanity at large, and the Christian commonwealth in particular, from the horrors that must attend upon a world war. There was reason to fear that the advice we gave, once it was made public, would be taken in bad part; that could not be helped. But our advice, respectfully listened to, was not taken'.

During the First World War Benedict XV had been criticized for refusing to pass moral judgments on unjust aggression. The same charge could not fairly be made against *Summi Pontificatus* which clearly, if not explicitly, condemned the political and religious policies adopted by the German and Russian Governments. On the other hand, Pius XII's condemnation of war seemed to lack the force and the urgency associated with Benedict XV. It was as if the later Pope discussed the issues in too general and too intellectual a way, though he did speak of the law of charity and human solidarity which resulted from the rational nature and common origin of all men whatever their race or nation and he also denounced totalitarianism which he argued was opposed to the principles of natural and international law. The re-establishment of a true and lasting peace depended on a new appreciation of the essential brotherhood of man and a recognition that the State as well as individuals were subject to the moral law: 'Whoever considers the State to be the end towards which all is directed, to which all must bow, is of necessity an enemy and an obstacle to all true and lasting progress among the nations. That is true whether this unlimited competence has been entrusted to the ruling power in the State by a decree of the nation or of some class within the nation, or whether that power has simply usurped the right to rule, regarding itself as the all-competent master of the situation, responsible to nobody'.

In view of later criticisms that Pius XII was always too neutral and general in his statements on the war, it is only just to point out that in this, his first encyclical, his criticisms of those Powers who broke their word or who resorted too quickly to threats and force applied more clearly to Germany and Russia than to any of the other combatants and that his remarks in this context were at least as direct as those of Benedict XV. In fact the Nazi authorities restricted the publication of *Summi Pontificatus* in Germany. At the same time the Pope had not explicitly condemned either side and it would also seem that he was not entirely convinced that the Allies could be trusted to conclude a just peace if only because he believed that their complacency since the end of the last war had been one of the causes of the present catastrophe. The encyclical was read in all Catholic churches on 29 October, the Feast of Christ the King; a feast which had been instituted by Pope Pius XI as a clear assertion of the supremacy of Christian morals over all other rival ideologies. On the same day Pius XII consecrated a number of missionary bishops from several nations as a sign of the universality of the Church. They included two bishops from Africa, one from India and another from China, a Mexican and an American, an Irishman, a Belgian and a Dutchman, a Frenchman, a German and an Italian.

In January 1940 Dr Josef Müller, who was personally acquainted with the Pope, approached Pius XII on behalf of a group of German generals who were planning a *coup d'état* against Hitler. The generals wished to make contact with the British Government in the hopes that the Allies would limit their military activities before the *coup* took place and promise to make a reasonable peace afterwards. The conspirators, whose plans were effectively defeated by the German military successes in France, were allowed to use Vatican officials including the Pope's personal private secretary, the German Jesuit Robert Leiber, as intermediaries with the Allies. However the British Government in particular was rather sceptical of these approaches and refused to promise or to discuss anything until Hitler had been eliminated. During the nine months of the 'Phoney War' the Holy See made three further efforts to mediate between the two sides but the Pope, and to a lesser extent the United States Government, did not seem to realize that it would have only been possible to re-establish peace at the time by accepting and recognizing a greatly enlarged and strengthened Germany.

In an allocution to the Cardinals on Christmas Eve 1939 Pius XII restated the five 'peace points' originally recommended by Benedict XV in 1917: the freedom and independence of nations, the need for progressive disarmament, the establishment of effective international institutions to arbitrate in cases of potential conflict, the peaceful and equitable revision of outdated treaties and the recognition of just national and racial demands, the general acceptance of Christian principles and a renewed spirit of goodwill and responsibility, justice and love. These five points were later accepted by the Cardinal Archbishop of Westminster, the Anglican Archbishops of Canterbury and York and the Moderator of the Free Churches in a letter to *The Times* which Bishop Bell described as 'a landmark in the history of Christian cooperation'. It was also at the end of 1939 that President Roosevelt sent his good wishes to the Pope and expressed the desire to work with him for the restoration of peace and the solution of post-war problems. The President proposed to send Myron C. Taylor as his personal representative residing at the Vatican, a proposal which was willingly accepted by the Pope.

The five 'peace points' provided a clear test by which to judge the aims and intentions of the conflicting nations and any remote possibility that they might be accepted or help to prevent an extension of the war disappeared with the German invasion of Denmark and Norway in April followed by the invasion of Holland, Belgium and Luxembourg in May. These invasions violated every one of the conditions laid down by the Pope who received many requests that he should condemn this unjust aggression. The Pope responded by sending three telegrams to the Queen of Holland, the King of Belgium and the Grand Duchess of Luxembourg in which he called for the 're-establishment of justice and liberty' in Holland, the 'complete liberty and independence' of Belgium, and the 'liberty and independence' of the people of Luxembourg. These telegrams, which were regarded as inadequate by the Allies at the time, were subsequently interpreted as expressions of sympathy with the victims of aggression rather than condemnations of the aggressors. Such interpretations, however, are unjust, though it is true that the Pope was not prepared to go as far as Tardini had wanted or as far as the Allies had requested.

The Pope's caution was probably the result of his desire to keep Italy out of the war and his fears that he might simply make the situation worse. Even so, Mussolini interpreted the Pope's telegrams as a political attack on himself. The *Regime Fascista* declared that the Pope had incited 'the Catholic King of the Belgians to cause the blood of his people to flow, in order to help the Jews, the Freemasons and the bankers of the City of London'. When Mussolini's Ambassador to the Holy See made an official protest, the Pope replied that he would not be influenced by threats, that Italy was compromised by being associated with the terrible crimes for which the Germans were responsible in Poland, that he himself had only maintained silence about events in Poland because he feared that a protest would make the sufferings of the victims even worse. He ended the audience with a warning: '. . . all of us will be subject to God's judgment. None will escape. No temporal success on earth can exempt us from this fearful judgment'.

The danger that Italy might enter the struggle inevitably increased with the military successes of the German armies in Europe and the Pope redoubled his efforts to preserve Italian neutrality. Pius XII had already publicly congratulated the Italians on their neutral stand on more than one occasion and he even left the Vatican in order to preach a sermon appealing for peace on Italian soil. He once had an interview with the King of Italy in an attempt to preserve Italian neutrality and in a joint effort with President Roosevelt brought pressure on Mussolini in order to achieve the same result. At the same time the Pope continued to promote the restoration of peace. At the beginning of 1940, with Myron Taylor and Sumner Welles, the Pope had examined the possibility of conciliation and before the invasion of the Low Countries, he gave his support to the offer made by the Queen of Holland and the King of the Belgians to use their good offices in an effort to open peace negotiations. The British and French promised to consider this offer if the two rulers were able to submit any German proposals 'of such a character as to afford real prospects of meeting with Allied desires'. The German Government simply interpreted this reply as a 'brusque refusal'. However by the end of May 1940 the French Ambassador to Italy reported: 'Pius XII did not conceal from me that he had used up all his credit, that the Duce refused to listen to him and no longer read his letters'.

The more neutral and moderate tone which was increasingly adopted by the Holy See at this time would seem to suggest that the ecclesiastical authorities no longer had any confidence that the Allies would be able to defeat or even resist the Nazi forces and that the Holy See must therefore learn to live in a Europe dominated by Nazism and Fascism. With the fall of France and the entry of Italy into the War, the Pope shared the opinion of most commentators outside Britain that the Hitler's Government could not now be overthrown except from inside Germany. He also might well have concluded that in these circumstances the consequences of further warfare would be even worse than peace in a Nazi Europe. Consequently Pius XII was willing to act on the advice of the American Minister to Belgium and attempted to persuade the British Government not to reject the moves in favour of peace that Hitler himself was making. At the end of June 1940 the Pope sent an appeal for peace to Italy, Germany and Britain, but, to the disappointment of the Vatican, the British Government dismissed Hitler's overtures as dishonest, deceitful and threatening and complained that they gave no guarantees to the nations which had been occupied.

With the entry of Italy into the conflict, the provisions of the Lateran Treaties safeguarding the independence and neutrality of the Vatican City State came into force and ensured that the Holy See would enjoy a greater degree of freedom than any other neutral agency. Although representatives of the Allies were technically entitled to remain in their official residences on Italian soil, they preferred to find accommodation within the Vatican and so established a means of communication between the Allies and the Holy See at a time when visits by foreign bishops were inevitably limited or restricted. Similarly at the beginning of June 1944 the German Ambassador moved into the Vatican as the British and French, Belgian and Polish representatives returned to Rome. The *Osservatore Romano* was free from Italian censorship, though copies might be confiscated, and it became the most widely read source of independent opinion in Italy. At one time the Italian authorities threatened to prohibit the circulation of the *Osservatore* in Italy unless it ceased publishing Allied war communiqués and details of the progress of the War and for a time the newspaper printed only religious news. At the beginning of the War the Vatican Radio was also a most important source of uncensored information, particularly about the persecution of the Church in Poland, not only to people in Italy but throughout the world.

Pius XI had been the first pope to use the Vatican Radio which became one of the chief symbols of the independence of the Holy See. Pius XII used the radio even more frequently than his predecessor in order to establish personal contact with the Church throughout the world, to preach the Gospel of peace to a world at war and to protest against any attacks on the Church itself. Although the Vatican Radio attempted to be neutral and unbiased during the later years of the War, it was the subject of a continuous struggle between the Foreign Offices in London and Berlin during 1940 and 1941. At this time the radio was experimental rather than established and unlike the *Osservatore Romano* did not come under the control of the Secretariat of State. As a result the British were able to exploit reports at which the Germans had officially protested. The radio was censored and jammed, quoted and misquoted, and even impersonated by secret transmitters. Reports on the radio were copied and distributed secretly while non-Catholics as well as Catholics in the occupied countries were imprisoned for having listened to it.

The point was that factual reports on the situation or conditions under National Socialism inevitably included accounts of religious persecution especially in Germany and Poland, and reports on the Church in Poland were broadcast as early as January 1940 on the instructions of the Pope himself. The Pope had already condemned the invasion of Poland in his encyclical *Summi Pontificatus* but it was the condemnation of an unjust act rather than of the unjust aggressor: 'The blood of countless human beings, including many civilians, cries out in agony, a race as beloved by Us as the Polish, whose steadfast Faith in the service of Christian civilization is written in ineffaceable letters in the Book of History, giving them the right to invoke the brotherly sympathy of the entire world'. The German authorities immediately forbade publication of the encyclical and feared that it would have a most damaging effect on world opinion. But the Poles themselves were not satisfied and the Allies also felt that the Pope's language was rather inadequate.

Cardinal Hlond, the Primate of Poland who had escaped to the West, submitted a detailed report on the persecution of the Poles and the Pope ordered that the facts should be broadcast on the Vatican Radio. On 22 January a broadcast claimed that Poland was in a state of terror and barbarism similar to that imposed by the Communists on Spain during 1936 and accused the Nazi authorities of using the same or even worse methods than those used by the Soviets. A few hours later a broadcast in English to North America described the deportation of Jews and Poles 'into separate "ghettoes" hermetically sealed and pitifully inadequate for the economic subsistence of the people destined to live there' and spoke of 'the cynical suppression of all but the merest suggestion of religious worship in the lives of this most pious and devotional of the peoples of Europe'. Similar broadcasts followed in French and Portuguese as well as German and Polish and the reports were also picked up by other foreign stations and newspapers throughout the world.

On 24 January the *Manchester Guardian* reported that 'Tormented

Poland has found a most powerful advocate. The Vatican broadcast, which has been issued in four languages, must make a deep impression on the consciences of the Christian world'. The broadcast was 'a warning to all who value our civilization that Europe is in deadly danger'. On the same day the *New York Times* informed its readers: 'Vatican City radio station made two broadcasts today, adding many details to the atrocities that supposedly are being committed in German-occupied Poland. It is now clear that the Papacy is throwing the whole weight of its publicizing facilities into an exposé of conditions which, yesterday's broadcast said, "profoundly pained" the Pope'. The Germans, on the other hand, delivered a strong protest to the Holy See and threatened that there would be reprisals in Germany if the broadcasts continued. Consequently the Pope suspended the broadcasts on Poland at least for the time being. When Tardini expressed the hope that they would soon be resumed, Pius XII smiled and agreed, though in the event broadcasts on Poland in this form were never carried again.

When Bishop Rarkowski, who supported the Nazis, published a pastoral on the first anniversary of the outbreak of war, the Vatican Radio commented: 'The German episcopate has so far avoided taking a position on this war that would transcend their pastoral duty towards the faithful. If the army bishop has read or heard what the Head of his Church has repeatedly and unequivocally said about the injustice done to Poland, he must be aware of the discrepancy between his position and that of the Holy See. Many Catholics do not at all share the political and historical viewpoint of the army bishop, but are convinced that Hitler's war unfortunately is not a just war and that God's blessing therefore cannot be upon it. . . . It almost looks as if the army bishop sometimes finds it easier to align himself with the Nazis than with his Church'. Inevitably and predictably the German Foreign Office protested to the Holy See.

Meanwhile Vatican Radio continued to carry reports on religious conditions in Germany and German policies in Alsace Lorraine. The Germans for their part continued to make official protests and threatened reprisals, and so the authorities in charge of the Radio were ordered to restrict all references to the bare facts without attempting to comment on or appraise them. The Radio authorities themselves decided to reduce the number of English broadcasts and to concentrate on Spain where the Germans were concentrating most of their propaganda at this time. The authorities tried to correct the false impression given in the Spanish press about religious conditions in Poland, Austria and Germany and continued to do so in spite of German protests. The Vatican Radio also transmitted the semi-official information that appeared in *Osservatore Romano*, reviews of Nazi literature and condemnations of racist theories. These criticisms were strongly reinforced by the Pope's own Easter broadcast in April 1941 when he warned the 'occupying powers' to treat with justice, humanity and foresight those peoples whom the fortunes of war had put at their mercy. Representatives of Germany and Italy, the only occupying powers at the time, immediately criticized the Pope, the Gestapo confiscated copies of the *Acta* in which the Pope's discourse was printed, and Goebbels expressed his determination to silence the Vatican Radio.

The British were not slow to seize on the opportunities presented to them by these Vatican broadcasts. The British Government recognized that the Vatican Radio was of incalculable importance in influencing Catholic opinion not only in North America but also in those territories occupied by the Germans whose citizens might otherwise be tempted to collaborate with their new masters. One official at the Foreign Office noted: 'The independent stand taken by the Vatican Radio is of the greatest importance to our propaganda generally and to our appeal to German Catholics in particular'. However the British were not simply content to repeat the Vatican broadcasts but 'reinforced' the German versions re-transmitted from London and tolerated the existence of secret radio stations, including one in London, which gave the impression that they were broadcasting on behalf of the Vatican. As a result the Pope was forced to take action and he decided that religious persecution in Germany should no longer be mentioned on Vatican Radio.

Not surprisingly the British Government was bitterly disappointed at these developments and the British Legation issued a strong protest to the Holy See in June 1941: 'His Majesty's Government have learned with astonishment, concern and deep distress that, towards the end of April, the Vatican Radio abruptly suspended all references to Germany, and all mention of German measures against the Church and the lying claims of German propaganda. This sudden silence on a subject of imperative concern to Catholics can only be attributed to successful pressure on the Vatican by the German authorities, and His Majesty's Government cannot but regard the decision of the Vatican to yield to this pressure as highly regrettable and inconsistent with the best interests of the Holy See and the Catholic Church. Such submission on the part of the Vatican means that the field is left open to the poisonous effects of Nazi propaganda among the Catholic population of the countries under German control. . . . There can be no doubt that, with the help of the United States, the Allied cause will prevail, and the Christian ideal triumph over pagan brutality. The day of the vindication of justice, fair dealing and human liberty may come sooner than might now be expected. What then will be the feeling of the Catholics of the world if it may be said of their Church that, after at first standing courageously against Nazi paganism, it subsequently consented, by surrender and silence, to discredit the principles on which it is based and by which it lives?'

The Holy See replied that the decision to end the broadcasts had been taken by the Pope himself and was not the result of any agreement with the Germans. Furthermore Catholics in the occupied countries had been made to suffer as a result of the serious distortions of the original broadcasts. At the same time officials at the Foreign Office were not as 'shocked' as the official protest seemed to suggest. Sir Alec Randall, who was in charge of Vatican affairs at the Foreign Office, commented in July 1941: 'The Vatican wireless has been of the greatest service to our propaganda and we have exploited it to the full. No other neutral power would, in the face of this, have persisted so long in furnishing us with useful material and risking violent criticism from powers with which it is in ordinary diplomatic relations'.

The persecution of the Church and people of Poland illustrated the impossible situation in which Pius XII found himself in attempting to decide whether or not to condemn German atrocities. Although communications between Rome and Poland were inadequate, the Holy See was well aware that priests and religious were being interned, religious services were restricted, Catholic organizations suppressed, seminaries and schools were closed, and ecclesiastical properties, including cathedrals, were being confiscated. Polish exiles begged the Pope to condemn the Germans and Polish troops fighting for the Allies were particularly bitter about the 'silence' of the Holy See. The Vatican received complaints from the Polish bishops, from the Polish Government in exile and from Cardinal Hlond who in August 1941 reported to the Secretary of State that the Polish people believed that the Pope had abandoned them and was even giving active support to their enemies.

Cardinal Maglione replied that the Pope had spoken clearly in his encyclical *Summi Pontificatus* which the Germans had succeeded in withholding from the Polish people. Subsequently the Pope had condemned the occupying Powers on no less than three occasions, but the Germans had done everything possible to conceal or to minimize the Pope's concern for Poland and to prevent the Holy See from sending material help to that country. Maglione also pointed out that the Polish bishops themselves were afraid to publish details of the German persecution in case of reprisals. In October 1942 Archbishop Sapieha of Cracow told the Vatican: 'We are alas unable to communicate publicly to the Faithful the contents of Your letters, because this would give rise to further persecutions. In any case, we are already suffering on account of our secret communications with the Holy See'.

The documents of the Holy See clearly reveal the extent to which Pius XII tried to mitigate the suffering of the Poles. In 1939 the Holy See attempted to send supplies to Poland but the Germans would not allow this. The Pope then tried to send money but the restrictions imposed and the unfavourable rate of exchange offered by the Germans were such that only a small proportion of the money would eventually reach the intended recipients. When the Germans agreed to allow the American Commission for Polish Relief to send supplies to Poland, the Holy See used this Commission as one of the agencies through which Vatican aid was sent to the Poles. Pius XII also organized the collection of money for Poland and in March 1940 Cardinal Maglione wrote to Bishop Hugh Boyle of Pittsburg: 'I am to tell you of the deep interest and appreciation with which the Holy Father is following the labours of your Committee in favour of prostrate Poland. Since the beginning of the war, the sad plight of this Christian people has been one of His heaviest preoccupations, and He has spared no efforts in providing alleviation for their sufferings. The burden has been greater than His resources, already strained by the numerous demands which the present untoward conditions in Europe have occasioned, would permit Him to expend; so that it was with heartfelt satisfaction that He welcomed the generous action of the American Bishops to raise funds for the relief of His beloved and sorely tried children in Poland'.

Pius XII finally spoke out on behalf of the Poles in an address to the Cardinals on 2 June 1943 which was then broadcast on the Vatican Radio. Fifty thousand copies of his speech were secretly distributed in Poland as well as among Polish exiles: 'No one familiar with the history of Christian Europe can ignore or forget the saints and heroes of Poland . . . nor how the faithful people of that land have contributed throughout history to the development and conservation of Christian Europe. For this people so harshly tried, and others, who together have been forced to drink the bitter chalice of war today, may a new future dawn worthy of their legitimate aspirations and the depths of their sufferings, in a Europe based anew on Christian foundations'.

Polish leaders throughout the world, including President Raczkiewicz and General Sikorski, expressed their gratitude to the Pope. Cardinal Hlond remarked: 'The Pope's words have placed before world opinion without ambiguity or doubt the sympathy of the Sovereign Pontiff for the cruel sufferings of the smaller nations'. Archbishop Sapieha wrote from Cracow: 'We thank Your Holiness for this speech in which You spoke so warmly of our unhappy nation. Hitherto, we have had countless demonstrations of the paternal love of the Holy Father for our nation – but this tribute is of historic importance. The Polish people will never forget the noble and holy words – which will also serve as an effective counter to the poison of enemy propaganda against the Holy See. If we obtain permission to print the speech, we shall do all we can to give the words of Your Holiness the greatest possible publicity. I say this under reserve, because every printed word must obtain the permission of the Nazi Party, under pain of severe penalties'.

From the very beginning of the conflict, Pius XII was almost totally preoccupied with a determination to do everything he could to limit the conflict and to end the fighting. But he felt that he could only hope to play an effective rôle as a peacemaker or a mediator if he enjoyed an undisputed reputation for neutrality and he was forced to adopt a most unenviable position in an effort to achieve this reputation. He had to avoid making specific judgments on the issues that had led to the conflict and cautious in expressing his sympathies with the victims of war. He had to avoid denouncing the crimes of the guilty or endorsing the accusations of inhumanity that came repeatedly from both sides. The Pope showed his total lack of bias towards those Catholics actively engaged in the struggle by never refusing to bless troops in uniforms whether they were fighting for the Allies or the Axis and on the whole he refrained from commenting on the military activities of either side. Similarly his efforts to assist the victims of war were fairly divided between the fighting nations. Thus the Pope felt constrained in condemning the German invasion of Poland or publicly demonstrating his sympathies with the Polish people, though it would also seem that he soon became convinced that public condemnations would have little influence on the Nazi authorities.

Of course such an approach involved considerable dangers and there are those historians who would argue 'that this carefully poised impartiality in the long run benefited the guilty rather than the innocent and so ceased to be impartial'. The Second World War differed fundamentally from the First in the sense that a compromise peace was never really possible. Papal appeals for peace on the basis of justice or frequent reminders of the sufferings caused by war left uncommitted observers cold or indifferent in a fight to the death between two irreconcilable rival ideologies. At the same time it is only fair to remember that the situation facing Pius XII was in some ways more difficult than that which had faced Benedict XV if only because the Holy See could not in the event ever seriously hope to influence or to moderate the claims of conquering Germans or victorious Russians.

The Pope and Vatican officials made no comment when Italy entered the war on 10 June 1940 but many Italian bishops and priests gave enthusiastic support to the national cause. Some bishops declared that obedience to the State during war-time was ordained by God and was a religious duty. A military chaplain proclaimed that: 'England is anti-Catholic and anti-Roman, with the morals of a pirate; a country of vast possessions and rich bankers, where the poor miners are left to rot in the mines. Her army is composed of mercenaries of every colour and she has taught the Australians to pillage. England's motto is, "First me, then my horse, then my dog, then everyone else"'. When the British Minister at the Vatican made an official protest, Mgr Montini showed himself to be 'most embarrassed and duly mortified' and shortly afterwards the chaplain concerned was suspended.

However, as the pattern of events unfolded, more and more Italian priests became increasingly disillusioned with the war and comparatively indifferent as to its progress or success. It became possible for a priest to proclaim: 'We Catholics have no enemies. All men are our brothers in our universal Faith, including the English, the Americans, the French and the Russians'.

Don Orione of the Angelicum told the readers of *Gerarchia*, a newspaper edited by Vito Mussolini, that Germany was no longer properly speaking a Christian nation. When Mussolini fell from power in 1943 he reminded the Holy See of the Concordat in the vain hopes that the Vatican would continue to recognize the Fascist régime. However the Vatican replied that the Concordat had been made with the Italian State and not with the Fascist Government and this refusal provoked bitter attacks in the Fascist press. At the same time the Vatican gave material help to those Italian troops who wanted to join the forces of the legitimate Italian Government and provided shelter for political refugees, including such leading Socialists and Communists as Nenni, Togliatti and Saragat, who were being pursued by the Germans.

During the early days of the War some of the Italian representatives of the Holy See throughout the world also revealed their sympathies and gave active support to the Italian cause and the British Government requested the recall or the replacement of a few members of the Vatican diplomatic service who were suspected or convicted of giving assistance to the enemy. At the same time the Holy See was understandably concerned to secure from both sides a recognition of the neutrality of the Vatican City State and a promise to safeguard the religious shrines and historic buildings of Rome. But any moves which Vatican officials made in pursuit of these aims were likely to be misunderstood and even misinterpreted by the Allies.

In December 1942 Osborne indicated some of the difficulties that might arise when he told Montini: 'I informed the Foreign Office that, in conversation with me, you had complained that His Majesty's Government seemed to display incomprehension and lack of sympathy towards the motives, interests and activities of the Holy See. I have now been instructed to reply that you entirely misinterpeted the sentiments of His Majesty's Government if you suppose that they feel any lack of sympathy towards the Holy See. On the contrary it is their earnest wish to maintain their traditional good relations with the Holy See. They find it, however, a little difficult to reconcile the position of the Holy See in regard to the bombing of Rome with their attitude in regard to the withdrawal of certain ecclesiastics of Italian birth from the Middle East. In the latter case the Vatican have based their reluctance to meet the requests of His Majesty's Government on the international character of the Catholic Church, its freedom from politics and its impartiality towards all belligerents. In the case of the bombing of Rome, however, the Vatican, far from adopting an international standpoint, would appear to be associating themselves with the interests of the Italian State'.

In due course both the Allies and the Axis declared their willingness to respect the neutrality of the Holy See but in the meantime the Allies asked whether the Pope had condemned the bombing of Allied cities and British cathedrals or the inhuman conduct of the Germans in the occupied territories. The Allies also warned the Holy See against the dangers of seeming to be too partisan. Roosevelt told the Apostolic Delegate in Washington that the Italian people had been made the instrument of Mussolini's pagan policy and that although there was no intention to damage the historic treasures of Rome, the military objectives in and around the city could not be ignored. Furthermore, the Allies suggested, information received would seem to imply that British aircraft and weapons captured by the enemy were being saved for the specific purpose of bombing the Vatican and placing the responsibility on the Allies. Nevertheless in December 1943 Air Chief Marshal Tedder, who was in command of the Allied air forces in the Mediterranean, gave assurances that his forces would abstain from flying over the Vatican City State.

Following the entry of Italy into the War, it seemed to some that the Roman authorities were dominated by 'an anxious neutrality' and that the Pope was unwilling – unlike his predecessor – to act as the moral conscience of the world. On 1 June 1940 Cardinal Tisserant told Cardinal Suhard of his fears that history would prove critical of the Holy See for having adopted an accommodating political line 'for its own exclusive advantage – and very little else. And this is extremely sad – particularly for one who has lived in the Reign of Pius XI'. Just over two years later Osborne described to Tardini how the position of the Vatican was seen at the Foreign Office: 'I would not like you to think that we are not aware that the Pope is being criticized by the Axis Powers, but you have summed up our chief criticism in the last words of your despatch, namely "the endeavour of the Vatican to maintain a precarious equilibrium outside of and above the war". In order to do this we feel that ever since the entry of Italy into the war the Pope has more and more assimilated himself to the status of a sovereign of a small neutral State in the geographical neighbourhood of Axis Powers, and, for worldly rather than spiritual reasons, has allowed himself, like others, to be bullied. In short, we feel that His Holiness is not putting up a very good fight to retain his moral and spiritual leadership, when he should realize that in Hitler's new world there will be no room for the Catholic religion and that if the Papacy remains silent, the free nations may find that they have little power to arrest the anticlericalism which may follow the war'.

A few months earlier, in February 1942, Osborne had made much the same point in a strong protest against the appointment of a Japanese Representative to the Holy See which, 'has caused a most unfavourable impression on His Majesty's Government who find it difficult to reconcile the decision with the frequent Vatican professions deploring the extension of the war. His Holiness' action is likely to be widely interpreted as a condonation of Japan's treacherous and unprovoked attack. In the absence of any indication of a suddenly increased importance of Vatican interests in the Far East such as to require the establishment of diplomatic relations with Japan, or of any development in the spiritual sphere that would justify the conferment upon Japan at this moment of a special sign of the Pope's favour, His Majesty's Government are reluctantly forced to conclude that His Holiness has again deferred to pressure from the Governments of the Axis Powers'.

However, it is important to remember that at this time, as Osborne himself told Maglione in September 1942, the British Government was most anxious to secure a public and specific papal condemnation of the Nazi treatment of the inhabitants of the occupied territories: the murder of innocent hostages, the extermination of peoples, the liquidation of local leaders, the suppression of religious freedom, the introduction of deportation, conscription and forced labour, and the persecution of the Jews. Although Osborne admitted that the Pope had already publicly denounced the moral crimes arising out of the war, the Ambassador argued that such denunciations were too general and had been superseded by 'the mounting record of Nazi crimes': 'It is affirmed that the mission of the Church is a spiritual one, that its primary purpose is the safeguarding of the faith throughout the world and that this imposes upon the Papacy political neutrality and supranational impartiality at all times, and more particularly in time of war between the nations. The Supreme Pontiff is, it is often asserted, the universal father whose charity and affection are impartially distributed among all peoples. But universal paternity and impartial charity need not exclude reprobation of offences against humanity and civilization by one nation at the expense of others. A policy of silence in regard to such offences against the conscience of the world must necessarily involve a renunciation of moral leadership and a consequent atrophy of the influence and authority of the Vatican; and it is upon the maintenance and assertion of such authority that must depend any prospect of a Papal contribution to the re-establishment of world peace'.

The Pope certainly had to struggle hard to maintain his neutrality but his determination to do so was the result of several factors. He believed, at least initially, that the very continuance of the war was a greater evil than an immediate peace and he still hoped to play a leading role as a mediator. He was aware of the limited effect that protests had on totalitarian régimes and wished to safeguard the position of European Catholics particularly in Germany where the future of the Church might be threatened either by persecution or by the establishment of a German National Church. Finally the Pope was alarmed by the increasing threat of Communism. Nevertheless there is no conclusive evidence that Pius XII allowed his fears of Communism to determine his attitudes towards Nazism or Fascism, though there is evidence that fears of a separate peace between Russia and Germany in 1943 might have influenced him and it is quite possible that he became increasingly preoccupied with the Communist threat to Eastern Europe. Certainly Vatican officials felt that the British were far too optimistic in their predictions about the behaviour and the attitudes of the Russians after the war and they failed to share the same sense of confidence in the ability of Britain to safeguard the future peace and security of Europe. In the event some of the statements made by British officials at the time proved to be remarkably over-optimistic. For example, at the end of May 1943 Hugh Montgomery, Secretary of the British Legation, assured Mgr Tardini 'that, whatever the exigencies of the War in the Far East, we should not dream of evacuating the defeated countries in Europe or of leaving Russia in exclusive control there'.

There are those historians who would argue that in time Pius XII began to recognize that Nazism rather than Communism was the greatest threat to the future of Christianity and civilization. What is certainly true is that the Pope made it perfectly clear that it was quite legitimate to resist German aggression even with the support of Russian Communists. When the Germans invaded Russia in 1941 the Pope rejected German requests, which were supported by the opinions of some prelates in France and Italy, that their invasion should be regarded as a crusade or at least a welcome attack on Communism. When the Italian Ambassador suggested that the Pope might issue a declaration in favour of the Axis forces fighting in Russia, he was asked for a word of explanation from those who had previously made treaties of friendship with the Soviet Union. Vatican officials consistently told German and Italian diplomats that if the Holy See was to condemn the religious policies of the Russian Government, it would also have to condemn the religious policies of the German Government.

A number of influential American Catholics were also opposed to Roosevelt's policy of supplying arms to the dictatorial and atheistic Government of Russia. Pius XI had clearly stated in *Divini Redemptoris* that no one who wanted to save Christian civilization could conceivably collaborate with Communism. The difficulties facing American Catholics were summarized by Mgr M. J. Ready in a memorandum to Sumner Welles: '. . . an objective view of the situation compels the admission that there is a measure of expediency in any policy of American aid to the Soviets – the expediency that suggests seizing the present opportunity to halt Nazi aggression and so enhance our national security. But to insure the support of Catholic citizens for this policy, it must be clear that it is not a question of expediency that is in opposition to the principle which forbids them in conscience to collaborate with Communism'.

Cardinal Spellman, who even then believed that America would eventually be forced to enter the war, explained the divisions among American Catholics and reported that 'things are in a turmoil here'. The Apostolic Delegate to the United States also appealed to Rome. President Roosevelt himself wrote to Pius XII expressing his belief that the survival of Russia would prove less dangerous to the future of Christianity than the survival of Nazi dictatorship. In an interview with the Pope, Myron Taylor outlined the situation in America and the attitude of the American Government to future developments. Taylor and the Pope also discussed an 'Interpretation of Encyclical of Pope Pius XI as not condemning the Russian people, but directed against Soviet practices in respect to individual liberty', and this conversation was faithfully reported back to Roosevelt. In September 1941 Cicognani was told that *Divini Redemptoris* was a condemnation of atheistic Communism and not of the Russian people and he asked the Archbishop of Cincinnati to publish a pastoral letter outlining the attitude of Rome which had proved entirely acceptable to the American Government.

However, the attitudes and approaches adopted by Vatican officials during the Second World War dramatically changed when the Pope was officially informed that the American Government would not engage in peace negotiations until Nazism had been completely destroyed. Until September 1942 and in spite of the persecution of the Church by the Nazis, the Pope had continued to receive leading members of the National Socialist Party and to send greetings to Hitler on his birthday. But on 19 September 1942 Myron Taylor had an audience with Pius XII in which he made it perfectly clear that the United States would continue the struggle until the Allies had achieved total victory over the enemy and would regard any 'Axis-inspired proposals of "peace"' as 'nothing less than a blow aimed at us': 'There is reason to believe that our Axis enemies will attempt, through devious channels, to urge the Holy See to endorse in the near future proposals of peace without victory. In the present position of the belligerents, we can readily understand how strong a pressure the Axis powers may bring to bear upon the Vatican. We therefore feel it a duty to support the Holy See in resisting any undue pressure from this source. It is for this reason that we feel impelled to make known our views on the subject of peace, and to point out that the growing power of the United States is now being applied to re-establish those principles of international decency and justice which have been so well expounded by the Holy See'.

In his reply the Pope remarked: 'We have read your Memorandum very carefully, and We have found it intensely interesting. The issues are so clear-cut; of the definite, determined stand of the United States Government it leaves no shadow of doubt'. The actual conditions of Unconditional Surrender were publicly announced at Casablanca in January 1943 but the Pope already knew that the Allies were determined to destroy Nazism and Fascism, and that as an incidental result Communism would not only survive but spread, and Soviet Russia would inevitably play a crucial rôle in the political life of the nations after the War.

Within a very short time, the Pope began to adopt a more definite line in his attitude towards the Nazis and he became more critical of their persecution of the Church. At the same time it is only just to remember that Pius XII's declarations on matters of principle, such as his Christmas messages, were frequently precise and definite. It is true that Pius XII's statement about peace in the Spring of 1941, for example, was an implicit rather than an explicit condemnation of Nazism while his practical recommendations seemed totally unrealistic at a time when Europe was dominated by the Nazis. However in his Christmas address to the Cardinals in 1940 he had outlined clearly, if in general terms, the principles of a 'new order' based on victory over international mistrust and the hatreds dividing nations, victory over national selfishness and the conflicts which resulted from an unbalanced world economy, and victory over the principle that utility was the basis and the aim of law. Over the years, the Pope outlined the bases of a sound international order. He defined the causes of conflict and urged nations to abolish the economic inequalities that existed between them. He defended the rights of minorities and warned against the dangers of totalitarianism and nationalism.

The Pope's condemnation of modern 'Statolatry' in his Christmas message of 1942 was clearly directed against the totalitarian régimes and his reassertion of the primacy of the Family over the State clearly contradicted the claims of the Fascists and the Nazis. Pius XII also made a clear reference to the Jews – though the Allies did not believe that he had been explicit enough – when he spoke of 'the hundreds of thousands who, through no fault of their own, and solely because of their nation or race, have been condemned to death or progressive extinction'. One German report commented: 'In a manner never known before the Pope has repudiated the National Socialist New European Order. . . . It is true, the Pope does not refer to the National Socialists in Germany by name, but his speech is one long attack on everything we stand for . . . God, he says, regards all peoples and races as worthy of the same consideration. Here he is clearly speaking on behalf of the Jews . . . he is virtually accusing the German people of injustice towards the Jews, and makes himself the mouthpiece of the Jewish war criminals'.

The German Ambassador was ordered to warn the Pope that the Nazis did not lack means of retaliation if the Holy See abandoned its neutral stand. This the Ambassador did, though he also reported to his superiors in Berlin that 'Pacelli is no more sensible to threats than we are'.

Inevitably many German Catholics were torn by divided loyalties during the Second World War though only a few of them could see the issues as clearly as Theodor Haecker did in May 1940: 'The leadership of Germany today, and of this there is not the faintest doubt, and it cannot be evaded, is consciously anti-Christian – it hates Christ whom it does not name. We are making war against peoples and States which although often only euphemistically Christian could not in any single instance be called definitely anti-Christian. And one cannot therefore avoid recognizing the fact, that over and above being a war of power – it is a war of religion. And we Germans are fighting this war on the wrong side! We are, as to the majority, making war as willing slaves, and as to the minority, as the unwilling slaves of a government that has apostatized, strong in the passion of its despair and in its despicable subjects, and all of us, the slaves of slaves without honour – *ruimus in servitutum* [are rushing into slavery]. From the very beginning, the repeatedly successful trick of these inhuman beings, sent to plague Europe, has been to combine, more or less, the special interests of their basely impulsive, greedy natures, with the true and genuine wishes and claims of the German people, combining them by an unprecedented skill in the art of lying. The climax of this hellish art has now been reached. Who does not love his country and his people *by nature*? There are innumerable people who love it more than their fathers or their mothers, their wives or their children, their brothers or their sisters, which is why it is always dangerous and almost a crime to over-excite this love. And who, then, will not *instinctively* wish his country to be victorious in a war? But: we Germans are on the side of apostasy. That is the German position'.

Christian resistance to National Socialism was often reluctant and disorganized and the gradual divorce between Church and State was a painful process. Individuals and groups first reacted against Nazi attacks on the Church before slowly beginning to question their basic attitudes towards the World War and the Third Reich. Even opponents of National Socialism were sometimes prepared to express their loyalty to the State or to the Führer and to support the War abroad, while Christian resistance to the Nazis was frequently a matter of self-defence rather than the result of an ideological or political opposition. Similarly although individual German Christians were immediately prepared to come to the help of the Jews, most Christians in Germany first protested against the persecution of their fellow Christians before finding the courage to condemn the persecution of the Jews. Furthermore it must never be forgotten that many of the limited successes which Churchmen enjoyed in dealing with the Nazis were frequently due to divisions among the National Socialists themselves rather than to their defence or assertion of Christian principles.

Nevertheless, with all their limitations, the Christian Churches showed a greater resistance to the claims of Hitler and the Nazis than any of the other great German institutions such as the judiciary or the universities. The German Trade Unions, for example, the largest and best-organized in the world were eliminated by a combination of threats and promises. Furthermore, as one commentator has pointed out: '. . . both in the case of active conspirators, such as those who partook in the 20 July 1944 revolt, and in the more passive but ideologically-orientated forms of opposition to Nazism, Christian ideals and idealism played a formative rôle'.

The real 'successes', like the real 'failures', of Christians in the struggle against National Socialism were perhaps inevitably on the individual rather than the institutional level. Could it not be that the lukewarm spiritual sentiments of individual Christians were ultimately responsible for the 'failures' rather than the opportunism or 'betrayals' of Church leaders though these too might be condemned? Was it not unfortunately true that too many individual Christians were more influenced by the fact of Nazism than by their Christian faith? Was it not also true that, as a commentator wrote in 1947: 'For the prophets to recall the Church to a higher standard of loyalty and behaviour is sure to bring about the reaction of the priests against the prophets, of the people against its origins?'

But, whatever criticisms might be made of the attitudes of Christians or their Churches towards the National Socialists, these should never be allowed to hide or conceal the very real witness and martyrdoms of so many Christians. If Catholics were humiliated by the behaviour of ecclesiastics like the Benedictine Abbot Alban Schachleiter, they could take pride in the courage of many other priests and layfolk. One Catholic priest was arrested in Düsseldorf for stating that it would not be so bad if the Communists did in fact come to power. Another priest was imprisoned for arguing that the bombing of Cologne was punishment for the destruction of Jewish shops before the War. A third priest found himself under arrest for maintaining that the German newspapers only spread lies and that Germany was responsible for the War. In Dachau alone over two thousand Catholic priests died or were murdered. During the War some 2,800 Polish ecclesiastics had been sent to Dachau of whom just over 800 survived. In 1942 of the 480 other ministers of religion in the camp, no less than 435 were Catholics. Many other priests and religious from France and Belgium, Holland and Luxembourg, Italy and Slovenia were also sent to Dachau after 1942 but only 350 of these had survived by the beginning of 1945. The Bishop of Clermont, for example, had been imprisoned there while another prisoner had been scourged and crowned with thorns.

In 1942 Franz Reinisch, a member of the Pallotine Order, was condemned to death for refusing to take the military oath of allegiance and was beheaded. He declared: 'The present government is not an authority willed by God, but a nihilistic government that has attained its power only through force, lies, and deceit. . . . The National Socialist principle, "Might before right", has forced me into a position of self-defence. Hence for me there can be no oath of allegiance to such a government'. Reinisch, as a soldier, was given permission to make a final statement: 'Since we are at this time engaged in a struggle against Bolshevism for the preservation of the Christian faith and the German fatherland, and, as the President of the Senate has himself declared in the General Assembly, for the preservation of a *Christian* Europe, the subject under sentence believes it imperative to abide unflinchingly by his previous demonstration of principle. For in our country this time of war is being used chiefly to tear from the hearts of the people, and especially from the hearts of youth, the belief in God incarnate, Jesus Christ . . . the prisoner under sentence believes that in refusing to give his oath of allegiance to the present government, he is more genuinely "loyal to the German nation in its fight for survival" than he would be in taking the opposite course. He is therefore ready and willing to sacrifice his life for Christ the King and for the German fatherland, in order that Christ the Lord may defeat the anti-Christian and Bolshevist powers and principalities not only abroad but also especially at home, that our people may become once more a strong and free nation of God amidst the nations of the Occident'.

In November 1943 four clergymen from Lübeck, including three Catholic priests, were beheaded in Hamburg. In their sermons, they had spoken of the burning of Lübeck after an air raid as a judgment of God. When Johannes Prassek heard his sentence, he wrote in his New Testament: 'The name of the Lord be praised! Today I have been condemned to death!' Hermann Lange wrote from his cell: 'I am perfectly calm . . . men are only tools in the hands of God. Hence, if God desires my death – his will be done. For me, it means that my life in this vale of sorrow is at an end . . . after all, death means homecoming. The gift we thereupon receive is so unimaginably great that all human joys pale beside it, and the bitterness of death as such – however sinister it may appear to our human nature – is completely conquered by it'.

Eduard Müller wrote: 'In the past I have always been greatly stirred by the heroes of our holy Church, by their readiness for sacrifice, and by their perfect devotion to Christ. Only now do I begin to apprehend their greatness, and I am filled with awe at their unsurpassable heroism. How far removed we are from their attitude! And now our Lord and Master receives us into his rigorous school; now he gives us a slight taste of what it means to follow Christ!

> *Lord,*
> *Here are my hands.*
> *Place in them what thou wilt,*
> *Take from them what thou wilt,*
> *Lead me where'er thou wilt,*
> *In everything – Thy will be done'.*

Bernhard Lichtenberg was Dean of the Cathedral of St Hedwig in Berlin. When the Nazis distributed anti-Semitic publications in October 1941, he ordered the following announcement to be read from the pulpits of all the churches in the diocese: 'An inflammatory pamphlet anonymously at-

Marshal Pétain and Pierre Laval receive Cardinals Suhard and Gerlier in Vichy in 1942 before the Germans entered unoccupied France

tacking the Jews is being disseminated among the houses of Berlin. It declares that any German who, because of allegedly false sentimentality, aids the Jews in any way, be it only through a friendly gesture, is guilty of betraying his people. Do not allow yourselves to be confused by this un-Christian attitude, but act according to the strict commandment of Jesus Christ: "Thou shalt love thy neighbour as thyself"'. He was denounced for reciting public prayers for Jews and for prisoners in concentration camps. When the Gestapo commissioner asked the Dean how he felt towards the Führer, he replied: 'I have only one Führer, Jesus Christ'. Lichtenberg was sentenced to two years' imprisonment and in September 1943 he wrote: 'When I look back upon the last two years, I desire and am obliged to thank God with all my soul, as well as all who have been instrumental in carrying out his holy will upon me. It is my firm resolution to keep, with the help of God, the vows that in his presence I made at the end of the thirty-day spiritual exercises. That is to say, I shall consider everything that happens to me, joyful or painful things, elevating or depressing, in the light of eternity. In my patience I will possess my soul. By neither word nor deed will I sin, and I will do everything out of love, and out of love I will suffer everything. I have enough courage to live for another twenty years, but should God will that I die today, may his holy will be done'. He died during the following month on his way to Dachau where he was being sent on the grounds that he was a danger to public order.

Some religious were themselves victims of Nazi racialism. On her conversion to Catholicism, Dr Edith Stein entered the Carmelite Convent at Cologne and took the name Sister Teresia Benedicta. In 1938 she was sent to Echt in Holland in order to protect her from persecution in Germany but in 1943 she was arrested and died in the concentration camp at Auschwitz. Other victims were simply priests or religious. In 1943 Alfons Maria Wachsmann who had been serving as a priest in Pomerania was arrested on the charge of undermining the morale of the armed forces. He was executed on 21 February 1944. Father Joseph Müller was arrested in May 1944 on the charge of being politically unreliable and was executed on 11 September. In November 1944 three priests who had been working in Stettin were executed following a large-scale Gestapo drive against the clergy of Mecklenburg and Pomerania. They were condemned 'not because they were criminals', as one of their judges admitted, 'but because it was their tragedy that they were Catholic priests'.

The Jesuit priest, Alfred Delp, was associated with the Kreisau resistance group which included Count Helmuth James von Moltke and Count Peter Yorck von Wartenburg. Without necessarily approving of the assassination plot against Hitler, most of the members of the Kreisau circle were familiar with the group of activists surrounding Count Claus von Stauffenberg who made the attempt on Hitler's life in July 1944. Delp was sentenced together with Moltke and was executed by hanging in February 1945. Delp expressed his conviction that 'God simply has completely cornered me' and spoke of his prison as the 'kindergarten of death'. He believed that 'God's strength accompanies me in all ways' and although he admitted that at times he had been 'nothing more than a bleeding, moaning mass', he always tried to bring this moaning into proper relation with 'the only two realities that make existence worthwhile – adoration and love'. At times he felt so tired and broken that he was no longer able to grasp the reality of the Eucharist. At the end of November, he wrote: 'Today is another very black day. God must really be very intensively concerned with me, in that he has thrown me so exclusively on my own resources. For some time now I have again been totally isolated. I am to learn what faith and trust mean'.

Delp spoke of the atmosphere during his trial being filled with 'hatred and animosity' and expressed the opinion that the outcome had been 'fixed'; 'My crime is that I had faith in Germany, a faith surmounting even a possible interim of desolation and darkness. That I did not believe in that insensate trinity of pride, arrogance, and force. And that I did this as a Catholic Christian and as a Jesuit'.

He told his fellow Jesuits: 'The actual reason for my sentence is that I am and remain a Jesuit. It was not possible to establish any connection with the event of July 20. Neither was the charge of a tie to Stauffenberg upheld. Other sentences demanded by the prosecutor, in cases actually involving knowledge of the affair of July 20, were much less severe and less biased. The air was so filled with hatred and animosity. The basic tenet is that a Jesuit is *a priori* an enemy and an adversary of the Reich. Thus in the one aspect the whole thing was a farce; in the other, however, it became a *pièce à thèse*. This was not a trial: it was simply a function of the will to annihilate'.

Father Rupert Mayer had received four decorations including the Iron Cross first class as a military chaplain during the First World War. In December 1916 a shell shattered his left leg and it had to be amputated. After the War Mayer became interested in the new Nazi Party largely as a result of his hostility to Communism. He addressed a public meeting in 1919 and was followed by Hitler himself who declared: 'Now that the priest has opposed Communism on religious grounds, I shall oppose it on political grounds'. However Mayer was quickly disillusioned and in 1923 spoke on the theme 'Can a Catholic be a National Socialist?' He was greeted with roars of applause but he told his audience that they were applauding too soon: 'Because I am going to tell you clearly that a German Catholic can never be a National Socialist'. He was then howled down and not allowed to speak and when the Party suffered its first defeat shortly afterwards, it was widely believed that Mayer was largely responsible. He ceased to subscribe to the war-veterans' associations when these were incorporated into the Nazi Party and gave up wearing his war medals as patriotism became identified with Nazism. Later, when he was released from the Landsberg Prison, he ostentatiously left his Iron Cross behind.

In May 1936 Mayer was warned that he might be forbidden to preach by the civil authorities. But when he was forbidden to 'speak' in public, he continued to 'preach', and when he was banned from preaching, he simply ignored the ban. He was arrested in June 1937 and the people of Munich decorated his confessional with flowers. Mayer wrote of his first imprisonment: 'I have now passed through the most beautiful period of my life. One would not believe that possible. I have been happy, completely happy, as never before in my life. In the course of these weeks the dear Lord has let me know – and I am a man of reason – that he is satisfied with me. That makes me happy; all else cannot disturb me. Prison is better for me than a thousand lectures on behalf of the Catholic community, on apologetics, on the Gospel – much better than if I were to lecture on heaven knows what'.

Mayer was released when he reluctantly agreed to accept the 'advice' of his superiors to stop preaching but when public opinion misinterpreted his actions he secured permission from his superiors to resume preaching, was immediately arrested and imprisoned in Landsberg am Lech. During his interrogation, he refused to answer several questions on the grounds that he could not do so without giving offence: 'I cannot and will not dissemble. Our beloved Fatherland would be ill served by hypocrites and cowards'. He himself later wrote: 'I spent Holy Week 1938 in prison. On Holy Thursday the parish priest got permission for the imprisoned Catholic priests to attend his Mass and receive Holy Communion. . . . The prison chaplain brought each one from his cell. I think there were eight of us. It moved us deeply and made an unforgettable impression'.

Eighteen months after his release from Landsberg, Mayer was arrested again, accused of homosexuality and charged with being involved in Monarchist plots. The reasons eventually given to explain his arrest were 'insubordination' and 'supporting aspirations hostile to the State'. In December 1939 he was taken to the concentration camp at Sachsenhausen where, by his own account, his treatment does not seem to have been as severe as that of many other prisoners and where: '. . . one good thing has come out of all this, I think I've come a good bit nearer God and,

147

spiritually, the same distance further from all worldly things. I cannot thank our Lord God sufficiently. So I'm not in the least worried about the future. I leave everything in God's hands'. He also recorded that during his imprisonment: 'I dreamt one time that I was about to be shot. At the same moment it became very noisy in the prison. I was still completely enmeshed in my dream and had no other thought than that they were coming to get me. Now suddenly there came over me a feeling of bliss such as I had never before experienced. I was utterly unable to comprehend that I had been chosen to die as a martyr. I had already got up, in order to be instantly ready – then the sound of steps receded from my room. That was a great disappointment, but the whole episode has often heartened me, since I actually would have been happy to die for the faith. But there was one other good thing about this occurrence: I had now experienced in my own being how easy God can make things, through his omnipotent grace, for those who must, or, better, are allowed to die for our holy faith'.

In August 1940 Mayer was released from prison partly as a result of the demands of public opinion and partly because of Nazi fears that he might become a 'martyr'. But the conditions which his religious superiors were forced to accept on his behalf were severe. He was to be confined in the Benedictine monastery of Ettal which he was not allowed to leave. His correspondence was to be restricted to personal and family affairs, a condition which was frequently circumvented by members of the local post office. He was forbidden to hear confessions or to conduct religious services in the presence of strangers. 'I am as the living dead', Mayer wrote: 'Yes, for me, so full of life still, this death is worse than the real death to which I had so often resigned myself. I can do the Gestapo and the whole movement no greater favour than to fade away here quietly, because to all Catholics, some of whom have not forgotten me, the Gestapo will come out of this well. The good people will say, "Oh, now that he's in the monastery he'll be quite all right, why, who knows what might have happened to him if he'd stayed in Munich". These people don't realize what the sort of life I have to lead here means to me. They don't realize that the air-raids affect me far more here than if I were in Munich'. Father Mayer was freed at the end of the War and died of a stroke on 1 November, the Feast of All Saints, 1945.

On the outbreak of war the German bishops issued a pastoral letter calling on Catholic soldiers to do their duty 'full of the spirit of self-sacrifice' and on 'all devout Catholics in civilian life to pray that God's Providence may bring the war to a victorious conclusion, with a peace beneficial for *Volk und Vaterland*'. Bishop Rarkowski, who described Hitler as 'the shining example of a true warrior, the first and most valiant soldier of the Greater German Reich', went even further. He demanded from Catholic soldiers unswerving loyalty to the Führer in all circumstances. This attitude, however, was not typical of the German bishops as a whole. In 1941 they issued another pastoral letter condemning both the continued persecution of the Church in Germany and Rosenberg's *Myth of the Twentieth Century*. The Nazi authorities interpreted this pastoral as a direct attack on the German State and Reinhard Heydrich commented: 'Here we see what a bitter and irreconcilable enemy we have in the Catholic Church'.

In 1940 Cardinal Bertram of Breslau sent a letter of congratulation to Hitler on his birthday from the meeting of the German bishops at Fulda. This action so infuriated Bishop Preysing of Berlin that he threatened to resign unless Bertram made it clear that the telegram of congratulation had been sent by him personally and not on behalf of the German episcopate. Pope Pius XII persuaded Preysing not to resign, but the Pope also made it clear that Preysing had been right to oppose Bertram's action. The Pope's letters to the German bishops during the War reveal his helplessness to do much more than offer words of sympathy and encouragement. Originally Pius XII gave his support to those bishops who tended to adopt an accommodating line with the Nazi authorities but he soon changed his mind and began to accept Preysing's advice when selecting episcopal candidates, excluding those whom Preysing regarded as too weak in their attitudes to the German Government.

On the other hand, and in spite of Preysing's complaints, the Pope did not remove Cesare Orsenigo, the Papal Nuncio in Berlin who was widely criticized as too accommodating in his dealings with the Nazi authorities. Orsenigo was undoubtedly treated in a most contemptuous way by the Nazis. He was not allowed to visit prisoners of war or to minister to their religious needs and his own servant was executed by the Gestapo. But to have removed Orsenigo might have brought into question the very existence of a Papal Nuncio in Berlin and Pacelli himself had once persuaded Pius XI of the value of a Nuncio in Germany as the only safe and secure means of communication between the German bishops and the Holy See. Furthermore Orsenigo proved to be the Vatican's best source of information on the situation in Poland and he was far more active and valuable than was generally supposed. He faithfully reported Nazi activities in Germany including their attempts to destroy the authority and influence of the Church, the confiscation of ecclesiastical property, the suppression of Catholic societies and the destruction of the Catholic press.

At the beginning of the War, Bishop von Galen of Münster boldly declared: 'We will do our duty out of love for our German Fatherland. Our soldiers will fight and die for Germany — but not for those men who bring shame upon the German name before God. Bravely we will fight against the foreign foe. But against the enemy in our midst, who strikes and tortures us, we cannot fight with weapons – only our stubborn endurance'.

Von Galen was perhaps the most outspoken member of the hierarchy in his condemnations of euthanasia, concentration camps, imprisonment without trial and confiscation of property. His condemnation of the euthanasia of mental patients so impressed the war hero Werner Molders that the Colonel asked Göring and Hitler whether the accusations were true, and both had to deny that euthanasia was part of the Nazi programme.

On one occasion Bormann remarked that von Galen deserved the death penalty but expressed the opinion that, in view of the existing military situation, Hitler was unlikely to consent to such a course of action at that time. Bormann's opinion was also shared by Goebbels: 'Simply to have Galen hanged would not be sufficient in this instance. If we hang him we can regard the population of Münster, and probably all Westphalia, as of no more use to us during the war. To postpone a measure however, is not to renounce it'. Von Galen was arrested after one of his sermons denouncing euthanasia but the public outcry was so great that he was released immediately and taken back in triumph to his palace at Münster.

Like Benedict XV during the First World War, Pius XII tried to unite Catholics throughout the world in a crusade of prayer for peace, recommending his predecessor's prayer for peace, and calling on them to provide money, food and clothing to relieve the sufferings of the victims of war. Within a few days of the outbreak of the War, Pius XII established the Pontifical Relief Commission and sent appeals for help to every Catholic diocese in the world. Relief agencies were set up in Norway and Denmark, France, Belgium and the Netherlands, Greece and Yugoslavia. When Italy entered the war, an office was established in Lisbon for the purchase and distribution of supplies from the United States. These agencies continued to work throughout the War and even as it came to an end, the Pope continued to work for the early repatriation of prisoners and displaced persons and he set up the International Committee of Catholic Charities with its headquarters in Paris to co-ordinate local and national efforts to assist the victims of war.

The efforts of the Holy See to secure food supplies for peoples in the occupied territories were frequently hindered by the determination of the Allies not to do anything that might help the German war effort or prolong the war. The Allies refused to lift the blockade against Germany and took the line that it was the responsibility of the occupying forces to provide for the material needs of those nations, such as Greece or Belgium, under their control. In August 1943 the British Government told the Apostolic Delegate in London: 'So long as the Germans have no hope of obtaining any supplies through the blockade they are obliged in their own interest to maintain a minimum standard of nourishment from the resources at their disposal in order to prevent the economic collapse of the occupied countries. The one country to which this argument does not apply is Greece, which is of little or no value to the Axis war effort, and it is for this reason that we have been able to make an exception to our general policy in respect of that country'.

Pius XII was also following the example of Benedict XV when he instructed bishops to appoint chaplains for prisoners of war and ordered his representatives throughout the world to visit the prison camps in the countries where they were working. He remarked in his Christmas allocution of 1940: 'We do not wish Christmas to pass without our representatives visiting the British and French prisoners in Italy, the German prisoners in England, the Greek prisoners in Albania or the Italian prisoners in the different countries of the British Empire, and giving them a sign of our tender care, some encouragement and our blessing. In the desire to share the troubles of the families who have lost touch with their relatives we have undertaken another responsible task; we have begun to transmit news for them as far as this is possible and permitted. This applies not only to a great number of prisoners of war, but also to refugees and to all those who, as a result of present vicissitudes, have been separated from their country and their families. It is a comfort to us that we have been able, by the help of our representatives and by our own subsidy, to give support to a great number of refugees, homeless and emigrants – including non-Aryans. Our task has been especially facilitated by the help given to us by our faithful sons in the USA'.

Papal representatives throughout the world provided social and pastoral care for prisoners and helped them to communicate with their families. A Vatican Information Service was established with different sections dealing with prisoners of war, refugees, deportees and missing persons, the sick and the orphaned, the provision of food and clothing, relief and medical supplies. Appeals for help came from all over the world and the Vatican Radio broadcast thousands of messages each month giving information about civilians as well as soldiers to their families and friends. At the same time parcels and medical supplies were sent to prisoners and other victims of the war in countries as far away as Finland and Ethiopia, Malaya and Greece. In March 1943 the British Foreign Secretary told the House of Commons: 'The Vatican have given such material aid and moral comfort to British Prisoners of War in Italy and in the Far East as it has been in their power to give. The humanitarian efforts to assist our Prisoners are much appreciated by His Majesty's Government'.

The Pope made special efforts to discover the fate of Polish prisoners deported to Russia and Lithuanians deported to Siberia. He appealed to the American Government and also sought permission to extend the Information Service to the United States.

The Pope and the Holy See were often asked to act as mediators during the War. In September 1941 the English Hierarchy asked the Holy Father to intervene in an effort to save the lives of twenty-five Belgian hostages sentenced to death at Tournay. In the same year the British Government asked the Holy See to use its good offices in order to secure an agreement with Italy for the exchange of sick and wounded prisoners of war. During the following year the British Government asked the Holy See to try to win the release of Poles interned in Spain and Allied prisoners threatened with deportation to territories occupied by the Germans and the Apostolic Nuncio in Madrid made repeated representations on their behalf.

It is, of course, impossible to know how successful attempts at mediation actually were or how influential in the event the Pope really was. However on one occasion the Deputy Prime Minister of Yugoslavia told the Apostolic Delegate in London: 'I have been informed that the Holy See graciously intervened in favour of the Slovenes who were condemned in Trieste by the special military tribunal on 14 December 1941. I am sure that it was only due to this high intervention that four of the nine men sentenced to death were graced. I have no words to express my gratitutde for this magnanimous act of the Holy See, which you inspired by your warm recommendation and which was effectual'. In October 1942 a British prisoner of war escaped and presented himself to the British Minister to the Holy See under the impression that he would be at liberty in the neutral territory of the Vatican City State. He was eventually exchanged for an Italian prisoner of war.

Pius XII was particularly concerned that the Church should provide shelter and protection for refugees from the War and victims of persecution. Church buildings in Rome which were outside the Vatican City State but which also enjoyed extra-territorial rights were frequently used to shelter political and Jewish refugees. The Holy See also encouraged other Catholic priests and religious to shelter Jews in spite of the risks to themselves and the result has been described as 'one of the finest examples of Christian charity in the whole war'. Roman churches and religious houses provided shelter for some 5000 Jews in 155 ecclesiastical establishments including several dozen in the Vatican itself. A Capuchin Father, Père Pierre Peteul Marie-Benoit, took care of 400 Polish Jews who had arrived in Rome at the beginning of September 1943. He also took steps to safeguard another 500 Jews from France by issuing them with permits to stay in Rome. He even secured the approval of the German Embasssy on the condition that the Secretariat of State also granted a letter of recommendation 'forgetting' to mention the fact that he was acting on behalf of Jews. After the War, Benoit was given a gold medal by the Italian Jewish Union; he himself paid tribute to Baron Ernst von Weizsäcker who was Ribbentrop's former under-secretary at the Foreign Office and was appointed German Ambassador to the Vatican in 1943 and 'who undoubtedly knew that the institutions of Rome were packed with Jews'.

On the day the German troops occupied Rome in September 1943, Father Rufino Niccacci was ordered by his Bishop to help a group of Jewish refugees, who had arrived in Assisi, to escape from the country. The Jews were first sheltered within the religious enclosure of a convent and the Mother Abbess, who originally protested, was reassured by the Bishop that he was acting on behalf of the Pope himself. As more and more Jews arrived, they were housed in the monasteries around Assisi where they were dressed as monks and taught to sing some plainchant. Father Rufino was helped by almost everyone, priests, nuns and laity, whose assistance he sought. The first refugees were sent with forged passports to Switzerland but, when this border was guarded more strictly, Rufino Niccacci personally escorted Jews dressed as monks and nuns across the Allied lines. In this way he saved some 300 Jews and scores of opponents of Fascism. When Father Rufino found himself under arrest, he was told by the Commander of the SS that 'the Catholic clergy is our enemy; we have shot 3000 priests in Europe so far', but he gave nothing away. Valentin Mueller, Commander of the Wehrmacht, did everything he could to help Niccacci and when he was 'ordered' to treat Assisi as an open city – an order forged by one of Father Rufino's own helpers – Mueller was able to force the SS to leave. It has been estimated that over 30,000 Jews were saved in Italy as a result of the assistance given to them by 'righteous gentiles'.

However, after the end of the War the question was raised whether Pope Pius XII had really done enough on behalf of the Jewish victims of Nazi persecution. The different approaches adopted by Pius XI and Pius XII were revealed at the end of 1938 when Cardinal Hinsley forwarded a request from Lord Rothschild asking the Pope for a declaration that all peoples are one in Christ. Cardinal Pacelli, then Secretary of State, replied that the Pope was very busy and not in good health. Cardinal Hinsley was authorized to interpret the Pope's mind and to express his approval of all the charitable help given to those who suffered unjustly. Such a diplomatic reply would seem to be more typical of Pius XII than Pius XI.

In 1939 Dr Isaac Herzog, Chief Rabbi in the Holy Land, who had previously been Chief Rabbi in Ireland, approached Cardinal Hinsley, Cardinal Joseph MacRory, the Archbishop of Armagh, and the Irish Minister to the Holy See, seeking an audience with Pius XII on 'certain matters of a non-political nature which are of most vital importance to Jewry'. However, Mgr Montini was only able to promise that if the Rabbi came to Rome he would be received by the Secretary of State; Herzog was received by Cardinal Maglione at the end of February 1940. In May 1940 Herzog again appealed to the Pope through Cardinal MacRory on behalf of Polish Jews in Lithuania who were threatened with repatriation to territories now occupied by Russia and Germany. But it might well be that at this time the Pope felt that he could only hope to intervene successfully in the case of those Jews who were also Catholics. In January 1939 the Vatican had requested several archbishops to establish committees to help Catholic Jewish refugees and unsuccessfully attempted to organize the emigration of some 3000 Catholic Jews from Germany to Brazil.

The Pope received many other requests to intervene on behalf of Jewish victims of persecution in the other occupied territories – from non-Catholics and Catholics alike, from Jewish Rabbis, Protestant Bishops and secular Governments. In June 1942 the Chief Rabbi of the British Empire, J. H. Hertz, appealed to the Pope on behalf of Jews deported from Slovakia. In September 1942 Myron Taylor informed the Pope that increasing numbers of men, women and children, and especially Jews, were being deported from Vichy France. He told Pius XII of the efforts to help being made by the American Government, efforts that included the possibility of seeking the intervention of the Holy See. In October a meeting of Jewish Deputies in Bloemfontein recorded 'with appreciation vigorous stand by Holy See against delivering Jewish refugees in France'. In December Hertz again appealed to Pius XII on behalf of Jews in Eastern Europe who were threatened with annihilation and at about the same time the Allies invited the Pope to endorse their Joint Declaration on the German persecution of the Jews or to use his influence with German Christians to restrain the excesses of the Nazis. In March 1943 the Rabbis of North America appealed to the Pope on behalf of Polish Jews.

The British Minister to the Holy See officially drew the Pope's attention to the persecution of the Jews at the beginning of 1943 and reported that the Pope had promised to do whatever he could on their behalf: 'I doubt if there will be any public statement, particularly since the passage in his Christmas broadcast clearly applied to Jewish persecution'. Some time earlier Osborne had reported: 'It is clear that the Pope regards his broadcast as having satisfied all demands for stigmatization of Nazi crimes in the Occupied Countries. The reaction of some at least of my colleagues was anything but enthusiastic. To me he claimed that he had condemned the Jewish persecution. I could not dissent from this, though the condemnation is inferential and not specific, and comes at the end of a long dissertation on social problems. . . . As a matter of fact his criticisms of the totalitarian systems were unmistakable, and, given his temperament, I think he deserves credit for much of what he said'.

In August 1943 the Pope received a plea from the World Jewish Congress: 'World Jewish Congress respectfully expressing gratitude to Your Holiness for your gracious concern for innocent peoples afflicted by calamities of war appeals to Your Holiness to use your high authority by suggesting Italian authorities may remove as speedily as possible to Southern Italy or other safer areas twenty-thousand Jews refugees and Italian nationals now concentrated in internment camps and residing in Northern Italy. . . . Our terror-stricken brethren look to Your Holiness as the only hope for saving them from persecution and death'. In September, A. L. Easterman, who had acted on behalf of the Congress, reported to the Apostolic Delegate in London: 'I have been informed that approximately 4000 Jews refugees as well as Yugoslav nationals, who were in internment camps and generally resident along the Dalmatian coast in formerly occupied Croatia, have been removed to the Island of Rab (or Arbe) in the Adriatic. As this Island has been captured by Yugoslav partisans, the Jews can therefore be regarded as removed from immediate danger. I am sure that your Grace will be glad to learn this news. I feel sure that the efforts of your Grace and of the Holy See have brought about this fortunate result, and I should like to express to the Holy See and yourself the warmest thanks of the World Jewish Congress. The Jews concerned will probably not yet know by what agency their removal from danger has been secured, but when they do they will be indeed grateful'.

In September 1943 the German Chief of Police in Rome threatened to send some 200 Jews to the Russian front unless they produced within 36 hours 50 kilograms of gold, or the equivalent in dollars or sterling, for the German Fatherland. The Chief Rabbi approached the Vatican which immediately placed 15 kilograms at his disposal and made the money available. The Jews were also told not to worry about the time needed to repay the loan. In the event the Jews succeeded in raising the money themselves. Nevertheless one of the main accusations levelled against Pius XII is that he failed to do anything for the Jews of Rome when more than a thousand of them were arrested in October 1943. However it is impossible to appreciate the evidence for or against Pius XII without first understanding the wider political situation in Rome at the time.

Baron Ernst von Weizsäcker, the German Ambassador to the Holy See, hoped to protect the Pope and Rome by representing their attitudes in the most favourable light possible for him, and by persuading his superiors that the Vatican was sympathetic to the German 'crusade' against Communism. At the same time Weizsäcker tried to persuade the Vatican to do as little as possible in order to avoid irritating the Nazis. The Ambassador preferred to make his own representations to Berlin rather than to forward the representations of the Holy See, partly in order to protect the Pope but also because he felt that he himself had more chance of succeeding with his superiors. Weizsäcker also became convinced that the Nazis intended to kidnap the Pope before the Allies reached Rome and therefore sent what his lieutenant Albrecht von Kessel later called 'tactical lies' to protect the Pope by persuading the Nazis that the Pope would not do anything to injure the German cause. On one occasion he wrote: 'A diplomat in close relations with the Vatican told me yesterday that the Pope condemned all plans which wanted to weaken the Reich. A bishop who is a member of the Curia said to me that in the Pope's opinion a strong Germany was absolutely essential to the Catholic Church. In a confidential text of an Italian journalist, I learned that when the Pope was asked, "What do you think of the German people?", he replied: "It is a great people, which in its fight against Bolshevism, sacrificed itself not only for its friends, but for its present enemies"'. Nevertheless, Weizsäcker, who was in close personal contact with Maglione and Montini, and therefore did not need to depend on such anonymous sources, did not record any of these opinions in his private papers.

When Montini approached Weizsäcker about German demands for 6000 hostages in retaliation for the murder of six soldiers, the German Ambassador did not make official representations to Berlin precisely because he wanted 'to keep the Holy See out of such questions' and feared 'that to talk about hostages in the name of the Holy See would provoke grave repercussions against the Holy See'. Montini recorded: 'I said forcibly that I could not accept this manner of thinking. The right of the Holy See to interfere in such a matter cannot be denied. The Pope is the common father of the faithful, he can intervene to defend them at any time and in any way. He is also the Bishop of Rome, and therefore has a special duty to plead for the members of his diocese'. Weizsäcker simply promised to do what he could privately. In the attempt to prevent the German occupation of the Vatican, Weizsäcker also tried to secure guarantees from the German Government in return for a declaration from the Curia praising the behaviour of German troops in Rome. However, the Pope was only willing to commend the behaviour of the German army as part of his expression of gratitude for the declaration of neutrality.

The Holy See and the Second World War

The Germans ordered the deportation of the 8000 Jews living in Rome at the beginning of October. The Secretariat had already expressed its fears that measures might be taken against Italian Jews, while Weizsäcker and Kessel had themselves warned the Jews to leave Rome. Pius XII was personally informed of the arrests on the morning they began by Princess Enza Pignatelli Aragona Cortes; he immediately contacted Cardinal Maglione, who at once invited Weizsäcker to come to the Vatican. The Secretary of State asked the Ambassador to intervene and threatened that the Holy See would issue an official protest if the arrests continued but Weizsäcker effectively silenced such a protest by promising to do what he could. On that day the Vatican received numerous appeals for information and help while Bishop Hudal, the Rector of the German church, sent a letter of protest to the German Commander in Rome.

It was on this occasion that Weizsäcker sent his infamous telegram to Berlin which did so much to injure the reputation of Pius XII but could be interpreted very differently if read in the light of Weizsäcker's private attitudes towards Berlin and the Holy See: 'The Curia is particularly shocked that the action took place, so to speak, under the Pope's window. The reaction would be perhaps softened if the Jews could be used for military work in Italy. The groups in Rome hostile to us exploit the action to force the Vatican out of its reserve. They say that in French towns where similar things happened, bishops took a clear position, and the Pope, as head of the Church, could not do less. People are beginning to contrast this Pope with his much more fiery predecessor Pius XI. Enemy propaganda abroad will certainly seize the occasion to provoke tension between the Curia and ourselves'.

In an effort to respond to so many emotional appeals for the intervention of the Pope and the Holy See, the *Osservatore Romano* published a leading article on 'The charitable work of the Pope' which has often been dismissed by contemporary and later commentators as too weak and indefinite, though this was not Weizsäcker's opinion. The Ambassador regarded it as sufficiently important and dangerous to send that report to Berlin which subsequently damned the Pope's reputation and is quoted as part of the conclusion to Hochhuth's play, *Der Stellvertreter*: 'Although the Pope is said to have been importuned from various quarters, he has not allowed himself to be carried away into making any demonstrative statements against the deportation of the Jews. Although he must expect our enemies to resent this attitude on his part, he has nevertheless done all he could, in this delicate question as other matters, not to prejudice relationships with the German Government. Since further action on the Jewish problem is probably not to be expected here in Rome, it may be assumed that this

157

question, so troublesome to German-Vatican relations, has been disposed of. On 25 October the *Osservatore Romano*, moreover, published a semi-official communiqué on the Pope's charitable activities in which the statement was made, in the style typical of this Vatican newspaper – that is to say, involved and vague – that the Pope extends his paternal solicitude to all men without distinction of nationality and race. There is no need to raise objections to its publication, since hardly anyone will understand the text as referring specially to the Jewish question'.

Yet at that very time, it has been estimated that more than half the Jews in Rome were being sheltered in ecclesiastical buildings that had been opened to them precisely on the instructions of the Pope himself. On 30 December one group of Jews expressed their gratitude to Pius XII: 'Moved with deep gratitude, the Jewish families who have been kindly sheltered at the Institute of Our Lady of Sion turn their thoughts to Your Holiness who has deigned to show them a new proof of your benevolence. And while they express their thanks for the speedy response to their appeal for aid, which was not addressed in vain to Your Christian charity, they wish above all to manifest their confidence and their faith for the Apostolic Blessing paternally bestowed on them'.

Another three thousand Jews were in hiding elsewhere in Rome but the last thousand were deported and killed. Weizsäcker himself was well aware of what was happening and that many Jews had been able to escape with Vatican papers. The Secretariat had even approached him to secure the release of individual Jews and had sent lists of 'baptized' Jews to him while retaining the actual certificates of baptism at the Secretariat.

At the time Jewish delegations publicly thanked the Pope for personally intervening with the authorities to prevent the deportation of Jewish refugees. The American Jewish Welfare Board wrote to Pius XII in July 1944 to express its appreciation for the protection given to Jews during the German occupation of Italy. At the end of the War, the World Jewish Congress expressed its gratitude to the Pope and gave twenty-million *lire* to Vatican charities. When the Chief Rabbi of Rome was received into the Church in 1945, he took the name 'Eugenio'. A former Israeli Consul in Italy has claimed that: '. . . the Catholic Church saved more Jewish lives during the war than all the other churches, religious institutions and rescue organizations put together. Its record stands in startling contrast to the achievements of the International Red Cross and the Western Democracies. . . . The Holy See, the Nuncios and the entire Catholic Church saved some 400,000 Jews from certain death'.

In November 1943 Chief Rabbi Herzog wrote to Monsignor Roncalli, then Apostolic Delegate to Turkey and Greece: 'M. H. Barlas, delegate of the Jewish Agency in Turkey, has brought to my knowledge the very valuable assistance you always give him in his efforts to come to the help of our unfortunate brothers and sisters who are in the Hitlerian hell, when it is a question of countries where the spiritual influence of the Catholic Church is strong enough. I well know that His Holiness the Pope is opposed from the depths of his noble soul to all persecution and especially to the persecution, unheard of in its ferocity and without parallel in the history of the human race, which the Nazis inflict unremittingly on the Jewish people, to whom the civilized world owes so much from the spiritual point of view. I take this opportunity to express to your Eminence my sincere thanks as well as my deep appreciation of your very kindly attitude to Israel and of the invaluable [so valuable] help given by the Catholic Church to the Jewish people in its affliction. Would you please convey these sentiments, which come from Sion, to His Holiness the Pope along with the assurance that the people of Israel know how to value his assistance and his attitude'.

As Anthony Rhodes has already shown, the Pope also protested, officially if only privately, against the persecution of Jews in those countries where he felt that he might have some influence. The deportation of Jews from Slovakia began in 1942 and the Secretary of State issued an immediate protest to the Slovakian Government. The President of that Government, Mgr Tiso, was a Catholic priest and he even contemplated offering his resignation, but his advisers persuaded him to avoid such provocative action and to use his authority to dispense from deportations, which he would seem to have done generously and for as long as he could. Nevertheless Charles Sidor, the Slovakian Envoy in Rome, was strongly criticized by Maglione, who described the deportations as a 'special stain on a Catholic country'. The Slovakian bishops issued a pastoral letter of protest, though this had to be modified before it could be published and some priests in parliament continued to vote in favour of anti-Semitic legislation. On 7 April 1943 the Pope himself wrote to the Slovakian Government: 'The Holy See has always entertained the firm hope that the Slovak government, interpreting also the sentiments of its own people, Catholic almost entirely, would never proceed with the forcible removal of persons belonging to the Jewish race. It is therefore with great pain that the Holy See has learned of the continued transfers of such a nature from the territory of the Republic. This pain is aggravated further now that it appears, from various reports, that the Slovak government intends to proceed with the total removal of the Jewish residents of Slovakia, not even sparing women and children. The Holy See would fail in its Divine Mandate if it did not deplore these measures, which gravely damage man in his natural right, merely for the reason that these people belong to a certain race. The pain of the Holy See is even more acute, considering that such measures are carried out among a people of great Catholic traditions, by a government which declares it is their follower and custodian'.

In July 1942 the Vatican representative in Zagreb, capital of the new state of Croatia established under Ante Pavelić, complained to the Chief of Police about the cruelties to which Jews were being subjected. The Chief then revealed that he had been ordered to send all Jews to Germany within the next six months and he reported that the Germans had recently killed two million Jews. The Police Chief explained that he was postponing deportations as long as he could and that he would welcome the intervention of the Holy See. The Vatican did intervene and at least initially gained an increase in the number of 'exceptions' that were granted. Nevertheless at the beginning of October Osborne still warned the Holy See of the dangers of granting a papal audience to Pavelić: 'I understand that Pavelić is likely to visit Rome shortly and it may well be that he will ask for an audience with the Pope. His reception in 1941 by His Holiness caused a very bad impression in official and unofficial circles in England where he is regarded as a regicide, or at any rate as the organizer of regicide. Since then the Croatian regime over which he presides and his Ustachi have been responsible for the murder of some 600,000 Serbs and at the present moment his troops are destroying Serbian villages in Bosnia and exterminating the Serbian population. Consequently his reception by the Pope, whether as a private person and a Catholic, as last time, or as head of the present Croatian régime, will undoubtedly arouse strong and adverse criticism in Great Britain'.

The Croatian Government attempted to identify two million Orthodox Serbs with the State of Croatia by forcing them to join the Catholic Church. The massacre of hundreds of thousands of Serbs during the Second World War was only surpassed in horror and violence by the extermination of the Jews and gypsies. The Orthodox were subjected to monstrous cruelties and suffered one of the bitterest persecutions in their history. 250 of them including their priest were ordered to dig a trench before being buried alive. 180 had their throats cut and their bodies were then thrown into a river. On 14 May 1941 hundreds of Serbs assembled for a religious service; a couple of them who had certificates showing that they were converts to Catholicism were allowed to leave, the rest were massacred. Catholic priests and the Franciscans in particular did not condemn these atrocities but actively supported and even participated in them.

Although Archbishop Ludwig Stepinac of Zagreb had publicly welcomed and thanked God for the Ustachi Government, he was not an uncritical supporter of its policies. The Archbishop was reported to have maintained that: '. . . the Church had its own laws of God . . . that the Church would always condemn measures which terrorized the public. The sole responsibility', said the Archbishop, 'for the growing and dangerous Communist partisan movement, for instance, would be laid at the door of the government who were acting too severely, even unlawfully, against Orthodox Serbs, Jews and gypsies, imitating the methods of the Germans. These people were being terrorized into taking to the woods and mountains and joining the resistance movements'. Another report also spoke of 'the personal intervention of the Archbishop in favour of Orthodox Serbs and Jews' and claimed that in a couple of sermons he had condemned racial and militaristic attitudes.

In 1943 on the Feast of Christ the King, Stepinac declared: 'The Catholic Church cannot admit that a race or a nation, simply because it is larger or stronger, can use violence against another which is smaller or weaker. We cannot admit that innocent people should be massacred simply because a soldier has been killed, perhaps in an ambush, even if it is claimed that he is a member of a superior race. A system which consists in shooting hundreds of hostages for a crime whose author has not been apprehended is a pagan system'. This sermon was repeated by his clergy on the following Sunday and thirty-three of them were arrested. The Archbishop also officially protested against the deportation of Jews and declared from his pulpit that: 'No civil power or political system has the right to persecute a person on account of his racial origins. We Catholics protest against such measures, and we will combat them'. Furthermore he revealed his opposition to forced conversions in a pastoral letter: 'Entry into the Catholic Church is welcomed only when the candidate has given proof of his honest and sincere desire to embrace the Faith, convinced of its truth as well as of its necessity for saving souls. Entry cannot be achieved through exterior constraints'.

On three occasions between 1943 and 1945, Pavelić requested that Stepinac should be replaced but on each occasion the Holy See refused. However, when the Communist partisans gained power in Yugoslavia all the members of the Church, innocent as well as guilty, became the victims of a new persecution and Stepinac himself was arrested. During his trial, Pius XII took the opportunity of defending himself and members of the Croatian hierarchy. The Pope referred to a reply from the Secretariat of State to the Yugoslav Legation in 1942 which promised that the Vatican would intervene with the Croatian bishops and which recalled measures already taken by the bishops to deal with the situation.

Although Hungary joined the Axis in the fight against Russia, the sermons and pastorals of the Prince Primate of Hungary during the War reflected his unflinching opposition to the Nazis and their policies. On New Year's Day 1943 Archbishop Seredi declared from the pulpit of St Stephen's Cathedral: 'There is no such thing on earth as a *Herrenvolk* – only those who serve God, and those who serve the Devil. No nation is inferior to another. . . . Murder is murder, and he who, for political reasons, orders mass executions will not receive the rites and consolations of the Church. Nor will the Church grant the sacraments to those who, on ideological grounds, abduct human beings for forced labour'.

Cardinal Seredi also protested in the senate against anti-Semitic legislation: 'Should your hearts, seized by race-hatred, drive you to vote for this law, hear my words – words which the Lord Himself suggests to me at this fateful moment. In truth I say to you: all the tears, all the victims, all the massacred martyrs will accuse you when your time comes to give an account before the Lord of your infamous act of this day. Remember the warning of Bernard of Clairvaux: "Do not touch the Jews for they are the apple of God's eye". In the name of Almighty God I shall vote against this infamous law'.

In April 1944 the papal representative in Slovakia received an eyewitness report from two Jews who had escaped about the exterminations of Jews in the 'labour camps'. The Pope immediately sent a telegram to Admiral Horthy, the leader of the Hungarian Government. The telegram did not actually mention the Jews but its message was clearly understood in Budapest: 'Supplications have been addressed to Us from different sources that We should exert all Our influence to shorten and mitigate the sufferings that have for so long been peacefully endured on account of their national or racial origin by a great number of unfortunate people belonging to this noble and chivalrous nation. In accordance with our service of love, which embraces every human being, Our fatherly heart could not remain insensible to these urgent demands. For this reason We apply to your Serene Highness, appealing to your noble feelings, in the full trust that your Serene Highness will do everything in your power to save many unfortunate people from further pain and suffering'. Horthy replied with understanding and gratitude: 'I beg Your Holiness to rest assured that I shall do everything in my power to enforce the claims of Christian and humane principles. May I beg that Your Holiness will not withdraw Your blessing from the Hungarian people in its hour of deepest affliction'. The Vatican also informed other countries about conditions in Hungary which was then subjected to mounting protests from many neutral as well as allied Powers.

When Horthy decided to sign a separate peace with the Allies, he was deposed by the Germans and replaced by a puppet régime. Seredi first attempted to persuade the new régime to withdraw the anti-Semitic legislation and when this move failed he issued a pastoral letter which was undoubtedly influenced by an open telegram to him from the Pope in which Pius XII expressed his sympathies for the Jews:'We do not question that certain elements among our Jewry may have had a demoralizing influence on Hungarian economic life, nor do we doubt that the Jewish question should be solved in a lawful, equitable manner. But we would forfeit our moral leadership and fail in our duty, if we did not demand that our countrymen should not be handled unjustly on account of their origin or religion. We therefore beseech the authorities that they, in full knowledge of their responsibility before God and History, will revoke these harmful measures'. This pastoral was read out in some churches before many copies were confiscated by the Government, which then put pressure on the Archbishop; he was forced to instruct his clergy to regard the letter as a personal one and they were ordered not to read it from the pulpit.

Nevertheless Mindszenty, then Bishop of Veszprém, believed that most of the Jews in Budapest had been saved from the gas chambers as a result of this strong protest by the Hungarian bishops: 'When innate rights, such as the right to life, human dignity, personal freedom, the free exercise of religion, freedom of work, livelihood, property, etc., or rights acquired by legal means, are unjustly prejudiced either by individuals, by associations, or even by the representatives of the government, the Hungarian bishops, as is their duty, raise their protesting voices and point out that these rights are conferred not by individuals, not by associations, not even by representatives of the government, but by God himself. With the exception of a lawful and legally valid decision by a magistrate, these rights cannot be prejudiced or taken away by any person and any earthly power'.

Many other individual Catholics as well as ecclesiastical institutions did what they could to save the Jews from further persecution and many priests and nuns were killed or imprisoned because of their efforts to help the Jews. Mindszenty himself was sent to prison for condemning the continuation of the war and for assisting the Jews.

Meanwhile the Vatican was able to publicize the Pope's efforts to help the Hungarian Jews. Seredi and the Papal Nuncio provided food and medicines carried in vehicles displaying the Papal insignia to the victims of the notorious 'Death March'. The Nuncio also signed several thousand blank passes giving safe-conduct to 'all persons of Jewish origin who enjoy the diplomatic protection of the Holy See' and as a result some 2000 Jews were able to escape. The Nuncio himself concealed about 200 Jews in his own palace and instructed other priests to follow his example. When a worker from the Red Cross complained that the use of blank or forged documents violated the terms of the Geneva Convention, the Nuncio replied that it was surely a virtue to rescue innocent men and women.

Unfortunately it proved much more difficult to assist the victims of persecution in Western Europe and the dangers which resulted from the unwillingness of Vatican officials to resist racist attitudes as strongly as they might were clearly shown in the case of the legislation adopted in Vichy France. When Léon Bérard, the Vichy Ambassador to the Holy See, was ordered to discover whether the new laws might create difficulties for the Vatican, Pétain was able to claim, unfairly but not without some justification, that the Vatican had adopted a careless or even an 'inhuman' attitude. It is only fair to point out that the Pope himself made a formal protest to Pétain against the persecution of the Jews, instructed the Papal Nuncio to the Vichy régime to issue another protest and recommended religious communities to provide refuge for Jews. But perhaps inevitably Pius XII seems to have been content to leave a great deal to be decided by the local bishops of Western Europe.

Pétain himself was not a devout Catholic but, rather like Maurras, regarded the Church as a politically useful organization. In 1940 the Primate of France, Cardinal Gerlier, Archbishop of Lyons, had enthusiastically welcomed the establishment of the Vichy régime but after a visit to Rome in January 1941 and with the increasing domination of the German authorities, he tried to prevent the Church from becoming too closely linked with French collaborators. The Cardinal was soon regarded by the press as one of the leaders of French opposition to collaboration and was nicknamed 'Primat des Gaullistes'. Gerlier's protest against the deportation of the Jews was read from every pulpit in his diocese and in spite of official censorship was broadcast throughout the nation. Gerlier declared that the French State and Church were now divided and he refused to bless those who volunteered to fight in the forces or to say Mass for those who had died in the fighting.

Other French bishops, especially Archbishop Saliège of Toulouse, also issued denunciations against the deportation of Jews. Saliège ordered an appeal to be read from all the pulpits in his diocese: 'That men, women and children can be rounded up like a herd of cattle, that members of the same family can be separated from one another and transported to unknown destinations – to live through this horror, is that what is reserved for us today? In the concentration camps of None and Recebedon disgraceful scenes have taken place. Jews are men too! Jewesses are women too! They too belong to the human race, they are our brothers and sisters. Let no Christian ever forget this!'

All the French bishops issued a more general protest to Pétain himself:

'The mass arrest of the Jews last week and the ill-treatment to which they were subjected, particularly in the Paris Velodrome d'Hiver, has deeply shocked us. There were scenes of unspeakable horror when the deported parents were separated from their children. Our Christian conscience cries out in horror. In the name of humanity and Christian principles we demand the inalienable rights of all individuals. From the depths of our hearts we pray Catholics to express their sympathy for the immense injury to so many Jewish mothers and children. We implore you, M. le Maréchal, to see that the laws of Justice and Right are not debased in this way'.

In Belgium, Léon Degrelle, the leader of the Rexist (*Christus Rex*) movement had been deeply influenced by Maurras and *Action Française*. In 1936 and at a time when women did not even have the vote, a quarter of a million Belgian voters had supported the Rexists but in the following year Catholics were forbidden to vote for Degrelle who immediately lost much of his political support and whatever influence he still enjoyed as a result of his collaboration with the Nazis. In February 1941 Cardinal van Roey again condemned the Rexists and in 1943 Degrelle, a regular communicant, was refused Holy Communion. The local bishop had ordered that Belgians wearing the Rexist uniform should not be admitted to the sacraments. In April 1944 Cardinal van Roey issued a pastoral letter denouncing Nazi racial theories and protesting against the deportation of Belgian workers. For their part the German authorities complained about anti-German statements made by certain Belgian priests who also refused to take part in requiem services for Belgian Nazis.

The Dutch bishops had warned their people of the dangers of National Socialism as early as January 1934 and two years later they ordered Catholics, under pain of excommunication, not to support Fascist organizations. During the German occupation of the Netherlands the Dutch bishops issued a pastoral letter condemning Nazism and prohibiting Catholics from cooperating with the Germans. Catholic journals were ordered not to submit to Nazi censorship, while Catholic radio broadcasts and trade unions were suspended as the Bishops refused to cooperate with the Nazis. The Catholic University of Nijmegen was closed when Catholic students were told not to sign the oath of loyalty to the Germans.

According to Fr Van Luenen, the strength of the Dutch bishops lay in their sense of solidarity. De Jong was the acknowledged leader of the five bishops who met on four or five occasions each year and were able to keep their discussions confidential. The former Chancellor of Germany, Heinrich Bruening, met de Jong several times before the War but always in secret because of the dangers involved. After the invasion, the Dutch bishops refused to speak with the German authorities except on those moral and theological matters within the bishops' competence. During the War, the Nuncio in Berlin was their only contact with Rome. They had no contacts either with the German bishops or with the Nuncio in Brussels. The Dutch bishops wrote many letters to the Nuncio in Berlin mostly about the conditions under which prisoners, especially political prisoners, were being held. None of these letters was ever acknowledged, but the Bishops heard from other sources that some of their letters had in fact reached their destinations.

In 1942 Christian churchmen in Holland agreed to issue a public protest against the deportation of Dutch Jews. The German authorities responded by promising to continue making an exception of those Jews who had been baptized Christians if the churchmen remained silent. The leaders of the Reformed Church in Holland agreed but in May 1943 the Dutch Catholic bishops issued their famous protest against the deportation of the Jews in the form of a pastoral letter which was read in all the Catholic churches: 'Deportation on such a scale has never been seen before in the Christian era. To find a parallel we must go back to the Babylon captivity, when God's Chosen People were led into exile. . . . This deportation, my Brethren, is not only a calamity, it is an injustice that cries to Heaven. . . .' The Germans continued to spare Protestant Jews but immediately began to arrest and deport Catholic Jews including the philosopher Edith Stein. However Fr Van Luenen does not believe that the condemnation of the persecution of the Jews significantly intensified that persecution because, he maintains, the persecution was escalating all the time.

Pius XII was obviously concerned to avoid provoking reprisals by a public condemnation of the persecution of Jews in Germany and Poland and was content to leave the responsibility for making such decisions to the local hierarchies. Early in 1943 the Holy See was informed by the Nuncio in Berlin and by Bishop Preysing about the deportations and executions of the Jews. It was also impossible to doubt any longer that the same persecution was being carried out in Poland. When Franz von Papen spoke to Mgr Roncalli in Istanbul about the massacre of thousands of Polish officers at Katyn, Roncalli replied 'with a sad smile that he had better first forget the millions of Jews sent to Poland and liquidated'. The correspondence and documents of the Holy See during the War reveal a growing sense of helplessness and frustration in the face of the persecution of the Jews in Germany and Poland. When the Papal Nuncio acting on instructions from Rome once raised the question of the Jews with the Führer himself, Hitler simply picked up a glass of water and with a motion of disdain flung it to the ground.

Towards the end of April 1943 the Pope wrote to Bishop Preysing: 'As

Supreme Pastor of the faithful we are also concerned that your Catholics should keep their convictions and their profession of these free from any accommodation with principles and actions which conflict with the law of God and the spirit of Christ and which indeed often treat these with contempt. To take a pertinent example, it has consoled us to hear that the Catholics, including especially the Catholics of Berlin, have shown much love for the so-called non-Aryans in their affliction, and in this connection we speak a special word of paternal recognition and of heartfelt sympathy to the Provost, Mgr Lichtenberg . . . We leave it to the pastoral authorities in each place to weigh whether and in what degree the danger of retaliatory measures and means of pressure following on episcopal declarations, and other circumstances arising perhaps from the length of the War and the mental attitudes which it produces, make it seem necessary, in spite of the reasons mentioned above, to exercise restraint *ad maiora mala vitanda*. In this there lies one of the reasons for which we impose restrictions on ourselves in our declarations; so far as we can see, our attitude is justified by the experience which we had in 1942 with papal documents released by us for distribution to the faithful. . . .'. [A direct reference to letters addressed to the Polish bishops] . . . 'In our Christmas message we have already said something about what is now being done against the non-Aryans in the area of German domination. This was short, but was well understood. We do not now need to give assurances that our paternal love and paternal care is due in increased measure to the non-Aryan or half-Aryan Catholics who are children of the Church like all the others, now during the collapse of their exterior existence and in their spiritual distress. With the situation such as it is at the moment, we can unfortunately provide them with no effective help except our prayers. We are determined, however, to raise our voice again on their behalf, according to what the circumstances demand or permit'.

Those who believe that Pius XII failed to denounce the crimes of Nazi Germany because of any sympathy for the authoritarian régime must explain why the Nazis themselves never regarded him as an ally and interpreted even his most moderate statements as expressions of hostility. The Pope felt obliged to adopt a different approach in dealing with different governments and in the case of Germany for example he was prepared to leave the ultimate decisions to the bishops most directly concerned. Pius XII undoubtedly believed, at least originally, that he would inevitably forfeit any claim to the role of peacemaker if he once modified his position of neutrality and as time went on felt unable to condemn the atrocities committed by one side without condemning those committed by the other. He also seems to have believed for a time, possibly quite wrongly, that the very continuance of the War was a greater evil than the horrors committed during it. He himself was very sceptical, probably rightly, about the influence of public denunciations on totalitarian régimes. Such condemnations were not only useless but might even provoke retaliation.

Pius XII was certainly concerned to safeguard German Catholicism from the threat of National Socialism and might even have been afraid of losing the loyalty of German Catholics. He was also anxious to avoid jeopardizing the position of Catholics in Germany and in the occupied territories. Judging from the Pope's correspondence with the German bishops, fears of reprisals would seem to have dominated his attitude towards the fate of Jews in Germany. The very evil to be condemned was sufficiently evil to be able to prevent its condemnation. But the Pope had to struggle hard to maintain his 'neutrality'. He was certainly well-informed and there is a suggestion of total helplessness in his letters in the face of such incredible evil. Even if he made the wrong decision in keeping 'silent', he cannot be accused of taking the decision lightly. Finally the Pope's own work on behalf of the Jews might have been endangered by a public denunciation of the Nazis, even though such a denunciation might have justified his moral reputation in the eyes of mankind. In this respect, at least, his choice was 'simple': was his own moral reputation more important than the life of a single Jew, or was the life of even one Jew more valuable than justifying his conscience in the eyes of the world? If Pius XII had spoken in this context, no doubt the case against him would have been that, by issuing moral platitudes, he had threatened the lives of others.

Pope Pius XII

Chapter V

From Pius XII to John XXIII

In spite of the cooperation – selective though it might have been – between Italian Catholics and the Fascist régime, the outburst of anti-clericalism which some had predicted and others had feared did not take place either with the establishment of the first coalition governments nor after the liberation of Italy. In fact during the two years between the overthrow of the régime and the liberation of northern Italy, Catholics cooperated extensively with the forces of the Left who seemed determined to avoid the anti-clericalism of the past if only because of the help given to the victims of persecution by priests and religious during the war. Although the resistance movements were often led by Socialists or Communists, most of the clergy had not opposed them while many religious had endangered their own lives by sheltering fugitives and helping them to escape. At the same time there emerged a group of Catholic politicians who were genuinely liberal and moderate in their political opinions and who sought freedom for the Church rather than ecclesiastical privilege or domination. Christian Democrats served on the Committees of Liberation established during the German occupation and the Christian Democratic Party at first seemed to embrace the political principles previously associated with the old Popular Party. Meanwhile the Italian people were less preoccupied with relations between Church and State and more concerned with the need for reconstruction and reconciliation. It is therefore hardly surprising that the demonstration of gratitude to Pope Pius XII in St Peter's Square after the liberation of Rome should have been attended not only by Catholics but also by Socialists and Communists.

Voting took place at the beginning of June 1946 to elect deputies for a Constituent Assembly and to determine the constitutional form of the new democratic State. In spite of the efforts of the Monarchists to win the support of the Holy See, the Pope remained neutral and Montini, then Sostituto at the Secretariat of State, gained the reputation for being 'progressive' or 'of the left', partly because of his refusal to support the campaign for the restoration of the monarchy at this time. The Christian Democrats gained 207 seats in the Constituent Assembly; the Socialists gained 115, the Communists 104 and the Liberals, the largest of the small parties, 41. However, all the parties proved to be cautious and moderate and were afraid of disturbing the newly re-established order. Neither the Socialists, the Communists or the Liberals ever proposed to suspend the Concordat or the Lateran Treaties or to adopt any other measure which might seem hostile to the Church. The only point at issue was whether the Lateran Treaties should be included as an integral part of the Constitution and in the event these were given constitutional status. But even those Italians who opposed this move were careful to manifest their great respect for the Church while those who were in favour also demonstrated their commitment to religious freedom and the rights of minority religions. The Assembly voted by 350 votes to 149 in favour of the following formula: 'The State and the Catholic Church are, each in its own sphere, independent and sovereign. Their relations are regulated by the Lateran Pacts. No amendment of the constitution is required in the event of any modification of the Pacts by mutual agreement.'

However, in adopting this formula, the Assembly had ignored the advice of one of the deputies who in the event might well have proved to have been more far-sighted than his colleagues: 'because it is in men's minds, in their hearts; because it pervades the consciousness of the people . . . because at a certain moment, in the years of most ruthless oppression, we perceived that the sole newspaper which still spoke with the voice of freedom – with the voice of *our* freedom, of the freedom that is common to all free men – was the *Osservatore Romano*; because we knew from experience that he who bought the *Osservatore Romano* was exposing himself to the risk of being beaten up . . . because, when the racial persecutions began, the Church ranged itself against the persecutors and took the part of the oppressed; because when the Germans were seeking out our sons in order to torture them and shoot them, they, whatever their party, found sanctuary . . . in presbyteries and monasteries . . . It was from these things, and not from the Lateran Pacts, that religious peace sprang . . . This brotherhood of the humble, the suffering and the oppressed in the face of the oppressors . . . has given back to Italy religious peace. That peace is in men's hearts. Do not destroy it, do not endanger it . . . by paltry, pettifogging subterfuges.'

The leader of the new Italian Christian Democratic Party after the War, Alcide de Gasperi, had never even visited the Secretariat of State during his political asylum in the Vatican City State. He was a devout Catholic, familiar with the social teaching of the Church, but determined to preserve the political independence of Italian Catholics and to prevent the Holy See from interfering in Italian politics either directly or indirectly through Catholic Action. The leader of Catholic Action at the time was Dr Luigi Gedda who enjoyed the confidence of Pius XII. Gedda has been described as 'the supreme example of what has come to be known as an "integralist"'; he favoured the formation of an anti-Communist front of Christian Democrats and parties of the right including the neo-Fascists. De Gasperi, on the other hand, was prepared to collaborate with modern Socialists or 'liberal' Republicans but he was not prepared to collaborate with the extreme forces of the right.

Inevitably relations between the Vatican and the Christian Democrats were not always smooth and friendly. Under de Gasperi, the Party refused to be controlled or directed by the Church as it tried to establish its legitimate position and authority within Italian society. Yet the Party enjoyed the support, if not the approval, of the ecclesiastical authorities, particularly at the local level, and largely depended on the support given by religious, Catholic organizations and even the committees organized by Catholic Action. Although Pius XII did not specifically approve of any particular party, his demand that Catholics should support only those parties which were fighting against the enemies of Christ coupled with the Church's opposition to Communism undoubtedly contributed to the early successes of the Christian Democrats. However the Party embraced different shades of opinion that could not easily be reconciled. De Gasperi himself had been the President of the first Congress of the Popular Party but in the disorganized state of Italian politics after the War, former Fascists and supporters of the right as well as those who were simply suspicious of change gave their support to the Christian Democrats, if only as the least of several evils. As time went on the forces of the left who had previously been members of the Popular Party lost control to those who were more willing to accommodate with the forces of the right and even with those who had previously been compromised by their association with Fascism.

The trend in Italian elections since the War dramatically illustrated the difficulties which faced Italian politicians and the ecclesiastical authorities. The Christian Democrats had secured an overall majority in the General Elections of 1948. However, in 1953 a third of the Italian people voted for the Communist Party and its allies and the Christian Democrats failed to secure an absolute majority in spite of introducing a voting system which had been designed to reduce the number of seats gained by the Socialists and the Communists. In May 1958 the Christian Democrats gained some 43% of the votes and was only able to form a Government with the support of the the Social Democrats. Some years earlier on the eve of the municipal elections in Rome in the spring of 1952, Pius XII had attempted to unite the Christian Democrats with the political forces of the right including the neo-Fascists, using the aged Don Sturzo as a rallying point. Sturzo, however, eventually refused to cooperate and the Pope, through Father Lombardi, attempted to put pressure on Signora de Gasperi who was both flattered and threatened in a vain effort to secure her husband's collaboration. Subsequently the Prime Minister was regarded as a rebel and he was refused a papal audience for himself and his family on the anniversary of his marriage and his daughter's profession as a nun. At the same time, the situation in Italy appeared to be paralleled, at least to some extent, by events in the rest of the world which seemed to the ecclesiastical authorities to prevent any possibility of collaboration between Catholics and Communists and even to force the Church into a position of uncompromising hostility.

The Pope could hardly be expected to ignore the Communist persecution of the Church in Russia, China and the countries of eastern Europe or the danger of the Communists coming to power in Italy, France or Greece. He, not unreasonably, excommunicated those Catholics who were associated with Communist attacks on Catholic bishops or who supported Communist efforts to establish schismatic churches. In July 1949 Catholics were also forbidden to join or to support the Communist Party, to publish or distribute, and to read or write Communist literature. Catholics who professed, defended or propagated the anti-Christian teachings of Communism were subject to excommunication and Communists were not allowed to be witnesses at Catholic marriages or to act as the godparents of Catholic children.

In April 1945 a confidential report had been sent to the Secretariat of State from the British Legation: 'At the request of His Majesty's Minister to the Holy See Mr Eden has instructed His Britannic Majesty's Ambassador at Moscow to forward, for communication to the Vatican, any information that may be obtainable (without approaching the Soviet authorities) regarding the situation of the Catholic Church, hierarchy and faith in Poland, Finland and the Baltic States. Sir D'Arcy Osborne has been instructed, in communicating any information so obtained to the Vatican, to stipulate that, if any use be made of it, His Majesty's Government should not be identified as the source. The following information has been forwarded to His Majesty's Minister from His Majesty's Ambassador at Moscow, who emphasizes, however, that all his reports on the situation in Poland are inevitably secondhand.'

The Ambassador reported that the Catholic Church was 'being very carefully handled' in Poland where the provisional authorities were at great pains to demonstrate the good relations existing between them and the Polish hierarchy. However, the situation in the Baltic States was to prove more typical of the future pattern of events. Although for the moment the organizations and hierarchy of the Church were still unaffected, seminaries were open and freedom of worship was allowed, it was impossible to contact the Vatican, religious books and pamphlets were no longer being published and religious instruction was forbidden.

In Poland itself during 1947 the Cominform replaced the Comintern – ostensibly dissolved in 1943 – which was then used in an effort to establish a schismatic Church, while the Orginform, an organization specifically directed against the Catholic Church, was established in 1950. Since the Vatican had continued to recognize the Polish Government-in-exile in London, the Communists retaliated by attempting to establish a Polish Catholic Church independent of the Holy See. The Communist Government unilaterally abrogated the Concordat and replaced it with an agreement with the Polish bishops that was much less favourable to the Church. In 1950 the State took over control of *Caritas*, a Catholic relief organization, and confiscated ecclesiastical property. Religious education was restricted, Catholic schools closed and religious publications suppressed. In 1952 the new Constitution of the Polish People's Republic separated Church and State but included guarantees of religious freedom which were soon shown to be useless. In the following year various Catholics, clergy and laity, were convicted as 'spies' acting on behalf of the United States and the Holy See, while those who were appointed to ecclesiastical office were forced to take an oath of loyalty to the State. In September 1953 Cardinal Wyszynski was confined to a monastery and prevented from exercising his office until these restrictions were removed following the riots of 1956, when he was restored to his diocese and the Government promised to safeguard religious freedom in return for Catholic recognition of the Communist régime.

In 1950, some eight months after the Holy See had ordered Catholics not to associate with the Communist Party, the Government of Czechoslovakia broke off diplomatic relations with the Holy See. Archbishop Josef Beran of Prague had been arrested in 1949 and was to be imprisoned for the next fifteen years. In the spring of 1950 over 300 priests and some 300,000 Catholics of the Diocese of Presov were subjected to pressure in an attempt to force them to join the Orthodox Church. Between March 1950 and the end of the following year all religious houses were closed while the religious themselves were imprisoned or sentenced to forced labour. By 1950 some 500 priests had already been sent to prison, an unknown number of religious had been deported and several dioceses were without resident bishops. A new constitution which was published in 1960 did not even recognize the Church as a society. When Cardinal Beran was allowed to leave for Rome in February 1965, he was told never to return. The short-lived religious liberties granted during the administration of Alexander Dubcek were repealed after the Russian invasion of Czechoslovakia, when further restrictions were imposed on members of the Catholic Church.

Since the time of St Stephen, who had been baptized and crowned by Pope Sylvester, the Archbishops of Esztergom held a unique position in the government of the State as well as the Church of Hungary. The archbishops were regarded not simply as representatives or advisers to the King but as defenders of the Hungarian constitution. In 1942 Cardinal Justinian Serédi declared: 'The Primate of Hungary combines two offices. He holds the highest rank in the Hungarian Church, and at the same time is chief guardian and interpreter of the law. Thus he symbolizes the dual nature – both spiritual and secular – of the Christian kingdom of Hungary ... ever since the days of St Stephen, the Primate has been the highest constitutional authority in the land after the King himself, second only to the head of the State.' These rights and duties, which were recognized in a new constitution established after the First World War, were not immediately challenged by the Provisional Government at the end of the Second World War.

The Communists gained only 17% of the votes in the General Election held towards the end of 1945 while the Smallholders Party gained over 57%. However as a result of pressure from the Russians, the Smallholders agreed that the Communists should hold three of the Ministries in a Coalition Government, including that of the Interior, while the Hungarian Bishops who had urged their people 'to vote only for those candidates who represent law, morality, order, and justice' were accused of attempting to prevent the democratic reconstruction of the country. The Russians also strictly controlled the activities of Catholic politicians at the same time as they were encouraging and actively promoting the interests of Hungarian Communists. Ecclesiastical properties, including most of the Church's schools, were confiscated, Catholic organizations were suppressed, and the number, size and content of Catholic publications were restricted.

In March 1947 the Government of the United States protested against the 'unjustified interference' of the Soviet authorities in the internal affairs of Hungary: 'Unable to achieve their political ends through normal constitutional processes, the Hungarian Communists together with other representatives of the leftist bloc have endeavoured to implicate a number of representatives of the majority Smallholders party in a recently revealed plot against the Republic and, by demanding the withdrawal of parliamentary immunity from Smallholders deputies, to weaken the parliamentary position to which that party was duly elected by the Hungarian people.

Simultaneously police and administrative authorities responsive to the dictates of these minority elements have utilized their powers of investigation of the conspiracy, not towards the expeditious judicial resolution of a threat against the state, but to conduct a general campaign against their political opponents.'

Episcopal appeals on behalf of prisoners, who might include former collaborators or Fascist supporters of the previous régime, were published in the press and deliberately misinterpreted. In October 1945 the Hungarian bishops had protested against the threatened deportation of the Hungarian Swabians: 'In the past, we obeyed our Christian duty and spoke out to protect both baptized and unbaptized Jews who were threatened with persecution. Nor can we keep silent now; for once again, people are being persecuted in this country. The new wave of persecution is not a direct result of the war. But ever since the war ended, some people in this country have been inflamed with hatred and a desire for revenge. We must all come forward and defend loyal Hungarians of German extraction who are being unjustly accused. We do not wish to absolve of war crimes those Germans who lived outside our borders. Nor will we defend war criminals who lived in Hungary itself. We condemned war criminals in the past and we condemn them now. But it is our duty to protest against the indiscriminate persecution of any racial or religious group'.

At the beginning of 1946 Cardinal Mindszenty, the Primate of Hungary, began to be subjected to those newspaper allegations of and 'spontaneous' demonstrations against his alleged Fascism that have become so characteristic of left-wing totalitarian régimes during the twentieth century. Nevertheless he continued to protest against deportations and in 1948 he declared: 'In August the Hungarian and Czechoslovakian Communist parties agreed to suspend the civil rights of 15,000 Hungarians, drive them from their ancestral homeland in Czechoslovakia, and confiscate their property. The two parties are vainly attempting to lend a semblance of legality to this atrocious persecution. Before God and our posterity I protest against the persecution of our innocent Hungarian people. The agreement between the Czechoslovakian and Hungarian Communist parties reveals a profound ignorance of the sufferings undergone by the deportees. Moreover, both parties are clearly determined to ignore the dictates of conscience'.

Mindszenty was eventually tried before a special branch of the Budapest People's Court, the President of which was a lapsed Catholic as well as a former member of the Fascist Arrow Cross Party. At the beginning of January 1949 Pius XII deplored Mindszenty's arrest in a letter to the Hungarian hierarchy and denounced his conviction at a secret consistory in the following month: 'This worthy prince of the church has been subjected to the worst humiliation. He has been sentenced to prison like a common criminal. We feel we must repeat Our solemn protest in the presence of you all. We utter this protest in defence of the holy rights of religion, which for so long were fearlessly and vigorously defended by this brave guardian of the Church. We join the universal outcry of all free nations and peoples, who have expressed their outrage in both the spoken and the written word'.

During the Hungarian uprising of 1956 the Hungarian Government solemnly declared that the charges made against Mindszenty in 1948 'lacked all legal foundation' and that the legal actions then taken against him were 'null and void'.

Meanwhile religious orders were dissolved and the religious themselves were expelled from their houses which were then confiscated. Those bishops and priests who were allowed to continue to exercise their ministries were closely supervised by the State which also restricted the religious activities of former monks and nuns. The Government also forced the Hungarian bishops to accept an unfavourable agreement and tried to extend its control over the Church by supporting the so-called 'peace priests'. Catholics who were willing to profess their faith jeopardized at least their jobs and their livelihoods as the Government attempted to suppress all religious education, even that given in private houses. In 1950 the Minister of Public Worship and Instruction told a Communist Party Committee that: '. . . any father who sends his child to religious classes, places it in the hands of the enemy and entrusts his soul and thinking to the enemies of peace and imperialistic warmongers . . . To send children to a reactionary pastor for religious instruction is a political movement against the People's Democracy, whether intentional or not. So far, we have applied the principle of optional religious instruction too liberally, and this we shall also change. Optional religious instruction cannot apply to technical and similar schools, even less so because the youth at these schools, if they wanted to, did attend religious instruction in the lower classes. No university has room for theological faculties any longer'.

Communism seemed to be threatening the future of the Church throughout the world and not only in eastern Europe. At the beginning of his pontificate, Pius XII had made what were considered at the time to be substantial concessions with regard to Chinese rites and ceremonies and the Holy See finally succeeded in establishing diplomatic relations with the Chinese Government. In 1945 the Pope set up a Chinese hierarchy of twenty archdioceses and seventy-nine dioceses, said to have been the largest in any country in the world, and created the first Chinese cardinal,

Thomas Tien, Archbishop of Peking. In 1946 the apostolic delegation was raised to the status of a nunciature and the Chinese Government sent an ambassador to the Holy See. At the same time plans were made to set up an Institute of Apologetics, a Secretariat of Agriculture and more industrial schools as well as to train more religious and laity for work in hospitals and dispensaries. By 1950 some 60 out of 146 bishops were Chinese, there were 2500 Chinese priests out of a total of about 5500 and there were over 3,250,000 Catholics. There were 4735 Catholic schools, 272 orphanages, 17 major seminaries, 3 universities, 216 hospitals and 847 dispensaries.

The People's Democratic Republic of China was proclaimed on 1 October 1949 and in the following year the Chinese Communists began to propagate their programme of 'Triple Autonomy', for self-support, self-evangelization and self-government, which inevitably questioned Catholic links with Rome. Official newspapers began to criticize Catholics in an effort to persuade them to accept the Three Autonomies which had already been imposed on the Protestant National Council. The real persecution of the Church began in 1951 with the liquidation of 'counter-revolutionaries', when twenty-two bishops were imprisoned and fourteen others expelled from the country. Over 1000 missionaries were also expelled while most of the other foreign missionaries were imprisoned or put under house arrest. When Pius XII condemned the Three Autonomies in his encyclical *Ad Sinarum gentem*, published in 1954, the Chinese Government retaliated with a second campaign against 'counter-revolutionary elements'.

In 1957 the Government set up the Patriotic Association of Chinese Catholics and over the next two years established a schismatic Chinese Church with twenty-six bishops. In the following year the Pope condemned the Patriotic Association as well as the unlawful consecrations of bishops which were by then obviously taking place, but the Vatican was in turn condemned as an agent of American imperialism. Meanwhile arrests and deportations multiplied in an effort to detach Chinese Catholics from the Church of Rome. At the beginning of 1962, when there were some forty-two bishops associated with the Patriotic Chinese Catholic Church, the Congress of the Patriotic Association declared that: '. . . the clergy and laity have come to recognize that the Catholic Church must be guided by the Chinese Communist Party along the road of socialism. They have also recognized the reactionary nature of the Holy See of Rome which, hand in hand with American imperialism, is plotting the destruction of the New China. With decisive action [the Association] has freed itself from the control of the Holy See . . . Many of the clergy and laity, having undergone courses of political indoctrination and labour exercises, in the face of socialist reality, have made considerable progress in reforming their political ideas'.

However, in the fight against Communism the Pope was always careful to avoid giving the impression that the Church was engaged in a crusade against Russia or the Russian people. As he explained in February 1946: 'We have wished never to say an unjust word, never to fail in Our duty to reprove every iniquity, every act deserving reproof; while avoiding – even when the facts justified it – any utterance likely to do more harm than good, especially to innocent people bowed under the yoke of an oppressor. Our constant aim was to stem a conflict so disastrous to poor humanity. That is why, particularly, We were careful, in spite of pressure, not to let fall one word of approval of the war undertaken against Russia in 1941. Assuredly no one would count on Our silence when the faith or the foundations of Christian civilization were in jeopardy. But there is no people to whom We do not wish with all sincerity a peaceful, dignified, prosperous existence behind their frontiers. We have tried only to lead people from the cult of force to the cult of right'.

In July 1952 Pius XII wrote 'to the most dear Russian peoples': 'No word came from Us that might seem unjust or bitter to any of the participants. Certainly We reproved iniquity or violation of rights, but so as to avoid (carefully and of set purpose) anything that might bring further hardships on oppressed peoples. And when in 1941 some tried to persuade Us to approve by word or writing war against the Russian people, We never would. Our exhortations, to peace, justice, are addressed to all. All know of Our strict impartiality during the war. The responsibility of Our office compels Us to condemn and reject the errors preached by atheistic Communism; We have had your good in mind in doing this. We know how many of you still nourish the Christian faith in your hearts. We pray it may be strengthened and increased and error repulsed'.

As a result of the emergence of the United States as the dominant power in world affairs following the Second World War, and of the size of the financial contributions given to the Church by American Catholics, it was inevitable that the Pope should wish to develop close relations between the Holy See and the United States – this quite apart from the sense of common interest which resulted from the events of the Cold War. However the 'foreign policy' of the Vatican could not really be accurately described as 'pro-American' or even less as 'supporting' NATO. Furthermore, although the Pope appreciated the positive qualities of the American people and proved willing to welcome American methods and techniques, he never regarded their way of life as either a pattern or an ideal for the rest of the world to follow.

The Pope was not only careful to avoid giving the impression of criticizing the Russian people but he also condemned the evils of capitalism and the tyrannies of the right as well as the left. In September 1950 he made it clear that in condemning Communism he was not identifying the Church with capitalism, as he urged the clergy to contrast and oppose both Communism and capitalism with the social and economic teachings of the Church. In his Christmas message of 1953 he reminded Catholics that: 'They must not close eye and mouth to social injustice, and so give occasion for doubting the social efficacy of Christianity. They must not forget that for the Christian the primary social factor is personal responsibility. This is too easy to forget in the impersonal atmosphere of many organs of modern democracy'. On the same occasion Pius XII calmly discussed the question of coexistence: 'It is hoped that present-day coexistence may bring men nearer to peace. The hope must be justified by coexistence in truth – a bridge between the two worlds which can rest only on the *men* of the two worlds, not on their régimes or social systems'.

On the whole the Pope's references to Communism were moderate and restrained in content and number until the Russians invaded Hungary in 1956, when he issued three encyclicals in ten days, culminating in a condemnation of the Russian action.

The Catholic Church in the modern age has been forced by practical considerations as well as its Christian ideals to work for the pursuit of peace; in view of the fact that the pontificate of Pius XII coincided with the events of the Second World War, the Cold War and the advent of the atomic age, it is hardly surprising that he should have been so deeply interested in the ideal of a world community and the attempt to establish an international agency to preserve peace. The Pope frequently referred to what he called the 'law of human solidarity and charity' and the fact that the earth was an inheritance shared among all men as a natural right, and he encouraged Catholic organizations to support and cooperate with other international agencies.

Unlike Pius XI, who was publicly critical of the League of Nations, Pius XII welcomed the advent of the United Nations and he expressed the hope that it might become a full and pure expression of international solidarity in peace. He also condemned all wars of aggression as sinful. In 1944 he declared: 'We have long maintained, that the notion of war as a suitable and proportionate means of resolving international conflict is already out of date'. However, the Pope modified his support for the United Nations with the development of the Cold War, and as the work of the Security Council was increasingly hampered by the Russian use of the veto. After the invasion of Hungary in 1956, the Pope declared: 'A unilateral outlook determined only by interest and force causes different charges of disturbing the peace to be treated very diversely and absolute standards are thus over-turned . . . UNO should have the right and the power to prevent every military intervention of one state within the boundaries of another, under whatever pretext, and also to undertake, with a sufficient police force, the keeping of order in a threatened state. If We make reference to these threats, it is because We wish to see the authority of UNO reinvigorated, above all by the achievement of general disarmament'.

The Pope frequently discussed the problems and difficulties preventing the establishment of peace both during and after the War. In the first sixteen months of his pontificate, he had appealed for peace on no less than thirty occasions and subsequently said more about peace than about any other subject that he discussed. During the War he had outlined possible solutions to the major problems of peace and war in his Christmas broad-casts. In 1939 he dealt with the pre-requisities for a new European order and in 1941 for a new international order. In 1942 he discussed inter-national relations, in 1944 dealt with democracy and in 1945 discussed the preconditions for a new peace. Subsequently he warned the Allies of the dangers of self-righteous vindictiveness and again attempted to outline the essential foundations of peace. He pointed out the errors of trying to secure peace at any price or of imagining that preparation for war was the only way to secure peace. He criticized those who depended solely on military deterrents and who failed to appreciate that better guarantees of peace were to be found in the restoration of Christian order, the abolition of hate and greed, the establishment of personal freedom and simultaneous and reciprocal disarmament.

The most significant development during the pontificate of Pius XII was the advent and then the spread of nuclear weapons. The first atomic bombs were dropped in July and August 1945 and in his Christmas message during the following year, the Pope spoke of the urgent need for disarma-ment in view of the new and terrible means of destruction which were now available. Nuclear energy, he pleaded, must be used in the service of mankind, not to bring about its destruction. He declared in his Christian message for 1950: 'In a war today arms would be so destructive as to render the world an empty waste, the desert not of its dawn but of its sunset. All states, all citizens would be involved, all institutions and values imperilled at once'. At the same time he exhorted scientists and men of good will to persevere in the study of nuclear energy, so that it might be directed towards securing the welfare rather than the destruction of humanity.

Two speeches given in 1953 and 1954 would seem to suggest that although the Pope was not willing to question the established principles of traditional moral theology, he was finding it difficult to adapt them to the new, appalling situation which was now facing the world. He continued to maintain the right to defence, apparently even with the use of nuclear weapons, but he also made it clear that if it became obvious that there was in fact no legitimate defensive use of such weapons, he would draw the logical conclusions. As he himself said: 'If the harm involved in the injustice is not comparable to the harm entailed by the defensive war, then it may be obligatory to put up with the injustice', and he made it clear that this applied especially to atomic, biological or chemical warfare. Furthermore, on the use of defensive weapons, the Pope declared: 'When this use extends so far as to escape the control of man entirely, then it must be rejected as immoral. Here there would no longer be question of defence against injustice or of necessary safeguarding of legitimate possessions, but of the annihilation pure and simple of all human life within the radius of action. This can be permitted on no grounds'. In short, Pius XII had recognized that a situation was possible and perhaps even imminent in which the use of nuclear weapons would be absolutely immoral.

Pius XII's consciousness of what he called 'the law of human solidarity' also dominated his political, social and economic thinking in which he showed a particular concern for international issues such as world poverty, imperialism and increasing urbanization as well as the tragic effects of war and the fate of refugees or displaced persons. Pius XII never issued an encyclical on social or economic reform which was as comprehensive as Leo XII's *Rerum novarum* or Pius XI's *Quadragesimo anno*. Possibly he did not feel that this was necessary in view of the comparatively recent statement by his immediate predecessor. However the Pope outlined 'the social teaching of the Church', an expression which had not been used by any of his predecessors, in radio addresses, allocutions and in public and private audiences. He was well aware, as he put it in 1947, that: '. . . while the Church condemns existing Marxist régimes, she can neither ignore nor refuse to recognize that the worker, in his efforts to improve his lot, confronts a social system which, far from being in conformity with nature, conflicts with the order established by God and with the purposes He ordained for the fruits of the earth'.

Pius XII condemned State totalitarianism and narrow individualism which both denied the dignity of the human person. He extended the concepts of social justice to relations between industry and agriculture as well as to the rights of each nation to share in the markets of the world. Christians were obliged to undertake the task of improving the conditions of the working classes as well as the reform of the complex structure of contemporary society. He called on the large land-owners in South America to pay a just wage to their workers and to improve their social and economic conditions. He reminded the colonial powers of their obligations and responsibilities and he himself recognized peoples' rights to self-determination. Pius XII opposed class warfare, favoured evolution rather than revolution, and showed himself to be unsympathetic to Socialism or nationalization. He advocated a community of interest and action, and defended the rights of private property as essential to human dignity.

Pius XII was suspicious of state intervention as a positive agent of reform rather than a negative instrument of defence. Consequently although he deplored the lack of Government legislation for the social needs of rural populations, he did not welcome the coming of the Welfare State and in 1945 expressed his fears at the provision of free education and free health services. The Pope's discussions on the rôle of women in the world were among his most sensitive and penetrating, though he again had several reservations. He was not convinced that the emancipation of women had proved to be entirely to their advantage and consistently maintained that the dignity of women was far more significant than the mere material domestic improvements that seemed to have become the ultimate concern of so many.

During the 1940s French Catholics in particular had become increasingly aware of the fact that industrial workers and the urban proletariat were largely indifferent or hostile to the claims of Christianity and the Church. This evidence of 'de-christianization' coupled with an apparently ever increasing shortage of priests suggested the necessity of adopting more radical methods of evangelization. The French bishops established special commissions with particular responsibilities for rural problems or workers in industry, religious education, social work or Catholic Action. They also encouraged the experiment of 'worker-priests' which was originally welcomed with enthusastic interest and optimism but this was to be followed by a sense of disappointment and even bitterness when the experiment was finally brought to an end.

The experiment of worker-priests developed from the *Mission de Paris* which had been established by Cardinal Emmanuel Caelestinus Suhard and was greatly influenced by the experiences of the twenty-five priests who had secretly been appointed as chaplains to accompany the hundreds of thousands of Frenchmen who had been sent to work in Germany during the War. The worker-priests tried to evangelize the working classes by sharing in their labours and the difficulties of their lives. By 1949 there were about 50 worker-priests including several religious and about 90 when the

Holy See prohibited further recruitment in 1951. However, it proved to be difficult to combine the secular and the religious rôles. Some of the priests found that they had not been sufficiently prepared – theologically, pastorally or even emotionally – for the tasks which faced them and they found themselves increasingly divorced from clerical attitudes and ecclesiastical structures. The Roman authorities first began to entertain their suspicions and doubts when it was reported that some of the priests had abandoned their priesthood and that others were associated with Communist movements.

The Apostolic Exhortation *Menti nostrae* on the sanctification of the priestly life, published in 1950, reflected the Pope's reservations and suspicions of the worker-priests. He was hostile to what he called the 'alarming spread of revolutionary ideas' among some of them who he described as 'not highly distinguished for learning or austerity of life'. Although Pius XII recognized that evil social conditions had led the French priests to adopt some radical views as well as their novel way of life, he complained that these were contrary to the dignity and the office of priests. But in spite of this lack of sympathy, the Pope was apparently content at the time to issue warnings and to leave the concrete decisions to the French hierarchy. Unfortunately it would seem that at this point relations between the worker-priests and their own bishops were deteriorating as their activities adversely affected relations between Church and State in France. Events such as the arrest of two priests during a demonstration against NATO reinforced the suspicions of the Roman authorities as well as the criticisms from right-wing forces in France.

In May 1953 the Pope criticized some of the positions adopted by the worker-priests and in August the seminary at Limoges, where clergy for the Paris Mission were trained, was closed and the French bishops and religious superiors were ordered to recall their priests. The French bishops were then ordered to end the experiment in spite of the protests of three French Cardinals, the leading members of the hierarchy, who personally appealed to the Pope. However in the following year the Pope allowed the worker-priests to continue though they were forbidden to work for longer than three hours a day or to join secular organizations, to engage in trade union activities or to live outside their community. These restrictions seemed so demanding that many of the worker-priests felt that the experiment itself had been brought to an end; others continued to hope that the restrictions might yet be lifted. The Holy Office, however, remained hostile and in June 1959 John XXIII, who had previously aroused the hopes of the worker-priests because of the sympathy he had shown as Papal Nuncio, endorsed the decision of the Holy Office to end the experiment which was described as incompatible with the spiritual life of a priest. At the same time, however, the *Mission de France* was given a new and original canonical status. It continued to train missionaries to evangelize France and on 25 October 1965 the French Bishops were allowed to issue a decree authorizing priests to work again full time in factories. Ten years later Jean Rémond, secretary of the *Mission de France*, was one of the first worker-priests to be consecrated a bishop.

The history of the worker-priests illustrated that the problems associated with 'adaptation' and 'response' were no longer simply of concern in the 'foreign' missions but were equally pressing in the 'missionary' territories of post-war Europe. It was in fact only in the course of the twentieth century that the Church effectively began to deal with two of the great difficulties involved in missionary activity or evangelization: the identification of the Church with the culture and nationality of the missionaries and the need to develop in indigenous clergy and a local liturgy with which the peoples of Africa or Asia could more easily identify. It was only in 1936 that Pius XI allowed Chinese Christians to use some of their national customs on the occasions of marriages and funerals. Three years later Pius XII allowed Chinese Catholics to venerate the dead, to honour Confucius and to attend civil and public functions of a religious nature. In 1944 the Roman authorities extended the authority of local bishops – and even occasionally of individual priests and laymen – to decide over similar controversial issues. As the Pope himself said at the time: 'The missionary is the apostle of Jesus Christ. His mission is not to transplant European civilization to missionary countries but rather to persuade their populations, some of whom enjoy the benefits of an age-old culture, to accept and assimilate the elements of Christian life and conduct, which should harmonize quite naturally and harmoniously with any healthy civilization'.

In the first encyclical of Pius XII's reign, the Pope declared: 'All who enter the Church, whatever their birth or native tongue, are to know they have an equal right of sonship in the Lord's household, where the law and peace of Christ prevail. In obedience to this law of equality, the Church makes it her constant concern to educate native clergy in a manner commensurate with their task, and to augment by degrees the ranks of the native episcopate. To give outward expression to our intentions, we have appointed the forthcoming feast of Christ the King as the day for raising to the episcopal dignity, over the tomb of the Prince of Apostles, twelve representatives from peoples, or groups of peoples of the greatest possible diversity'.

Subsequently, the Pope consecrated twelve bishops from every continent and all parts of the world including the first African from south of the Sahara since the first half of the sixteenth century. Some fifty-one ecclesiastical territories were in the care of local bishops at the end of 1945. By 1951 there were ninety-one and on the death of the Pope in 1958 there were 139. Pius XII himself had created eighty-five new bishoprics and archbishoprics and some 123 vicariates and prefectures apostolic by the end of 1951. 162 archbishops and bishops residing in their sees were of Asian or African origin at the end of 1961 and the number had risen to 228 by the time that the Second Vatican Council came to an end.

The establishment of an indigenous clergy and native hierarchies was obviously an important factor in attempting to deal with the effects of the decline of imperialism on the missionary activity of the Church. In 1951 and 1957 the Pope also issued two encyclicals, *Evangelii praecones* and *Fidei donum*, in which he called on Catholics throughout the world to support the missions particularly in Africa. In the first he reminded the missionary: '. . . to regard the country to which he goes bearing the light of the Gospel as his second fatherland, and to give it the love which is its due; thenceforth he will seek no earthly benefits, whether for his country or for his religious institute, but only what is needful for the salvation of souls'.

At the same time, although Pius XII was not in favour of colonialism, he was sometimes forced or prepared to be unduly tolerant to some of the colonial régimes. In 1958 there was only one native auxiliary bishop in the former Belgian Congo where there were some 5,000,000 Catholics.

Pius XII held only two consistories in nineteen years but on each occasion he increased the international representation in the Sacred College of Cardinals so that, as he himself said, it might become 'a living image of the Church's universality'. He tried to demonstrate that universality in 1946 by creating thirty-two cardinals from eighteen nations only four of whom were Italians. Previously there had been twenty-three Italian cardinals and only fifteen from other nations. The first name on the list was that of the Patriarch of the Armenians of Cilicia and there were also cardinals from several European countries, from the United States and Canada, from five Latin American republics, from Mozambique, China and Australia. For the first time there were fewer Italian Cardinals than non-Italians. However, many of the new cardinals came from traditional cardinalitial sees, and they had little influence on the central administration of the Church since the Curia was still dominated by Italians.

The Roman Departments remained firmly under the control of Italian cardinals while the College of Cardinals never met to discuss or to deliberate with the Pope but simply to listen to and approve his words and actions. Nevertheless the Pope's actions reflected the dramatic shift in the numerical strength of Catholicism from Europe to other parts of the world because thirteen prelates from outside Europe received the red hat. In a second consistory in 1953 Pius XII created another ten Italian cardinals, four of whom were curial officials and four of whom were diplomats, out of a total list of twenty-four. At the time of his death there were only fifty-two cardinals including sixteen Italians and fifteen cardinals in the Curia. The only non-Italian who was regarded as a serious candidate for the papacy was Cardinal Agagianian who had lived in Rome since leaving Armenia as a boy.

The significance of Pius XII's reforms in general as well as his reforms of the College of Cardinals and of the Curia have sometimes been exaggerated. Although the Pope allowed the re-establishment of some national episcopal conferences and even permitted the establishment of a continental episcopal conference in Latin America, he did this without modifying in any way the authority of the Roman Curia or the Papal Nuncios. Furthermore it is arguable whether all the reforms of Pius XII were really adequate to meet the needs of the time. For example, in the apostolic constitution *Sponsa Christi* published in 1950 he dispensed enclosed nuns from their obligation to live in seclusion so that they might take a greater part in the active apostolate. He also recognized the need to change traditional customs and practices including religious habits which put unnecessary restrictions on some forms of apostolic activity. And he tried to promote collaboration and to co-ordinate the activities of different religious orders in an effort to avoid wasting resources and to achieve a better distribution of effort. But was this really enough?

The problems of evangelization had a direct effect not only on pastoral theology but on other developments such as the liturgical movement and the growth of ecumenism. At the beginning of the century a number of influences were already at work that would ultimately transform the spiritual and liturgical lives of Catholics throughout the world. Those Catholics who actually practised their religion showed an increased sense of religious and pastoral commitment. There was a new emphasis on the need for frequent Communion and devotion to the Eucharist, a greater reverence for the Sacred Heart of Jesus and the Virgin Mary. At the same time the Liturgical Movement was growing with its awareness of the importance of conscious and public worship.

The original centres of the Liturgical Movement in the Catholic Church were to be found in monasteries such as Maredsous or Solesmes. Encouraged by the liturgical reforms of Pius X, German liturgists organized the first Liturgical Week for laymen at Maria Laach in the Holy Week of 1914 when the dialogue Mass was introduced into Germany. This was followed by similar Liturgical Weeks and conferences, the establishment of commissions and institutes, and scholarly publications, all of which helped in the necessary task of informing and influencing other Catholics. The first Eucharistic Congress after the First World War was held in Rome in 1922 and subsequent congresses were held in Amsterdam, Chicago, Sydney, Carthage, Dublin, Buenos Aires, Manila and Budapest before they were again suspended by the outbreak of the Second World War. In 1922 the Roman authorities also gave formal approval for dialogue Masses and six years later Pius XI published a *Constitution on Sacred Music* in which he strongly recommended the active participation of the laity: 'It is absolutely necessary that the faithful should attend the sacred actions, not as outsiders or silent spectators, but thoroughly imbued with the beauty of the liturgy . . . so that they may join their voices to those of priest and choir in accordance with antiphonal rules'. The First International Liturgical Congress was held in Antwerp in 1930.

In his first encyclical, Pius XII promised to follow the example of his predecessor in adapting local customs and cultures for use in the Catholic liturgy. The Second World War gave a great impetus to the development of the Liturgical Movement as millions of Catholics found consolation and strength in the reception of the sacraments. Meanwhile thousands more Catholics enduring persecution or life in prison camps rediscovered the meaning and reality of the Church and its liturgy. Obviously the progress of the Liturgical Movement varied from country to country. But by the middle of the twentieth century liturgical and biblical developments were already helping to reduce the popularity of some forms of devotion that were not only untheological but even unorthodox. Some priests were saying Mass more slowly and distinctly, the use of missals and dialogue Masses became more widespread, the number of liturgical centres and Bible societies, publications and conferences increased and the Liturgical Movement was beginning to develop in spite of occasional excesses and aberrations.

In his two great encyclicals, *Mystici Corporis* published in 1943 and *Mediator Dei* published in 1947, Pius XII gave his official approval to the Liturgical Movement but at the same time warned against exaggerations or unintelligent deviations. He made it clear that he did not regard liturgical reform as a panacea for spiritual ills and although 'the Christian community is in duty bound to participate in the liturgical rites according to their station', he was determined to safeguard the Church from 'excess or outright perversion'. The Pope emphasized the significance of the ordained priesthood and the authority of the hierarchy, he commended private Masses, private devotions and private prayers, he defended the practice of

189

reservation and Eucharistic devotions outside Mass such as Benediction, he strongly recommended the practice of frequent confession, he opposed the abolition of black vestments or 'unsuitable' Old Testament readings, he condemned the unauthorized use of the vernacular, and disapproved of the use of 'table' altars.

In the years after the War, the Roman authorities granted concessions to various countries in an effort to encourage the liturgical participation of the laity. In 1947 a bilingual Ritual was approved for use in France while the Belgians were allowed to have evening Masses on Sundays and Holy Days. In the following year the Japanese bishops were allowed to approve of evening Masses under certain conditions, while some Polish priests were allowed to say evening Masses every day. In 1949 the Holy Office authorized the translation of the Roman Missal, except for the Canon, into Mandarin Chinese while the Indian bishops introduced evening Masses and reduced the Eucharistic fast in some of their dioceses. In 1950 the German bishops were given concessions to permit the use of some traditional customs in the administration of the sacramental rites.

The Easter Vigil was restored, at first experimentally, in 1951 and this was followed by the reform of the Holy Week liturgy. In 1953 evening Masses were approved for the Church throughout the world and the Eucharistic fast was drastically modified. *Christus Dominus* illustrated Pius XII's determination to adapt old Church laws to new and different circumstances. He referred to 'new conditions of time', 'grave difficulties apt to deter people', 'travel . . . health . . . labours . . . missionaries . . . late hours . . . workmen in factories . . . mothers . . . children' as well as the need 'to promote the reawakened devotion toward the Eucharist'. Over the next few years the rules in fasting were further modified, the rubrics of the Mass and the Office were simplified, the practice of concelebration was reintroduced and permission was given for the use of vernacular hymns during Mass.

But in spite of these reforms the Pope remained cautious. In an address to the International Conference on Pastoral Liturgy held at Assisi in 1956 he warned against novel opinions on the nature of the Real Presence and the celebration of Mass, he supported Eucharistic devotions such as the Forty Hours and the practice of reservation in an immovable tabernacle at the centre of the high altar. He also maintained 'the unconditional obligation of the use of Latin for the celebrant'. Two years later the Holy Office issued further warnings against the practice of changing the prayers or readings at Mass, defended the practice of baptizing children as soon as possible, and re-asserted the authority of the Holy See and the Bishops over liturgical developments.

The growth of Catholic Action and the liturgical movement were part cause and part effect of a new awareness of the rôle of the laity and an appreciation of the Church as the mystical Body of Christ and the community of the faithful. This understanding of the Church and the laity, with all its pastoral and liturgical implications, proved to be one of the most fruitful developments during the first half of the twentieth century. In 1943 the Pope issued his encyclical, *Mystici corporis Christi*, in which to some extent he endorsed ecclesiological developments that had occurred during the nineteenth century particularly under the influence of John Adam Möhler. The Church was the mystical body of Christ, visible, indivisible and organically compact. The Church established by the preaching of the Gospel and the redemption of the Cross and spread throughout the world following the gift of the Spirit at Pentecost was entrusted with the sacraments of Christ as the means of salvation. But the Pope also emphasized that the Church was identical with the Roman Catholic Church as well as the hierarchical nature of ecclesiastical authority. He warned against the notion of an invisible Church of all men of good will in mystical union with Christ which might be contrasted with the visible institutional Roman Catholic Church led by the Pope.

This encyclical marked a crucial stage in the Church's understanding of the rôle of the laity, though it was not entirely free from those clerical and authoritarian sentiments which were typical of Pius XII. After the war the Pope increasingly recognized that the laity would have to play a greater part in the life of the Church. He described the layman 'as a kind of *minister Christi*'. The laity not only belong to the Church, 'they *are* the Church – that is, the community of the faithful in earth under the direction of the common head and the bishops in communion with him'. He told the first World Congress of the Lay Apostolate in 1951: 'If the Church is kept in the sacristy anywhere it is by force: she should be doing all that is possible to extend her influence outside'. By this time Pius XII was conscious, if suspicious, of the increasing significance of the laity in the life of the Church. He did not particularly like such phrases as 'lay theology', 'emancipation of the laity' or even 'the priesthood of the laity'. He preferred to speak of the 'collaboration' or 'aid' rather than the 'participation' of the laity in the apostolate of the hierarchy and constantly emphasized the need for Catholic organizations to work in harmony with the bishops.

Nevertheless Pius XII enlarged the notion of Catholic Action as defined by Pius XI and extended it to all organized actions of the Catholic laity in the pursuit of apostolic ends. Furthermore in a speech given to women only a week before the second World Congress of the Lay Apostolate in 1957, the Pope declared: 'Although the Church refuses to see the sphere of her authority unduly limited, she neither represses nor diminishes thereby the liberty and initiative of her children. The ecclesiastical hierarchy is not the whole Church, and it does not exert its power in external affairs as does, for example, a civil authority, on the juridicial plane alone. You are members of the Mystical Body of Christ, grafted on to Him as on an organism animated by one single Spirit, living one and the same life. The union of the members with the head in no sense implies that they abdicate their autonomy or that they renounce the exercise of their functions; quite the contrary, it is from the head that they are always receiving their impulses'. It would seem that the Pope was undoubtedly aware of the rôle of the laity, and even prepared to accept some of its implications, without finding it possible to reconcile or resolve all the tensions involved in this crucial development.

The development of the ecumenical movement, the liturgical movement as well as forms of Catholic Action like the Young Christian Workers helped to encourage the study of the scriptures among many ordinary Catholic priests and laymen. In the encyclical *Spiritus Paraclitus* published in 1920, Benedict XV had modified some of the more extreme positions adopted by Leo XIII in *Providentissimus Deus*, but both encyclicals took a rather conservative stand. It was Pius XII who first encouraged the use of critical methods and by implication gave his approval to the development of biblical theology, the study of the doctrinal and religious significance of scripture. In fact his encyclical on biblical studies *Divino Afflante Spiritu*, published in September 1943, has been described 'as probably the greatest single achievement of Pius XII's reign and one of his assured titles to a place in history'.

The Pope encouraged biblical scholars to translate the Bible from the original languages rather than from the Vulgate and to use scientific methods in determining more accurately the original text of scripture. He recognized that advances in the study of ancient languages, the discovery of new texts and a better understanding of patristic exegesis had added new dimensions to biblical studies. Scholars should use all the resources of history and archaeology, philology and allied sciences in order to give the people of God a better understanding of the theological content and meaning of the sacred writings. The Pope emphasized the importance of determining the authors' meaning and gave his qualified approval to the use of Form Criticism. Finally Pius XII ended on a positive note of freedom that some consider to be unique in Roman documents: 'There remain many things, and of the greatest importance, in the discussion and exposition of which the skill and genius of Catholic commentators may and ought to be freely exercised, so that each may contribute his part to the advantage of all, to the continued progress of sacred doctrine and to the defence and honour of the Church'. This statement was widely regarded as a major breakthrough and one which freed Catholic scholars from the dangers of fideism or biblical fundamentalism.

It is perhaps significant that an Instruction of the Biblical Commission in 1964 would restrict this freedom to work for the progress of doctrine and the defence of the Church by adding the phrase, 'to the preparation and further support of the judgment to be exercised by the ecclesiastical magisterium'. Meanwhile, however, Pius XII announced that work was to begin on a new translation of the psalter in an effort to promote liturgical as well as biblical reform. And in 1948 the Biblical Commission sent a letter to Cardinal Suhard which also adopted a positive approach towards the dating of the *Pentateuch* and the interpretation of *Genesis*.

During the later pontificate of Pius XII, the Pope and the ecclesiastical authorities succeeded in inhibiting various theological and biblical, pastoral and liturgical developments which had sometimes begun even before the War and which other Catholics felt to be long overdue. In particular the publication of the encyclical *Humani Generis* in 1950, which revoked some of the concessions made in the field of biblical studies, marked the return to a more intransigent approach which was made even worse by the over-enthusiastic and intemperate way in which this encyclical was sometimes applied on the local level. The encyclical was not unfairly seen as an attempt to moderate what the Pope himself seems to have felt were exaggerated interpretations of *Divino Afflante Spiritu* and the letter to Cardinal Suhard. Even at the time *Humani Generis* was compared, not always seriously, with *Pascendi*, the encyclical which condemned Modernism, though in fact Pius XII's encyclical, as one would expect, was a much more balanced document.

Nevertheless *Humani Generis* was one of the strongest condemnations of theological error since the condemnation of Modernism. Among those important aspects of the faith that the Pope felt were being questioned were biblical inerrancy, the nature of creation and original sin, the existence of angels and devils, the Real Presence, the significance of tradition in determining questions of morality, the necessity of the Church for salvation and, perhaps most important of all, the authority of the ecclesiastical hierarchy as the ultimate authority in matters of faith and morals. As it was stated in the encyclical, 'lovers of novelty pass from disdain of scholastic theology to neglecting and even despising the magisterium of the Church which bestows high authoritative approval on that branch of theology'.

The Pope warned against the dangers of rationalism and neo-

Pope John XXIII

Kantianism, Modernism and Marxism. He attempted to check what he saw as a relativism which emphasized evolutionary development at the expense of divinely revealed doctrine and an over-emphasis on an existential or irenic rather than a scholastic approach. He was critical of those who tended to accept theories or hypotheses which resulted from historical criticism as if these were demonstrated conclusions or who adopted the view that Christ had not established the Church as the unique depository and interpreter of the Word of God. In the following year the Pope again emphasized the importance of dogmatic formulations and the dangers of kenoticism in his encyclical, *Sempiternus rex Christus*, commemorating the Council of Chalcedon.

The Pope published *Humani Generis* during the same month that he announced his intention of defining the Assumption of the Blessed Virgin. Pius XII had a particular devotion to the Virgin Mary. In 1942 he consecrated the human race to the Immaculate Heart of Mary, in 1953 he proclaimed a special Marian year to commemorate the centenary of the definition of the Immaculate Conception and in 1950 he solemnly defined the dogma of the Assumption of Mary into heaven. The Pope's attitude towards ecclesiastical authority and theological research was clearly revealed in this definition: '. . . theology, even when positive, cannot be equated with a purely historical science, since God has given His Church, together with these sacred sources, the Living Teacher to illustrate and develop those truths which are contained only obscurely and as it were by implication in the store-house of faith'.

Although the ecclesiastical authorities in the first half of the twentieth century had tended to avoid issuing those great condemnations associated with their nineteenth-century predecessors, Joseph Wittig was inexplicably condemned in 1926 while Pierre Teilhard de Chardin was restricted in both his writing and his teaching. Furthermore such illustrious theologians as Chenù, Congar or de Lubac were among the victims of a 'witch-hunt' conducted by more conservative theologians that did not entirely cease even with the pontificate of John XXIII. But with the more general decline of the extreme opponents of 'Modernism', theological developments in the Catholic Church became increasingly influenced by an awareness of the significance of the Christian sources, scripture and tradition, and of the need to apply the message of Christianity to the problems of the contemporary world. Between 1930 and 1960 Catholic theologians became more conscious of the apostolic, pastoral and missionary dimensions of their work.

As a result of the earlier 'anti-Modernist' reaction, Catholic theologians had largely directed their attention to less 'dangerous' — and by definition less significant – issues. During the first half of the century the popes continued to follow the example of their predecessors in supporting scholastic theology and this support was reflected in different ways by Catholic writers and thinkers throughout the world who regarded Aquinas either as a barrier or as a light, to use Lacordaire's image later taken up by Cardinal Mercier. But the revival of neo-Thomism supported by Pius XI in *Studiorum Ducem* or by Pius XII in *Humani generis* was not always reflected in the scholarship of a Gilson or a Maritain and ignored the reaction against scholasticism which had been prompted by a greater appreciation of the Fathers and the medieval Augustinian tradition, Orthodox and Protestant theologians, and even the work of non-believers. Gabriel Marcel and Michael Schmaus continued to discuss the problems of eschatology and the philosophy of history. Pastoral and liturgical theology continued to develop with writers like Yves M. J. Congar and Josef Jungmann. The work of theologians like Friedrich Wilhelm Maier or Romano Guardini, Erich Przywara, Otto Karrer and Karl Adam both illustrated the weaknesses of the scholastic approach and prepared the way for new theological insights associated with names like Rahner or de Lubac who, at least in the opinion of one historian, 'effected the biggest revolution in theology since the baroque age'.

It has been said that Pius XII did not dominate or 'manipulate', but conserved and delayed; he was not a politican but a diplomat. It would seem to be true that as a result of concentrating on important public or diplomatic issues, the Pope found that he had too little time to give to the everyday government of the Church and its internal welfare. In particular he failed to establish and foster good relations between himself and his own departments or with individual bishops and seems to have been unduly influenced by that small group of people around him who were not very popular in Rome. It was the Pope himself who said that he wanted 'executors' not 'collaborators'. But in spite of his enormous capacity for work and his incredible self-discipline, such a personal system could not work for long. Originally he tended to concentrate the government of the Church in his own hands. He frequently reserved crucial decisions to himself or else circumvented the usual channels. When Cardinal Maglione, the Secretary of State, died in 1944, Pius XII resumed the position he had held between 1930 and 1939. However, during his later years as Pope even Pius XII found it impossible to carry the burdens he had imposed upon himself. He became increasingly reluctant to receive Heads of Congregations in audience and frequently referred them to the Secretariat where the officials concerned were not always empowered to deal with the issues being raised. This concentration of authority coupled with its increasing ineffectiveness also adversely affected the authority of bishops who were frequently ignored by the Pope or humiliated by his officials.

Perhaps the Pope's most noticeable defect was that he liked to give his audiences the impression of being astonishingly competent in their particular fields of work or knowledge and he even at times attempted to give professional advice with the result that he was occasionally simple to the point of being banal. He spoke on sporting events, systems of communication, types of footwear, the history of mineral extraction, recent developments in surgery or pharmacy, nuclear physics, cinema techniques, newspaper production, information agencies, hotels and tourism, railways and postal services, and animal slaughter. If Pius XI had issued a record number of formal publications, his successor gave a record number of addresses and allocutions to specialized audiences. In the month of October 1953 Pius XII gave addresses on neuropsychiatry, the nature of crime and punishment, human factors in business, the lawfulness of amputation, the need for evaluating scientific progress, the acquisition and use of medical knowledge, international travel as well as addressing a delegation of scientists from Denmark and the faculty and students of the Gregorian University.

In May and June 1955 he wrote a letter to the third Congress of the International Federation of Christian Workers' Movements in Düsseldorf, gave a speech to farm workers, sent a radio message to Catholics in Southern Rhodesia, addressed rose-growers and participants in the International European Symposium for the study and production of antibiotics, sent directives for the fifteenth Spanish Social Week, wrote a letter to the Kolping Association in Germany and addressed the directors and employees of the Bank of Naples, delegates attending the fourth World Congress of Petroleum as well as representatives of the Italian film industry. Inevitably some of the Pope's advice was not always particularly valuable. In September 1957 he spoke to dentists about the 'deforming pressures tending to excessive enlargement of the upper jaw so that the teeth close badly' and suggested ways of correcting children who continued 'sucking their thumbs beyond their early years'. In May 1957 he advised scientists, who were dealing with the problems of the stars, that: '. . . the sun deserves not to be neglected, for besides the influence it exercises on the earth and its inhabitants, it also by reason of its nearness more readily reveals the secret of its behaviour; thus study of the sun will never cease to be an essential branch of astronomy'.

The best allocutions of Pius XII were in the field of moral theology, and although he was hardly revolutionary in his attitude to sexual morality or the theology of marriage, he was unusually frank and open in his discussions of medical ethics. This openness could be seen in his lecture on the regulation of births given to the Italian Catholic Obstetric Union in October 1951, his address on medical treatment to the International Histopathological Congress in 1952, on psychoanalysis, relations between doctors and patients, and the principles of genetics in 1953, and on painless childbirth and the use of analgesics in 1956.

The style of government adopted by Pius XII was not only authoritarian but even triumphalist, and his spiritual supremacy was reinforced by claims of supernatural experiences and reports of papal visions. In October 1951 a Papal Legate revealed to a Portuguese audience that the Pope had on four occasions witnessed a similar phenomenon to that which had been reported to have occurred at Fatima. In December 1954 it was stated in the press that Christ had appeared at the bedside of the sick Pope. A Protestant who had intended to make an attempt on the Pope's life was apparently converted by a vision of the Blessed Virgin. It was arranged that the would-be assassin should be present at the Vatican Radio while the Pope recited the rosary and that he should then hand to the Pope the dagger with which he had intended to kill him. These and similar reports were received without question or even surprise by the majority of Catholics at the time.

However, any appraisal of Pius XII must first take account of the significance of a war that was not only massive in scale and enormous in its sufferings but tragic in its consequences. The most promising missionary fields as well as traditional strongholds of Catholicism seemed threatened if not irretrievably lost to the Church. Secondly in his later years the Pope was suffering from severe illnesses which severely weakened his physical and mental strength and which may well have led him to overestimate his own undoubted abilities. Finally – and this may well have been a result of the first two points – there does seem to have been a contrast between the more positive and progressive approach which the Pope was sometimes prepared to adopt during the earlier years of his pontificate and the more negative or cautious policies which he endorsed or tolerated later. Certainly the publication of *Humani Generis* and the way in which this was applied by enthusiastic integrists to hinder theological and biblical research as well as the Pope's own speech to the Assisi conference might be used as evidence of a more conservative approach than he had previously shown in dealing with contemporary problems. It could be that Pius XII felt that he had gone far enough and had achieved what was necessary and was afraid to let developments slip from his control. But it could also be that as a result of his natural conservatism, his ultramontanism and sense of *Romanità*, he ultimately failed to sympathize with theological or disciplinary pluralism and became suspicious of biblical and ecumenical, liturgical and pastoral developments, though these had long since become realities which he had previously been too sensitive and intelligent to ignore.

When Pius XII died on 11 October 1958 many non-Catholics as well as Catholics believed that his death marked the end of an epoch; they were right, though hardly in the way that they had expected or imagined. In 1956 Daniel-Rops reflected the almost unanimous opinion of Catholics throughout the world when he wrote: 'I often find myself thinking of a lighted window high up in the dark façade of the Vatican. It looks down each evening upon the Piazza of St Peter's; behind it a man sits at work, keeping watch and ward. There are countless men whose labours are prolonged far into the night, and many windows shine through the long silent hours. But this light is symbolic: a beacon amid the wilderness of Earth; a guarantee of certitude written across the winding scroll to time; a signal of hope, an earnest of better things to come when the dark shadows have dispersed'.

It seems almost incredible now to recall that there were Catholics at the time who were unable to conceive of a Church without Pius XII, though few Catholics could have imagined that within a year of his death the high reputation of the late Pope would not only be questioned but so challenged that he would then seem to have been to some but a symbol of dead hopes and abandoned dreams.

Almost within hours of Pius XII's death unwelcome stories were reported of scandals involving his nephews and the influence of a Sister Pasqualina. The Pope's doctor tried a new method of preserving his body which failed. Decomposition set in even before the lying-in-state was over and members of the Noble Guard were said to have fainted at their posts. The same doctor sold his diaries of the Pope's last days to the newspapers, complete with photographs, and called a press conference to explain his failure. Later some serious and significant criticisms began to appear. Had the late Pope been indecisive as well as autocratic? He had laid down detailed rules governing a papal interregnum, but never made the necessary appointments to carry them out; the chamberlain's duties were clear enough, but unfortunately there was no chamberlain. In a discourse on the first anniversary of Pius XII's death, Cardinal Tardini revealed to the world what he had endured during the last pontificate and catalogued the more exasperating habits of an apparently fussy and fastidious Pope. Other questions were then being raised. Had Pius XII not only been aloof and inaccessible but even psychologically and physically unwell during the years immediately before his death, and how far had these factors influenced some of his decisions?

When the Cardinals arrived in Rome for the Conclave, many of them became very conscious, if they were not already aware, of the over-centralization of ecclesiastical authority and the sterility of a pontificate that had hitherto been concealed only by the prestige and the personality of the dead Pope himself. It was not without significance that in his speech on choosing a pope, Monsignor Antonio Bacci should have emphasized the need for the pope to be a 'pastor of souls': '. . . he will be ready to receive and welcome the bishops as his collaborators in the government of the Church of God; he will be ready to give them counsel in their doubts, to listen to and comfort their anxieties, and to encourage their plans . . . his heart will feel movements of particular tenderness for peoples oppressed by an absolute, tyrannical, and persecuting power; and equally, too, for those social classes that still find themselves in such straitened conditions and poverty that not even by the sweat of their brows can they procure for themselves and their children sufficient food and a sheltering roof . . . May the new Vicar of Christ be like a bridge between heaven and earth . . . a bridge between the various social classes. . . . A bridge between nations, even between those that reject, rebuff, and persecute the Christian religion, and may he seek to rebuild between them that true peace which is the only source of prosperity, tranquility, and progress'.

There were not many obvious 'candidates' for the papacy among the Cardinals. The last consistory had been held in 1953 and the Pope had not filled any vacancies in the Sacred College since then. It was even suggested that members of the Conclave were thinking of electing Archbishop Montini of Milan who was not yet a Cardinal but on the eleventh ballot they elected Angelo Roncalli who took the name, John XXIII. In electing Roncalli, the Cardinals were choosing one of the most experienced diplomats among them. He had been Apostolic Visitor to Bulgaria, Apostolic Delegate to Greece and Turkey, and Nuncio in France. This last appointment had been an extremely sensitive one in view of the fact that de Gaulle's Provisional Government wanted to remove those French bishops who had supported the Vichy régime. In the event only three of the thirty-three bishops involved were asked to resign. Roncalli's piety was well-known, he was universally liked and he had had pastoral experience as Patriarch of Venice. Finally he had not been associated too closely with his predecessor and was old enough to be regarded as a 'transitional' pope. As the new Pope himself commented later: 'When on 28 October 1958 the Cardinals of the Holy Roman Church designated me for the supreme responsibility of governing the universal flock of Jesus Christ, there was a widespread belief that I would be a provisional, transitional Pope. But instead, here I am on the eve of the pontificate's fourth year, with an immense programme of work in front of me to be carried out before the whole watching, waiting world. As for me, I am like St Martin: he neither feared to die nor spurned to live'.

The background of the new Pope was at once both traditional and yet sufficiently different from that of his immediate predecessor to suggest the possibility that he might adopt a different and a more personal approach. Unlike Pius XII, John XXIII was not a 'Roman'. The new Pope had been born in the north of Italy and had served as a chaplain in the Italian army. He had been the secretary and the biographer of the liberal Bishop Radini Tedeschi of Bergamo, one of the leading Italian disciples of Leo XIII. Radini Tedeschi was a friend of Pope Benedict XV who first invited Roncalli to work in Rome. Pius XI, who assisted Roncalli when he was working on the papers of St Charles Borromeo, sent him as Visitor to Bulgaria. Inevitably Roncalli's experiences of life in Italy during war and peace, the different attitudes towards the Church and the papacy which he had encountered in Bulgaria, Greece and Turkey, the problems and difficulties of French Catholics would play their part – or so it was hoped – in the formation of his policies as Pope.

At the same time Roncalli had proved to be a devoted and loyal servant of the Pope and the Church throughout his career. He once noted in his Journal: 'I am always thinking of Pius IX, of saintly and glorious memory; and, imitating him in his sacrifices, I would like to be worthy of celebrating his canonization'.

It would have been ironic indeed if the Pope of the First Vatican Council had been canonized by John XXIII during the Second Vatican Council and it is tantalizing to speculate what impact this might have had on the latter's subsequent reputation. John XXIII also admired and respected Pius XII and constantly quoted from him. For example a good deal of *Pacem in Terris* was taken directly from Pius XII's Christmas broadcasts between 1939 and 1941. Furthermore, although Roncalli as Patriarch of Venice had received delegates from a Communist women's organization and warmly welcomed a Socialist Party Congress, he had also clearly disowned a group of progressive Catholics and given his full support to Pius XII's political boycott of Communists and Socialists. Archbishop Roncalli had not then been particularly sympathetic towards moves in favour of cooperation between Catholics and Communists or even Socialists. He warned his people to: 'Beware of pacts and compromises, of understandings founded upon dreams, upon promises of respect for liberty made by those who trample truth, justice, and liberty under foot without scruple'. However, after he became Pope, he tended to avoid making pronouncements on Communism and it was widely believed that he quietly discouraged the Italian bishops from giving political instructions.

Many contemporary and later commentators – possibly unduly influenced by events which had occurred during the second and more intransigent period of Pius XII's pontificate – have exaggerated the contrast between Pius and John, whose basic conservatism and sense of authority have often been seriously underestimated. His consciousness of the dignity of the papacy was revealed in his Journal when he wrote: 'Peter's successor knows that in his person and in all he does there is the grace and the law of love, which sustains, inspires and adorns everything; and in the eyes of the whole world it is this mutual love between Jesus and himself, Simon or Peter, the son of John, that is the foundation of the Holy Church; a foundation which is at the same time visible and invisible, Jesus being invisible to the eyes of our flesh, and the Pope, the Vicar of Christ, being visible to the whole world'.

John believed that the Pope was not only the centre of unity, but that 'the supreme and infallible magisterium was reserved by the Lord to Peter personally and to his successors' and that this was 'the essential bond of visible unity of the Church'. As the Pope himself said: 'It is indispensable to the unity of the faith that there be union among the teachers of the divine truths, that is, the harmony of bishops among themselves in communion and submission to the Roman Pontiff'.

The early moves of the new Pope did not foreshadow the dramatic changes that were to come later. In April 1959 the Holy Office endorsed Pius XII's ban on giving political support to the Communists and in June John XXIII supported the decision of the Holy Office to end the experiment of the worker-priests in France. Pope John, like his predecessor, deplored the persecution of the Church by Communist régimes and wrote letters of sympathy to churchmen such as Mindszenty, Stepinac and Beran who were victims of Communist persecution. The new Pope appointed the rather conservative Cardinal Tardini as Secretary of State and although he created more Cardinals than ever before, he also increased the percentage of Italian Cardinals in the Sacred College. Pope John showed his favour to some of the professors of the Lateran, who were well known for their traditional views, and supported the continued use of Latin in the study of theology as well as the liturgy of the Church. In an Apostolic Constitution, *Veterum Sapientia*, the Pope warned bishops and religious superiors against those who opposed the use of Latin in the liturgy or in sacred studies and ordered that those lecturers in universities and seminaries who were unable to teach in Latin should be replaced.

There is no evidence that John XXIII reformed either the College of Cardinals or the Curia. He simply increased the number of Cardinals and in the case of the Secretariat for Christian Unity, which he established later, tried to circumvent the Curia. Pope John created twenty-three Cardinals within two months of his election of whom fourteen were Italians and eleven members of the Curia. In the following year he created another eight Cardinals, three of whom were Italians and seven members of the Curia. In 1960 he created another eight Cardinals with only one Italian member of the Curia. In 1961 four more Cardinals were appointed with one Italian curial official and in 1962 eleven new Cardinals of whom eight were members of the Curia and four came from Italy. In short more than half of the fifty-four Cardinals created by John were members of the Curia and most of these were elderly and rather conservative. John himself had been elected by fifty-two Cardinals of whom fifteen were in the Curia. Pope Paul would be elected by over eighty Cardinals of whom thirty-three were members of the Curia.

John XXIII first made an impact on public opinion throughout the world by showing himself to be a pastor and a common father. As a young seminarian, he had written: 'Did You not say, O Lord, that Your yoke is easy and Your burden is light? Is it not written in Your Scriptures that to serve You is to reign? Is it not the greatest honour for a holy man if people say of him that he is the servant of God? Surely Your Pontiff, Your Vicar on earth, is proud to be called by this name: the servant of the servants of God!'

At his coronation, Pope John declared that the true ideal of a pope was to 'realize first and foremost in himself the splendid image of the Good Shepherd'. Two months after his election he paid a Christmas visit to the children in the Hospital of the Infant Jesus and the Hospital of the Holy Spirit. During the afternoon he welcomed the boys from the Villa Nazareth and Don Gnocchi's little cripples to the Vatican. At eight o'clock on the following morning he made his world-famous visit to the prisoners in the Regina Coeli. At the same time he was visiting as many parishes as he could in the diocese of Rome. His religious sincerity and pastoral zeal coupled with his open and spontaneous personality inevitably captivated his audiences. Meanwhile he was re-establishing the normal government of the Holy See without making any dramatic changes. He established relations with the Curia and regularly received Prefects in audience. He allowed the third meeting of the Episcopal Council of Latin America to meet in Rome and approved of its results. He also proposed that the Italian episcopal conference should be given greater autonomy.

Consequently few contemporaries were expecting any particularly dramatic announcement when on the afternoon of 25 January 1959 the Pope went to the Basilica of St Paul's Without the Walls to celebrate pontifical vespers on the Feast of St Paul, the apostle of the Gentiles, and to conclude the octave of prayer for Christian unity. This was his tenth official appearance outside the Vatican in ninety days. John XXIII addressed the seventeen cardinals then present in Rome who had been summoned to attend by the Master of Ceremonies. It was there that the Pope announced his intention of calling an ecumenical council, with the promotion of Christian unity especially with Christians in the East as one of its objects, of holding a synod for the religious needs of the people and the diocese of Rome, and of reforming the Code of Canon Law and publishing the Canon Law of the Oriental Churches. This programme has not unnaturally been compared with that of his predecessor who declared that the three main aims of his pontificate were a new translation of the Psalter, the definition of the Assumption of Our Lady and the excavation of the tomb of St Peter.

The Roman Synod passed off without achieving anything of great significance or interest and was in fact completed within a week in January 1960. The Synod reasserted the Church's right to remind Catholics of their obligations at election time and called on all the faithful to cooperate in the defence of their religion and the Church. Priests were forbidden to witness the marriages of those who held Communist or other principles opposed to Christianity. The Synod repeated the Church's condemnation of abortion, direct sterilization and artificial insemination. Priests were instructed to explain the sacrament of Extreme Unction, to conduct funerals with dignity and without the use of lavish decorations, and not to charge the poor for burials. The faithful were encouraged to sing at religious services. Pope John himself was not any more effective in pursuing his third aim. He simply appointed a Commission of thirty Cardinals to revise the Code of Canon Law on 29 March 1963.

It was only with the opening of the Council that the Pope clearly revealed his determination to associate bishops throughout the world with the authority and the responsibilities of the Bishop of Rome, to initiate the pastoral reform or *aggiornamento* of the Catholic Church itself and to work for the restoration of Christian unity. The Pope's intention of calling a General Council was neither particularly novel nor unique. Pius XI had contemplated resuming the First Vatican Council that had been brought to an abrupt end by the events of 1870 and Pius XII had also thought about the idea in 1948 but in both cases work was suspended as a result of divisions of opinion. Pope John himself had only vague ideas about what the Council might actually achieve but he certainly hoped to adapt the pastoral mission of the Church to the modern world and to work for Christian unity. In 1959 he declared: 'The Council will certainly present an admirable spectacle of truth, unity, and charity. We have confidence that such a manifestation will be for Christians separated from Rome a gentle invitation to seek and find that unity for which Christ offered to His Father such an ardent prayer'.

In June 1961 the Pope expressed the hope that the Council would help to promote the sense of brotherhood and peace of mankind but he also claimed that the two first tasks of the Council were the *aggiornamento* of the Catholic Church and preparing the way towards the reunion of Christians.

The events and the sufferings during the Second World War coupled with the challenge of Communism, materialism and scepticism which followed had given a great stimulus to the development of ecumenism. In 1945 the Holy Office gave its approval to the Braunshardter Conferences between Catholics and Lutherans and in the same year Father Charles Boyer established the Unitas Association in Rome which worked for the reunion of all Christians with the Catholic Church. However the official attitude of the Church towards the Ecumenical Movement remained one of cautious reserve, of neutral if not suspicious interest. The ecclesiastical authorities were reluctant to participate in case official representation might seem to imply the recognition of other Christian Churches.

Furthermore the promulgation of the dogma of the Assumption on 1 November 1950 was described by Father Congar as 'a cruel blow to ecumenical activity; in many places groups which had been full of life ceased to exist'. On the other hand it was perhaps not untypical of Pius XII that he should have expressed his 'fullest confidence that this solemn declaration and definition of the Assumption will greatly help towards the advance of society'. Roman Catholics had become accustomed to hearing the Pope speak so authoritatively on such a great variety of subjects that even a solemn definition of Mary's Assumption into heaven was taken almost as another matter of course. A thousand bishops, the entire diplomatic corps representing fifty nations and almost a million people from practically every country in the world were present in St Peter's Square when the Pope defined that 'the Immaculate Mother of God, the ever Virgin Mary, after completing her span of life upon earth was assumed to the glory of heaven in body and soul'. Other Christians, however, were most disturbed and even the Greek Orthodox Churches protested.

Yet Pius XII himself had made several important contributions to the development of the Ecumenical Movement within the Catholic Church by promoting liturgical and biblical reform, by his acts of charity during the war and his work for peace throughout the world, and by his willingness to receive so many different individuals and groups of people in papal audiences. However he seems to have been content to issue general appeals to other Christians to return to the unity of the one Church. For example in his encyclicals *Orientalis Ecclesiae* and *Sempiternus Rex* on the anniversaries of the death of St Cyril of Alexandria and the Council of Chalcedon, he simply appealed to the Orthodox Churches to return to the one fold. He told a German audience in November 1948: 'We know how urgent among many of your people, Catholics as well as non-Catholics, is the aspiration toward unity in the Faith. And who could feel more intensely this desire than the Vicar of Christ himself? . . . [However the Church must remain] . . . inflexible before all that could have even the appearance of a compromise, or of an adjustment of the Catholic Faith with other confessions . . . [because the Church] . . . knows that there has always been and always will be one sole infallible and sure rock of the whole truth and of the fulness of grace come to her from Christ; and that this rock, according to the explicit will of her divine Founder, is herself and simply herself'.

In 1948, on the eve of the first meeting of the General Assembly of the World Council of Churches in Amsterdam, the Dutch bishops ordered a day of prayer that the Holy Spirit might enlighten the minds of those taking part but no Catholics were officially authorized to attend any of the meetings. At the same time the Holy Office reminded Catholics of the prohibition against worshipping, *communicatio in sacris*, with non-Catholics as well as the canonical rules governing discussions and congresses with non-Catholics which required the permission of the Holy See. This warning was directed to Catholics in Germany and more specifically to members of the Una Sancta movement. A further instruction from the Holy Office warned Catholics not to exaggerate the faults of their predecessors or to reduce the guilt and responsibility of the Protestant Reformers.

Eighteen months later, however, the Holy Office conceded that the Ecumenical Movement was the work of the Holy Spirit and gave a very modified word of encouragement to Catholic ecumenists who were allowed to engage in conversations and even to say approved prayers with other Christians. However these conversations were to be supervised by the local bishop who was required to report on them annually to the Holy Office. At this time the task of Catholic ecumenists was not an easy one as the career of a theologian like Father Congar or the history of such publications as *Irenikon*, *Unitas* or *Istina* would show. But in 1949 the Holy Office was also prepared to condemn Father Feeney's extreme views on the impossibility of salvation outside the Catholic Church and in 1951 Bishop Willebrands succeeded in establishing the International Catholic Conference for Ecumenical Questions. In 1952 the Vicar Apostolic of

Sweden gave permission to four Catholic 'observers' to attend the Third World Conference on Faith and Order at Lund. However two years later there were no Catholic observers at the World Council at Evanston which was probably as well in view of the bitter attack on the Church made by the Methodist Bishop Santos Barbieri of Argentina. In 1957 two official observers attended the North American Study Conference on Faith and Order.

The possibility of calling a General Council or arranging a meeting between Pius XII and the Patriarch Athenagoras had been suggested on a few occasions in 1946, 1954 and 1957. But relations between the Orthodox and the Catholic Churches were complicated by political developments as well as historical or theological divisions and by the existence of the Uniate Churches. Reaction to events which occurred during the Second World War and various manoeuvrings during the Cold War had further soured relations between the Catholic and the Orthodox Churches. Since 1945 Uniate Churches in the Ukraine, Rumania, Bulgaria and Czechoslovakia had come under attack from the Communists, an attack which was sometimes supported by the Orthodox authorities. On the other hand, in 1957 and in spite of appeals from the Faculty of Theology in Athens, Pius XII had appointed a successor to the deceased Exarch of the Greek Uniate Church and even arranged to have him consecrated in Athens.

Consequently, the Ecumenical Movement seemed to have made little progress in the Catholic Church by 1960. However, by then, non-Catholics were being attracted by the personality of the new Pope, his openness and charity, his humility and rejection of triumphalism, his confidence and trust in God and in Divine Providence. Patriarch Athenagoras I of Constantinople described the Pope as 'a man sent from God whose name was John'. The Patriarch praised the attitude of 'the new Pope of Rome, John XXIII who is so well-known, loved, and respected in our ecclesiastical jurisdictions'. Athenagoras welcomed the calling of the Council, though other Orthodox Patriarchs were more reserved. Archbishop Fisher of Canterbury also welcomed the Council and called on the Pope in December 1960. This was a quiet and formal but significant meeting. For the first time since the Reformation the Pope had met an Archbishop of Canterbury.

Pope John not only received prominent members of other Christian Churches, but invited non-Catholics to attend the Council as observers and, perhaps most important of all, established the Secretariat for Promoting Christian Unity under Cardinal Augustine Bea to guide the Catholic Ecumenical Movement throughout the world. The establishment of the Secretariat illustrated the Pope's awareness of the fact that the Curia was not equipped to deal with all problems and of the necessity of establishing an administrative body independent of curial control. In the event, the Secretariat took the lead, in spite of opposition from the Curia, in improving ecumenical relations and influencing the Fathers at the Council. In 1961 when the World Council of Churches met in New Delhi, the Pope gave permission for five Catholic observers to attend and this paved the way for the attendance of non-Catholic observers at the Council itself. The vast difference between the Decree on Ecumenism which would be published in 1964 and the Instructions of the Holy Office in the late 1940s would prove to be the measure of the achievement of Pope John, Pope Paul and the Second Vatican Council, many of whose decrees – on Revelation and the Liturgy, on the Church and the Oriental Churches, and on the Training of Priests – would also be imbued with the spirit of ecumenism.

When Pope John first announced the Council, the *Osservatore Romano* 'hid' the announcement between a couple of much less important and even routine items, while *Civiltà Cattolica* did not even mention the subject until four months later. In view of later events, it was not without significance that one of the most positive and enthusiastic welcomes should have come from Cardinal Montini, then Archbishop of Milan: 'The Council will make Rome the spiritual capital of the world from whence the light will spread upon those places and institutions where men are working for the union of the peoples, for social peace, for the welfare of the poor, for progress, for justice, and for liberty'.

Montini produced a statement so prophetic and remarkable that it seems to summarize the whole of his later aspirations and achievements as Pope: 'An event of the utmost importance has become reality. It is not the importance of an event which spreads hate or terror like a fearful war; it is not the importance of earthly politics or secular civilization, like the transitory importance of so many human gatherings; here is none of the importance of scientific discoveries or of temporal concerns, as it is with so many events of our civil life. This event will be important for peace, truth and the spirit; important for the present, important for the future; important for nations and for the hearts of men; important for the Church and for the whole of humanity. It will be the greatest Council the Church has ever held in the whole of the twenty centuries of its history; even as to numbers it will be the greatest spiritual assembly of its hierarchy in the utmost peace and unity; it will be the greatest Council in the catholicity of its extent, which truly covers the whole of the civil world and the whole of our planet. Before our very eyes history is opening up enormous prospects for centuries to come'.

The announcement of the Council was also welcomed, perhaps inevitably, by Catholic hierarchies throughout the world but it was given a particularly positive welcome by the bishops of France and Belgium, Holland, Germany and Austria. Bishops from the developing countries also manifested a special interest as did other Churchmen, such as Cardinal Léger of Montreal or Cardinal Lercaro of Bologna, who were well-known for their 'liberal' and enlightened views. Many other bishops, however, as Cardinal Heenan admitted of the bishops in the English-speaking world, were quite unprepared for the sort of Council that was being planned by their European colleagues while the suspicions of some of the other 'conservative' bishops would in due course give way to outright hostility.

It was perhaps inevitable that at least initially the preparatory work for the Council should have been controlled and even dominated by members of the Curia. In 1960 ten Preparatory Commissions and two Secretariats were established along with a Central Commission of Bishops from about sixty countries who were responsible for the work of co-ordination and drawing up the standing orders of the Council. These Commissions paralleled the existing Roman Congregations and were each led by the same curial Cardinals. Furthermore members of the Commissions were largely sympathetic to the Curia, though there were a few independent bishops and theologians. Between the autumn of 1960 and the autumn of 1961 the Commissions and the Secretariats produced some seventy drafts on a variety of subjects which, in the words of Father Chenù, lacked 'any reference to the needs of the contemporary world' and in the event none of them survived. As a result the Pope has been accused of failing to give the leadership required during the preparations and proceedings of the First Session of the Council and of following the disconcerting line he had adopted in Paris: 'a half turn to the right, a half turn to the left'. However it must be remembered that, in spite of considerable opposition as well as apathetic ignorance, the Council did take place and the fact that Pope John had been able to bring together bishops from throughout the world – even from Communist countries – in order to see the Church and the World from a different perspective was one of his greatest achievements.

The Second Vatican Council officially opened on 11 October 1962 in the presence of some two and a half thousand Fathers from practically every part of the world and non-Catholic observers from other Christian Churches. At the end of the Council there were no less than ninety-three observers representing twenty-eight Churches who, by then, were both consulted and able to comment on the proceedings. The Council itself consisted of four sessions which were held during the autumn of every year

The Papacy in the Modern World 1914–1978

from 1962 to 1965, though some of the most critical moments occurred when the Council was not actually in session and when the bishops were away as members of the Curia tried to regain control of a situation which they felt they were in danger of losing.

The Pope himself outlined the aims of the Council in his official opening address, which was delivered on 11 October 1962, when he criticized the more intransigent conservatives in the Church: 'It often happens that, in the daily exercise of Our apostolic ministry, We are shocked to discover what is being said by some people who, though they may be fired by religious zeal, are without justice, or good judgment, or consideration in their way of looking at matters. In the existing state of society they see nothing but ruin and calamity; they are in the habit of saying that our age is much worse than past centuries; they behave as though history, which teaches us about life, had nothing to teach them, and as though, at the times of past Councils, everything was perfect in the matter of Christian doctrine, public behaviour, and the proper freedom of the Church. It seems to Us necessary to express Our complete disagreement with these prophets of doom, who give news only of catastrophes, as though the world were nearing its end. In the present state of affairs, now that human society seems to have reached a turning-point, it is better to recognize the mysterious designs of divine Providence which, passing through the different ages of man, and his works, generally against all expectation, achieve their purposes and guide all events wisely for the good of the Church – even those events which seem to conflict with her purposes'.

The Pope went on: 'The salient point of this Council is therefore not the discussion of this or that theme of the Church's fundamental doctrine. . . . But, setting out from a renewed, serene, and tranquil adherence to all the teaching of the Church . . . the Catholic and apostolic Christian spirit of the whole world now awaits a leap forward towards a doctrinal penetration and a formation of consciences corresponding more completely and faithfully to the authentic doctrine, which itself should be explained and elucidated in accordance with the methods of research and literary formulation familiar to modern thought. It is one thing to have the substance of the ancient doctrine of the *depositum fidei* but quite another to formulate and reclothe it: and it is this that must – if need be with patience – be held of great importance, measuring everything according to the forms and proportions of a teaching of pre-eminently pastoral character'.

The first meeting of the General Congregation was intended to deal with elections to the Commissions of the Council but Cardinal Liénart, Archbishop of Lille, pointed out that to proceed at once would prejudice the elections in favour of the existing members of the Preparatory Commissions, a factor of which members of the Curia were presumably not unaware. It was therefore decided that the elections should be delayed in order that the necessary consultations might take place and the Commissions became much more truly representative. At the beginning of December the Pope announced the formation of a special Commission to control and co-ordinate the work of the other Commissions in an effort to reduce the number of *schemata* and to ensure that they followed more closely the aims set out in his opening speech. By then it was evident that the Council had been able to assert its autonomy against the Curia and that a substantial 'majority' had emerged in favour of the *aggiornamento* who were able to define their aims and, at least to some extent, to establish the means to achieve them. In general the 'majority' were more ecumenical, pastoral and willing to adapt to the modern world than the 'minority' who were concerned to safeguard the faith and stability, the tradition and authority of the Church.

The first vote which was taken, on the renewal of the liturgy on 14 November, illustrated on which 'side' the sympathies of the 'silent majority' lay. Forty-six Fathers found themselves opposed by 2162. These divisions were revealed even more dramatically in the debate on the second *schema*, on the sources of Revelation, when, by a vote of 1368 to 822, the Fathers remitted the rather conservative and narrow document submitted to them. The point was that many of the original *schemata*, especially many of those submitted by the Theological Commission, were inadequate or mediocre and even provocative to other Catholic theologians as well as to the representatives of other Christian Churches. The original *schema* on Revelation was described as 'excessively professional and scholastic, not pastoral, excessively rigid, theologically immature, incomprehensible to non-Catholics, unsympathetic to scientific research in theology and exegesis, too evidently reflecting certain schools of thought'. Although the number of Fathers opposed to the *schema* on Revelation did not reach the required two-thirds, the Pope himself intervened and returned the *schema* not to the Doctrinal Commission but to a special mixed Commission which included representatives of the Secretariat for Unity.

A hasty examination of two rather ordinary *schemata* on the Mass Media and the Eastern Churches was followed by the debate on the *schema* on the Church. The Fathers accepted a suggestion from Cardinal Suenens, who was warmly supported by Cardinal Montini, that the subject of the Church was central to the work of the Council and particularly such issues as the reform of the Church, its relations with the world and with other Christian Churches. Once again in the debate on the *schema* on the Church, the approach adopted by officials of the Curia was rejected by the Fathers in Council. One very important reason which helps to explain this unexpected determination of the Fathers to question and to challenge the line laid down by members of the Curia was the influence of the many theologians from all parts of the world who were advising their Bishops and the various Commissions.

Any discussion of the Church – as of the Liturgy – inevitably raised the question of the rôle of the laity. John XXIII shared many of his predecessor's reservations about the rôle of the laity and he often stressed the need for obedience to Bishops and hierarchies. However John had none of the clericalism associated with Pius and many other ecclesiastics and, as a result of his past experience, he was well aware of the dangers which might result to the Church from adopting too conservative or intransigent attitudes. In the event the Council ensured that many of the developments on the rôle of the laity to which Pius XII had given a guarded welcome, would become part of the ordinary teaching of the Catholic Church. As the Chapter on the Laity declared: 'Pastors know that they were not instituted by Christ to take upon themselves the whole salvific mission of the Church to the world, but that their proud duty is so to tend the faithful and acknowledge their ministrations and divine gifts that all may unanimously cooperate, each in his own fashion, in the common task'.

Pope John also caught the imagination of the world through his encyclicals, though his first encyclical, *Ad Petri Cathedram* which was published on 29 June 1959, was an extremely cautious document and passed without comment. John defended the traditional prerogatives of the See of Rome, endorsed his predecessor's warnings against Communism and exhorted the faithful to obey the discipline of the Church. But although John was as uncompromising as his predecessors, his appeal for Christian unity was much warmer and more friendly than theirs: 'You will allow Us to call you, with ardent desire, brothers and sons. Allow Us to nourish the hope of your return – a hope We cultivate with fatherly affection'. His encyclical on missions, *Princeps Pastorum*, which was issued in November, was also widely ignored though it was a worthy successor to *Maximum Illud* which it was intended to commemorate. However the publication of *Mater et Magistra*, on social justice and international relations, on 15 July 1961, created a sensation.

Mater et Magistra was published on the seventieth anniversary of *Rerum Novarum* and the thirtieth anniversary of *Quadragesimo Anno* and did not really mark a radical departure from the support for moderate reform which had developed in Catholic social teaching since the time of Leo XIII. Pope John's defence of the dignity of labour and support for the wider distribution of property, though developed in contemporary terms,

From Pius XII to John XXIII

were taken from the teachings of his predecessors. But the Pope's obvious concern for social and material welfare, peace and international reconciliation, human and political rights as well as Christian unity evoked a wide response and not simply from Roman Catholics. The Pope seemed to be more sympathetic to modern man than many of his predecessors had been and he adopted a more positive approach to contemporary political, social and economic reforms. He recognized the role of the State as an active agent in the promotion and development of the human personality and human welfare, in the improvement of health and living conditions, and the provision of education and leisure activities: 'Turning to the political field we observe many welcome changes. In a number of countries all classes of citizens are taking a part in public life, and public authorities are taking a keener interest in social and economic matters. We are witnessing the breakaway from colonialism and the attainment of political independence by the peoples of Asia and Africa. Drawn together by their common needs, nations are becoming daily more interdependent'.

At the same time the Pope was critical of the 'neo-colonialism' of the Communist and the Western Powers: 'There is a further temptation which the economically developed nations must resist: that of giving technical and financial aid with a view to gaining control over the political situation in the underdeveloped countries, and furthering their own plans for world domination. Let us be quite clear on this point. A nation that acted from these motives would in fact be introducing a new form of colonialism – cleverly disguised, no doubt, but in no respect less blameworthy than that from which many nations have recently emerged'.

On 9 April 1963 John XXIII signed his encyclical *Pacem in Terris* at a ceremony which, for the first time in history, was televised. In some ways this encyclical was also a very traditional document. Pius XII was quoted about thirty times and *Pacem in Terris* covered much the same ground as *Mater et Magistra*: social and economic problems, colonialism and the problems of development, the United Nations and international peace. The first section dealt with order between men; the second with relations between the State and its subjects; the third with relations between different States; the fourth with the world community; the fifth and final section consisted of 'Pastoral Exhortations'. However, *Mater et Magistra* had been addressed to the Catholic faithful, whereas *Pacem in Terris* – one of the most comprehensive papal discussions of political and social problems – was addressed to 'all men of good will' as John XXIII reasserted the Pope's responsibility to promote political, economic and social harmony throughout the world: 'We therefore consider it Our duty as Christ's vicar on earth – Christ, the Saviour of the world, the Author of peace – and as

213

the interpreter of the most ardent wishes of the whole human family, in the fatherly love We bear all mankind, to beg and beseech men, and particularly statesmen, to be unsparing of their labour and efforts to ensure that human affairs follow a rational and dignified course'.

The Pope distinguished between false philosophies or ideologies and their political, economic and social programmes. Theoretical objections did not necessarily exclude the possibility of practical cooperation such as the urgent need for disarmament in view of the dangers of nuclear conflict: 'in this age, which boasts of its atomic power, it no longer makes sense to maintain that war is a fit instrument with which to repair the violation of justice'; 'by meeting and negotiating men may come to discover better the bonds that unite them together, deriving from the human nature which they have in common'. Christians above all should work energetically for 'the establishment of such a world community of peoples as is urgently demanded by the requirements of the common good'. The Pope gave his support to the work of the United Nations, defended the rights of all peoples to political independence, condemned economic and cultural as well as political imperialism, manifested his personal concern for the interests of developing countries, and called on wealthier countries to assist the development of the less fortunate while respecting their political freedoms and their local cultures. In short, the Pope condemned the abuses of authority either by oppression or by neglecting to promote the welfare of men and women throughout the world. Communism was never explicitly mentioned.

In distinguishing between error and people in error, the Pope went so far as to claim that: 'Catholics who, in order to achieve some external good, collaborate with unbelievers or with those who through error lack the fulness of faith in Christ, may possibly provide the occasion or even the incentive for their conversion to the truth'.

He was therefore prepared to tolerate some degree of cooperation between those who might be opposed ideologically but whose political programmes were worthy of support and, according to some contemporaries, effectively lifted the ban which had prohibited Italian Catholics from supporting the parties of the left. Perhaps as a result of his experience of French politics, Pope John proved willing to allow the Christian Democrats in Italy to form a coalition with the Socialists and when, in February 1962, Fanfani attempted to form a centre-left coalition of Christian Democrats and Socialists, most of the Italian hierarchy, under instructions from the Pope, did not protest.

Within weeks of the publication of *Pacem in Terris*, increasing numbers of Italians took the opportunity of voting in favour of the Communist

Party, but it is only fair to add that the Communist Party had made consistent gains in Italy over the past ten years. Furthermore the Communist threat seemed reduced during John's pontificate by the official rejection of policies associated with Stalin, by the apparent end of Communist expansion into Eastern Europe and by the increasing prosperity of the West. Meanwhile Catholics like Aldo Moro, Secretary of the Christian Democrats and later Prime Minister, had continued the unenviable task of attempting the political education of Italian Catholics. However the Socialists and Christian Democrats did not remain united for long. The Italian Bishops were frightened once again into giving their support to the Christian Democrat Party which was able to form a Government dependent on the small political groups of right and centre, and opposed by Socialists and Communists. Nevertheless during the reign of Paul VI, Pietro Nenni, one of the leaders of the Socialists, went, with the approval of the Pope, to address a conference of the United Nations on the significance of *Pacem in Terris* and was received in a long private audience on his return.

There are several possible reasons which might help to explain why *Pacem in Terris* was given such an enthusiastic reception in the East as well as in the West. It has been argued that the encyclical had such an impact because people were generally unfamiliar with what Pius XII had actually said in his numerous speeches over some twenty years. On several occasions Pius XII, like some of his predecessors and other ecclesiastical authorities, had defended the rights of Catholics and made it clear that the Church only wanted from 'liberal' or from Communist régimes the opportunity to operate in freedom. However, John XXIII was careful to avoid the rather triumphalist and even apocalyptic language that had so often alienated non-Catholics and he concentrated on criticizing opposing philosophies and ideologies rather than 'opponents' as such.

Furthermore, in *Pacem in Terris* Pope John defended the right of man 'to worship God in accordance with the right dictates of his own conscience and to profess his religion both in private and public'. Unlike Pius XI, John XXIII implicitly accepted freedom of speech and freedom of the press and welcomed the advent of the democratic form of Government. For the first time, a Pope was recognizing, and not merely tolerating, the conscientious rights of all men and not simply of Catholics. Finally, the encyclical was published at a time when the interest of the world in the papacy had been aroused by the opening of the Council and the force of John's own personality, his evident sincerity and unselfish work for peace. It seemed to many that the Pope was developing and expounding more traditional Catholic principles in such a way that the Church appeared to be far more concerned with human problems than the World had ever imagined. As one left-wing contemporary writer observed: 'John XXIII's claim to go down in history will rest not so much on his title "pope of peace" – what pope has wished to be known otherwise? – but on his merit in having matched the peace of God against the realities of our time'.

When the peace of the world was threatened by the building of the Berlin Wall in 1961, Pope John issued one of his famous appeals for peace; an appeal which was addressed: '. . . to all Our sons, to all those whom We feel the right and the duty to call such, to those who believe in God and in His Christ, and also to the unbelievers, because all belong to God, and to Christ, by virtue of their origin and their redemption'.

Kruschev described the Pope's appeal as 'a good sign': 'John XXIII pays his homage to sound reason when he warns those who govern of the danger of a general catastrophe and appeals to them to take into account the enormous responsibility which they bear towards history'. In spite of Kruschev's crude attempt to take advantage of the propaganda value of the Pope's appeal as a warning to the Western Powers, the first point of contact had been established between the papacy and the Russian leader. The Pope made another public appeal for peace during the Cuban crisis in October 1963.

The Pope's obviously sincere concern for the preservation of world peace was a crucial factor in the improvement of relations between the Kremlin and the Vatican and the cautious interest which the Russian press began to show in the Second Vatican Council. The account of the Pope's opening address in the Soviet newspapers was not unfriendly in spite of his references to the absence of bishops from Eastern Europe and from China. In fact the improvement in relations between Rome and Moscow as well as suspicions between the Orthodox Churches themselves were to occasion an unfortunate misunderstanding between the Roman Catholic and the Orthodox Churches. Originally the Patriarchate in Moscow, like the Orthodox Churches in the non-Communist world, had decided not to send representatives to the Council. But following the first session of the Council and after receiving certain reassurances about the religious and political implications, two observers from the Russian Orthodox Church were allowed to attend. In February 1963, as a result it would seem of the good offices of the Russian observers, the leader of the Ukrainian Church, Archbishop Joseph Slipyi of Lwow who had been in a Soviet prison since 1945, was released and allowed to return to Rome. In March Kruschev himself sent a message of appreciation when the Pope was nominated for the Balzan Peace Prize and John XXIII received the votes of all four Soviet representatives. During the same month Kruschev's daughter and son in law, Alexis Adjoubei, the editor of *Izvestia*, were received in audience by the Pope. Incidentally the last occasion on which Pope John left the Vatican was when he went to receive the Balzan Peace Prize on 11 May 1963.

Pope John died less than two months after the publication of *Pacem in Terris* but at least he had given his last message to the world: the Church, renewed by the Council, must strive – with the help of other Christians and of all men of good will – to establish the unity and the peace of all mankind. He himself, during the last few months of his life, attempted to bring to an end the oppression of Catholics under Communist régimes by establishing new political and diplomatic relations with countries of the Communist world. He continued to receive prominent members of other Churches, and raised the status of six Uniate Patriarchs by making them 'associated members' of the Congregation for the Eastern Church. He spoke to various groups of pilgrims and broadcast to peoples in other parts of the world. He visited Roman parishes and universities, seminaries and religious institutions, and re-visited the children in the Hospital of the Infant Jesus. He won not only the respect and admiration of the world's political leaders but the love and affection of ordinary people. When he went into the streets of Rome, crowds flocked to meet him as the political parties covered their posters and cinemas removed their placards. His final agony which lasted three days and three nights, was shared by millions of people throughout the world.

The coming of John XXIII had at once coincided with and helped to create a new sense of optimism and mood of hope following some of the worst years of the Cold War. But if Pope John was a humble priest of simple piety, he was also a realist. He was a shrewd observer of the contemporary scene and a man of clear vision with a strong sense of confidence in divine providence and a robust sense of history. John XXIII did not feel any great nostalgia for the past but gave an optimistic welcome to the present and to the future. He happily accepted the modern world and gave his support to contemporary notions of social justice and the unity of mankind, on colonialism and the exploitation of the third world. He differed from his predecessors in his conviction of the extent to which it was still possible to influence the world for good and his *aggiornamento* was but a means of enabling the Church to deal more effectively with the modern world. Pius XII often dealt with contemporary problems in the light of Natural Law and addressed the world on such problems. However it was John XXIII who was able to convince the world that the Holy See was not solely or even primarily concerned with the interests and the claims of Catholics and the Church, but with the needs of all men.

Furthermore, there was something curiously remote and even impractical about Pius XII's approach to contemporary problems and his pronouncements lacked the prophetic inspiration that seemed to mark those of John XXIII or even Paul VI. One of the basic differences between Pius XII and his successor was that the former never forgot the significance of his position as Pope whereas John XXIII always seemed much more personal in his approach and men throughout the world responded enthusiastically to his bold, direct and simple language. The world listened, not necessarily because Pope John was saying anything substantially new, but because *he* was saying it and in his own personal way.

Without ever modifying the external forms of triumphalism associated with the modern papacy, non-Catholics and unbelievers as well as Catholics were able to recognize in John XXIII that sense of service, pastoral zeal and sense of detachment that has always been typical of the saints among the servants of the servants of God. As he himself wrote in his *Journal*: 'The sublime work, holy and divine, which the Pope must do for the whole Church, and which the Bishops must do each in his own diocese, is to preach the Gospel and guide men to their eternal salvation, and all must take care not to let any other earthly business prevent or impede or disturb this primary task. . . . They are to preach to all alike, and in general terms, justice, charity, humility, meekness, gentleness and the other evangelical virtues, courteously defending the rights of the Church when these are violated or compromised'.

In a very real sense, John XXIII had enabled the Catholic Church to rediscover its pastoral mission to bring Christ to the world and incidentally helped to bring Catholics out of a state of 'splendid isolation' by working for the reunion of Christians and uniting with all men of good will in pursuit of the common good.

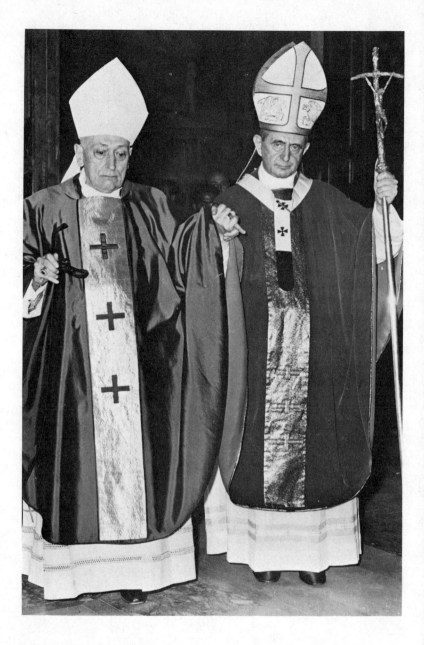

Pope Paul VI and Cardinal Mindszenty leave the Sistine Chapel in 1971

Chapter VI

Paul VI and the Second Vatican Council

The opening of the second session of the Council had originally been fixed for 12 May 1963, but was postponed until 8 September as a result of the serious illness of the Pope. When John XXIII died on the evening of Whit Monday, 3 June, one of the most revolutionary pontificates in the modern history of the Church had come to an end. Pope John had put himself at the disposal of the age in order that he might allow the Spirit of God to 'blow where it listeth'; would his successor attempt to continue along similar lines or simply try to restore the *status quo ante*? Giovanni Battista Montini, the Cardinal Archbishop of Milan, madé his own position quite clear in a sermon which was interpreted by the secular press, inevitably if unjustly, as a declaration of his own candidature. John XXIII 'has shown us some paths which it will be wise to follow. Can we turn away from these paths so masterfully traced? It seems to me we cannot'. Montini then continued to discuss the rôle of the bishops in the government of the Church: a theme which he himself had emphasized both before and during the Council.

Montini had spoken only briefly and rarely in the Council, though he did deliver three major addresses on the Council and his Lenten pastoral of 1962 was regarded as the most significant statement on the subject by any of the Italian bishops. His most important intervention was in support of Cardinal Suenens on the collegiality of the episcopate and on ecumenism. Montini kept the people of his diocese fully informed of the Council's progress by writing a weekly report, *Letter from the Council*, to the Milan newspaper *Italia*. His lodgings during the Council were with Pope John who had already confessed in his private diary that it was Montini whom he would like to succeed him as Pope. On his election the London *Times*, *Le Monde* and the *New York Times* unanimously proclaimed that the cardinals had chosen a pope who was closest to the thinking of his predecessor and who was the most likely to pursue the policies of John XXIII. It was also such a predictable election that the Italian newspapers were claiming that Montini had been elected at least two hours before the announcement was made. When Cardinal Ottaviani announced the result, he got no further than the Christian name before the roar of the crowd showed how popular as well as anticipated the election had been.

It has been said that Pope John could call a Council, but not finish it, and that Pope Paul could finish what he would never have begun. The irony goes deeper. John had to die within a short space of time if the integrity of his 'idea' of unity was to be preserved. Had he lived as long as Paul it might have been destroyed by the accumulation of administrative details and demands. These were precisely what Pope Paul had been trained to master, and it is typical of him that within a few days of his election, he had reconvened the Council which met shortly after the date fixed by his predecessor. Furthermore, as Professor Marty once remarked: 'The first session under John XXIII was not considered much of a success; reforms looked like window-dressing, progress seemed slow and the old guard was in control. The second session, which opened on 29 September 1963, soon dispelled doubts about Paul's leadership. Change was coming and Paul VI was not entirely closed to change.'

On the day after the election of the new Pope, Paul VI declared in a radio address that 'the principal work' of his pontificate would be the continuation of the Second Vatican Council. But nothing had really been decided during the first session of the Council, and it was not impossible for the Pope to modify seriously or even to reverse the intentions of his predecessor. However, although Paul VI was certainly prepared to intervene in the debates of the Fathers, he quickly showed that he was prepared to allow their deliberations to produce decrees that could scarcely have been imagined when the Council first opened and which paved the way for an irreversible change in the attitudes and practices of Catholics throughout the world.

In the opening address of the second session of the Council, Paul VI paid a moving tribute to Pope John: 'We cannot recall this event without remembering our predecessor of happy and immortal memory whom we greatly loved, John XXIII. To all of us who saw him in this seat, his name brings back the memory of his lovable and priestly image. When he opened the first session of this Second Vatican Council on 11 October last, he gave a speech which appeared to be prophetic for our century – not only for the Church, but for the entire society of mankind. That speech still echoes in our memory and conscience while it directs the path the Council must take. It frees us from all doubt and weariness which we may encounter on this difficult journey. O dear and venerated Pope John! May gratitude and praise be rendered to you. Surely under a divine inspiration you convoked this Council to open new horizons for the Church and to channel over the earth the new and yet untapped spring waters of Christ our Lord's doctrine and grace.'

Paul described the objectives of the Council as: 'the self-awareness of the Church; its renewal; the bringing together of all Christians in unity; the dialogue of the Church with the contemporary world.'

At the end of the first session of the Council, the number of *schemata* had been reduced and commissions were instructed to redraft the rest of the *schemata* in the light of Pope John's opening address to the Council. These commissions were to act under a new co-ordinating commission most of whose members were not associated with the Curia. These reforms were not interrupted by the election of Paul VI and he himself set up a College of Moderators – Cardinals Agagianian, Doepfner, Lercaro and Suenens – to supervise the discussions and debates. The second session was dominated by the debate on the *schema* on the Church, to which the *schema* on the Blessed Virgin was also attached. There were long and sometimes fierce discussions on such issues as the restoration of the permanent diaconate and episcopal collegiality. In fact the opposition to the chapter on religious liberty and the declaration on the Jews was so strong that they had to be revised and resubmitted at the next session, while some observers feared that they might even be suppressed altogether.

By the declaration on definition of religious liberty, the Council intended to recognize the free exercise of religion in society, not to free human beings from their responsibilities to the authority of God. Religious liberty was doctrinally justified on the grounds of the absolute dignity of the human person created according to the image of God. The deliberate and explicit rejection of anti-semitism, widely regarded as a crucial test of the *aggiornamento*, was opposed by some Catholics on the 'right', Christians in Middle Eastern countries and Arab nationalists opposed to the State of Israel. The declaration was eventually passed in November 1964 by a majority of 1893 to 99. Meanwhile the Pope increased the number of elected members in each commission in order to overcome the obstacles created by members of the Curia and abolished a number of restrictions on episcopal authority which went far beyond the proposals in the *schema* on the bishops.

In December 1963 the *schema* on the liturgy was approved almost unanimously. This marked the first real achievement of the Council and revealed the extent of the progress that had been made. In *Mater Ecclesia*, John XXIII spoke of the need to preserve the essentials of the liturgy, while expressing 'the new forms of life introduced into the modern world'. At the time of the Pope's death, the Council had achieved little more than the insertion of St Joseph's name in the Canon of the Mass. However, Pope John had succeeded in bringing the question of liturgical reform before a Council of the Church and so set the stage for a radical change. At first sight the reforms of the liturgy at the Second Vatican Council appeared to be more revolutionary than they actually were. The reforms were based on the experiences and developments of the previous fifty years and were in many ways less radical than some of the reforms adopted at the time of the Counter-Reformation. At the Council of Trent it seemed vitally necessary to establish a pattern of liturgical unity and even uniformity. The Second Vatican Council, on the other hand, simply tried to develop diversified patterns of worship within an essential unity. Latin was no longer the only language of worship even in the Roman Church and the Council officially recognized the crucial rôle of local bishops' conferences in the implementation of liturgical reforms.

According to the Constitution on the Liturgy, the Christian liturgy is the public worship of Almighty God, in which the whole Mystical Body of the Church, Christ the Head and the Faithful as members, gives honour and thanks to God, seeks His mercy and the help of His grace in order that the Faithful might be directed in the way of salvation. The Fathers at the Council laid down the norms for reforming the pattern of Catholic worship in order to meet the needs of contemporary society. In future, the liturgy was to be more evidently pastoral and didactic, biblical and communal. The Fathers strongly re-affirmed the authority of the Holy See and of the local hierarchies. However, since conscious and active participation in the liturgy was the right and duty of all the baptized, the Fathers also sanctioned the use of the vernacular, the adoption of regional or traditional customs, the simplification as well as the reform of the liturgy and the removal of artificial distinctions and barriers.

In the spirit of the Council's decrees, the Pope later authorised the most complete and fundamental revision of the sacramental rites and the *Roman Missal* since the Council of Trent. In May 1969 the Congregation of Rites was divided into the Congregation for Divine Worship and the Congregation for the Causes of Saints and on the following day the new Roman Missal was published revising the Order of Mass and the Church's liturgical year. But the development of the liturgical movement was paralleled and sometimes confused with other, particularly theological, developments as happened in the controversy over the Dutch Catechism in 1966, and then in the case of Archbishop Lefebvre with his specious and ostensible demands for the right to celebrate the 'Latin Mass'. The first controversy was heightened by those whose suspicions were raised by the pastoral rather than the theological emphases which they saw in the revised liturgy. In 1969 several theologians, who believed that the New Form of Mass differed strikingly from the theology of the Mass formulated at Trent, published their criticisms and Cardinal Ottaviani sent a personal letter of protest to the Pope.

In the Decree of Ecumenism published in 1964, the Fathers of the Council hoped to lay down the practice and principles of the Catholic approach to ecumenism without in any way jeopardizing the traditional claims of the Church. Ecumenism was a movement inspired by God which embraced all 'the initiatives and activities, planned and undertaken to promote Christian unity, according to the Church's various needs and as opportunities offer'. As Cardinal Archbishop of Milan, Paul VI had sponsored meetings between Catholic and Orthodox theologians and as Pope he was determined to develop ecumenical relations, not only with other Christian bodies, but with non-Christians and non-believers. The Secretariat for Non-Christians was established in 1964 and the Secretariat for Non-Believers in the following year. The Pope committed himself to promoting Christian unity at the beginning of the second session of the Council when he declared: 'If among the causes of division any fault could be imputed to us, we humbly beg God's forgiveness and ask pardon too of our brethren who feel offended by us. And we willingly forgive, for our part, the injuries the Catholic Church has suffered and forget the grief endured through the long chain of dissensions and separations'. He also expressed his sorrow in his first encyclical: 'That We, who promote this reconciliation, should be regarded by many of Our separated brothers as an obstacle to it, is a matter of deep distress to Us'.

The Pope was particularly concerned to heal the breaches with the Orthodox and with the Anglican Churches. In December 1963 he announced his intention of going to the Holy Land on pilgrimage and within a few days the Patriarch of Constantinople expressed his desire to go with the Pope. This move infuriated the Archbishop of Athens who appealed to the monks of Athos to defend Orthodoxy from the ecumenical schemes of the Patriarch. Pope and Patriarch met in January when Paul presented Athenagoras with a chalice and was given a pectoral medallion of the Blessed Virgin. The meetings between the two leaders marked a dramatic turning point in relations between their two churches and the speed with which they developed a new understanding and even a new ecclesiology in their correspondence after 1963 is quite remarkable. In September 1964 the Pope returned the head of St Andrew to the Orthodox church and in the following November he sent an official message to the Third Pan-Orthodox Conference at Rhodes in which he addressed the bishops as his equals.

In December 1965 the mutual anathemas and excommunications that, according to the Orthodox, 'barred the road toward dialogue on equal terms' were solemnly lifted by Pope and Patriarch: 'They regret the offensive words, the reproaches without foundation, and the reprehensible gestures which, on both sides, have marked or accompanied the sad events of this period. They likewise regret and remove, both from memory and from the midst of the Church, the sentences of excommunication which followed these events, the memory of which has influenced actions up to our day and has hindered closer relations in charity; and they commit these excommunications to oblivion. Finally, they deplore the preceding and later vexing events which, under the influences of various factors – among which, lack of understanding and mutual trust – eventually led to the effective rupture of ecclesiastical communion'.

The suspicions of many Orthodox Christians made it almost impossible for the Patriarch to visit Rome in case this was interpreted as a sign of submission. Paul VI therefore proposed to visit the Patriarch in Istanbul in a letter which seemed so incredible that Athenagoras had to read it three times before he could believe it. During the visit, which took place in July 1967, Athenagoras described Paul 'as the Bishop of Rome, the first in honour amongst us, he who presides in love'. The two leaders subscribed to a declaration of principle in which they testified to 'rediscovery as sister-Churches', accepted 'diversity of customs in the unity of faith' and demanded 'the sacrifice and suppression on either side, in a spirit of total abnegation, of everything which in the past had seemed to contribute to the unity of the Church but which tended in reality to create a gulf difficult to bridge'. This mutual recognition as sister-Churches marked a striking development from the universal jurisdiction that the Church of Rome had claimed for over a thousand years. The papal visit also had the practical effect of giving international support to the Patriarch at a time when he was experiencing difficulties with the Turkish authorities.

In October 1967 a Patriarch of Constantinople visited the Pope in Rome for the first time since 1451. The Pope also received the Armenian Catholicos Khoren I in 1967 and the Armenian Catholicos Vazken I in 1970. In the following year he received the Patriarch of the Syrian Orthodox Church of Antioch and the first Coptic Patriarch since the separation of the Churches. In 1973 Pope Paul and the Coptic Patriarch, Pope Amba Shenouda III, issued a joint declaration of one faith in the Person of Jesus Christ, God Incarnate, and so took a major step in healing the division that had taken place in 451 between the Church of Rome and the Coptic Church of Alexandria. Paul's gesture of humility in 1975, kissing the feet of the Metropolitan Meliton, drew an immediate response from the Patriarch Dimitrios I: 'Paul VI has gone beyond the papacy and has joined the Fathers who founded the Church': 'The Pope has proved to the Church and to the whole world that he is what he should be: a Christian bishop and above all the first bishop of Christendom, the Bishop of Rome, that is a reconciling and unifying bridge between the Church and the world'. In December 1975 Pope and Patriarch announced the formation of a commission for dialogue between their two Churches.

In 1966 the Pope received Archbishop Michael Ramsey and embraced him as a brother: 'By your coming you rebuild a bridge which for centuries has lain fallen between the Church of Rome and Canterbury'. The reception of the Archbishop was incomparably more warm and friendly than the earlier occasion on which Archbishop Fisher had called on Pope John. At that meeting not even a photograph had been taken, whereas Archbishop Ramsey joined with the Pope in a public service of prayer in Saint Paul Without the Walls. The success of this meeting led to the establishment of the Anglican/Roman Catholic International Commission which subsequently produced three so-called 'agreed Statements' on the Eucharist, Ministry and Authority. A body to study contacts between Catholics and Lutherans had already been established in July 1965. If relations between the Pope and Archbishop Coggan seem to have been somewhat less cordial, this was largely as a result of the Archbishop's campaign for immediate intercommunion and the ordination of women.

At the canonization of the English and Welsh martyrs in 1970 the Pope himself added a significant passage about the Anglican Church to his address: 'May the blood of these martyrs be able to heal the great wound inflicted on God's Church by reason of the separation of the Anglican Church from the Catholic Church. . . . Their devotion to their country gives us the assurance that on the day when – God willing – the unity of faith and life is restored, no offence will be inflicted on the honour and sovereignty of a great country such as England. There will be no seeking to lessen the legitimate prestige and usage proper to the Anglican Church when the Roman Catholic Church – this humble "servant of the servants of God" – is able to embrace firmly her ever-beloved sister in the one authentic communion of the family of Christ: a communion of origin and faith, a communion of priesthood and rule, a communion of the saints in the freedom and love of the spirit of Jesus'.

Paul himself perhaps most clearly defined his attitude to unity and diversity in *Evangelii Nuntiandi* published in 1975 where he spoke of its being 'among the tendencies of our time to appreciate the special qualities of the individual Churches'. Anticipating the Agreed Statement on Authority issued by the joint Anglican/Roman Commission, the Pope spoke of the dangers when an 'individual Church cuts itself off from the universal Church', since, in doing so, 'its ecclesiastical status is impoverished'. It is tempting to speculate how far these attitudes influenced his thinking on the question of intercommunion and the ordination of women.

Several of the debates during the Council, particularly those on collegiality and the rôle of the laity, also had an immediate bearing on relations with other Churches, while many of the 'disciplinary' reforms made over the next few years again reflected a more ecumenical approach. Mixed marriages could take place without a priest acting as witness, non-Catholics were no longer required in writing to promise to bring up their children as Catholics, while Catholics were even allowed to marry before non-Catholic ministers. A new and more solemn form of the rite was introduced for mixed marriages and the celebration of Mass was allowed in the case of a marriage between a Catholic and a baptized Christian. At the same time bishops were instructed to establish diocesan ecumenical commissions, the indiscriminate conditional baptism of converts was discouraged, Catholics were allowed to pray with other Christians and to attend non-Catholic liturgical services, while non-Catholics were admitted to the sacraments of the Church if only in exceptional circumstances.

In the years following the Council, the fall in the numbers of adult converts or children attending Catholic schools, the decline in specifically Catholic publications and traditional devotions as well as more radical theological trends were seen by some commentators as the unfortunate 'side-effects' of an unhealthy preoccupation with ecumenism. And it cannot be denied that the Pope himself later expressed some reservations. In 1969 he declared: 'Those who see everything perfect in the camp of the separated brothers, and everything heavy and blameworthy in the Catholic camp, are no longer able to promote the cause of union effectively and usefully. As one of the best contemporary ecumenists, a Protestant, pointed out with sad irony, "the greatest danger for ecumenism is that the Catholics should become enthusiastic about everything that we have recognized as harmful, and abandon everything which we have rediscovered as important".'

Meanwhile, however, the Decree on Ecumenism and the Constitutions on the Church and Revelation were completed without further difficulty during the third session of the Council in 1964. This fact illustrated how far some of the bishops had moved during the previous two years. However, the Pope himself modified the *schema* on ecumenism after this had already been approved by the assembly and 'explained' the true meaning of collegiality in relation to papal primacy. He also proclaimed on his own initiative that Mary was Mother of the Church. Nevertheless, in spite of papal interventions and modifications, the work of reform went on. The last weeks of the Council in 1965 were undoubtedly rushed as the bishops raced against the clock to vote on the remaining texts. The Decrees on Bishops, Religious and Seminaries, as well as the declarations on Christian

Education and Non-Christian Religions were promulgated in October. The Decrees on Divine Revelation and on the Laity were published in November, while the Decrees on Mission and Priesthood, the declaration on Religious Liberty and the Constitution on the Church and the World were promulgated at the beginning of December.

It is not easy to summarize why and how the Second Vatican Council had the dramatic impact that it undoubtedly did but it might be possible to illustrate the wider situation by concentrating on the approach which the Fathers finally adopted towards missionary activity since this Council went further than any other in formulating a missionary approach and reflecting the changing composition of the Catholic Church throughout the world. The African and Asian bishops arrived for the opening of the Council with no clearer ideas of what they hoped or expected to achieve than bishops from Europe or America. However, the missionary bishops quickly appreciated that they were not an insignificant force as they discovered that the more active bishops were busily canvassing for their votes and as a result many of them became closely involved in the theological discussions taking place among the Fathers. Furthermore the debates on the reform of the liturgy clearly showed that the bishops were no longer content with a uniformity imposed by regulation but were demanding a degree of pluralism in which the missionary situation would obviously play a crucial part in determining more general rules. It is significant, for example, that the Fathers should have ignored a personal appeal on the part of the Pope to give their approval to a *schema* on the missions which they regarded as inadequate.

The actual Decree on Missions, *Ad Gentes*, was a rather equivocal document reflecting the transition from the missionary activities of the nineteenth century to the greater awareness of the missionary role of the whole Church which was developing during the twentieth century. However in order to discover the teaching of the Council on missions it is necessary to take account of all its proceedings and documents. In the first place the Council marked a crucial stage in the development from the idea of 'foreign missions' to that of 'local churches'. Secondly the Council restored and re-emphasized the idea of missionary activity as an essential characteristic of the whole Church. The Council also brought about an important change in relations between Christian missionaries as mission became a spur to ecumenism. Finally the declarations of the Council on the rôle of the laity, relations between the Church, other Christian bodies and the World, and the declaration on religious freedom inevitably had a dramatic impact on missionary developments.

The Fathers defined missionary activity in terms of the obvious historical and theological developments that had taken place – the decline of imperialism and a better understanding of God's universal salvific will in the work of salvation. Non-Christians had the right to hear the Gospel of Christ as well as the choice of believing in him and receiving his baptism. God desires that those who have received the Christian faith should share its fulness with others and baptism into the Church was the divinely established means of achieving salvation. The Fathers also discussed how Christian faith and morals might best be presented to non-Christians without repelling them by its novelty or alienating them from their cultural backgrounds. Of course the problem of adapting Christianity to conditions in Asia or Africa is further complicated by the increasing attempts to westernize Asian and African societies. However missionaries were instructed to share in the social and cultural lives of those among whom they worked, to make themselves 'familiar with their national and religious traditions, gladly and reverently laying bare the seeds of the Word which lie hidden in them'; an obvious reference to the possibility that God had already in some ways revealed Himself to all mankind.

During the Council there were the inevitable clashes, tensions and delays of which the Pope himself was well aware. On one occasion, he was quoted as saying: 'You think that things are not moving fast enough? Be patient! True, we could make many reforms immediately, but they would all come to nothing if the minds and the personalities had not changed. For this one needs time. Such is the law of history'.

As Pope, Paul was very conscious of the fact that 'When a step forward is taken, some find the step is timid, that it has changed nothing; others, that it is too bold, that it changes everything too much'. In the event, the conservative opposition which at first had proved to be so influential largely melted away, a fact which would seem to justify the Pope's own attitude to the tensions of the Council as revealed in conversation with Jean Guitton: 'Many possible crises were avoided. One of the most visible results was that the Council took place without too many upheavals. It was never suspended, interrupted. It arrived, in some ways beyond all hopes. It is possible to say that the bishops as a whole set themselves to learn and to listen, and many were surprised how in four years their point of view changed and broadened, how they sometimes accepted what before the Council they would have judged unacceptable or too rash. This action of the Council upon itself was a sign of the divine presence'.

On 4 December 1965 there was a farewell service for the observers to the Council, the first occasion on which a Pope had joined in worship with non-Catholics, and the closing ceremonies took place on 8 December in the presence of delegations from 81 governments and nine international bodies. No secular government had been represented at the First Vatican Council. The Pope told his audience: 'This is a unique moment, a moment of incomparable significance and riches. In this universal assembly, in this privileged point of time and space, there converge together the past, the present, and the future. The past — for here, gathered in this spot, we have the Church of Christ with her tradition, her history, her councils, her doctors, her saints. The present — for we are taking leave of one another to go out toward the world of today with its miseries, its sufferings, its sins, but also with its prodigious accomplishments, its values, its virtues. And lastly the future is here in the urgent appeal of the peoples of the world for more justice, in their will for peace, in their conscious or unconscious thirst for a higher life, that life precisely which the Church of Christ can and wishes to give them'.

Paul himself summarized the main thrust of the Council when he said: 'Never before perhaps, so much as on this occasion, has the Church felt the need to know, to draw to, to understand, to penetrate, serve and evangelize the society in which she lives; and to get to grips with it, almost to run after it, in its rapid and continuous change'. The Pope was also aware of the dilemma which faced himself and all Catholics at the end of the Council. He made it clear that he could not approve of those who hoped that they could simply return to their former religious attitudes now that the Council was over. On the other hand, he did not approve of those who continued to 'bring into perpetual discussion truths and laws already clarified and established' or who wanted to introduce 'innovating or subversive criteria into the analysis of the dogmas, statutes, rites, and spirituality of the Catholic Church in order to bring its thoughts and life into line with the spirit of the age'. The true task was to study, to understand and to apply the work of the Council, and this involved the continuing work for reforms in the Church. Meanwhile the Pope's own personal determination that the Church should seek the world, to make it listen and respond, explains the enormous range and extent of his work and travels which can best be focused on his implementation of the Council, his work for Peace and Justice, and in his dealings with secular governments and especially with Communist régimes.

On the day before the Council ended, 7 December 1965, the Pope revealed his intention of reforming the Curia by abolishing the Congregation of the Holy Office with its Inquisition and Index of Forbidden Books and replacing it with the Congregation for the Doctrine of the Faith. This move was widely interpreted as showing that Paul VI clearly recognized the distinction between the truths of faith and the manner in which these might be expressed. However the Pope only changed the personnel of the

Congregation some three years later and they were therefore able to moderate the force of the reforms which he had initiated. In fact Pope Paul's reforms of the Curia often seemed to be too moderate or insufficient and this was especially true of the reform of the Holy Office in 1965.

Paul VI always proved to be reluctant or unwilling to dismiss or replace curial officials and perhaps especially those who had been involved in the alleged machinations that had forced him out of the Curia in 1954. At the same time Pope Paul has also been accused of being too diffident in supporting his friends such as Cardinal Lercaro, Archbishop of Bologna, who was forced to resign as a result of questionable accusations of financial maladministration. The Pope himself was not unaware of his own reluctance to deal firmly with officials in the Curia and he advised his successors to wait three months before making any permanent appointments. He also introduced five year tenures without the right of reappointment for all officials at the Vatican as well as the rule that all of them should lose their positions on the death of a Pope. However, in 1973 he himself simply reappointed those who had been given positions in 1968. And it was perhaps not untypical of Paul VI that although he had established the age of retirement for bishops at seventy-five and that for cardinals at eighty, he himself did not resign at either age.

The reforms of the Curia announced in August 1967 were also potential rather than real. Pope Paul tried to introduce a degree of collective responsibility by ordering heads of departments to meet periodically under the chairmanship of the Secretary of State. He reduced the number of Congregations from eleven to nine, changed some of the names of the Congregations, appointed non-Italians to influential posts in the Curia and centralized finances. In January 1968 Archbishop Giovanni Benelli, the Pope's *sostituto*, began to introduce distinguished foreign Cardinals such as Garrone and Villot, Seper and Willebrands, though many of the 'foreign' Cardinals found it difficult to resist adopting the old 'Roman' ways and their introduction into curial positions proved less effective than many Catholics hoped at the time. The Pope tended to be content with bringing more progressive churchmen into influential positions rather than attempting to achieve radical structural changes. He seems to have believed that new persons within the old structures would have the desired reforming effect and he was not always well-served by the men he appointed. In the event the extensive reorganization of the Curia would seem to have had less effect on the life of the Church than the regulations governing the restoration of the permanent diaconate which were promulgated on 27 June 1967.

There were other 'failures'. One of Pope John's aims in calling the

Second Vatican Council was in order to revise Canon Law and he established a Pontifical Commission to achieve that aim only two months before his death. However nothing has yet been produced and it would seem that the process of revision is likely to take twice the time that Cardinal Gasparri spent in producing the Code of Canon Law published in 1917. Several different reasons have been suggested to explain the delay but it is no secret that a basic difference has emerged over the revisions produced so far which have been criticized as little more than modifications of the existing Code. In October 1977, 300 of the 1200 members of the Canon Law Society of America formally declared at their annual convention that the present drafts seen by their colleagues, with the exception of the draft on religious life, were 'unacceptable in their very substance'.

Other reforms, however, were more immediately effective. Paul VI was essentially a simple man who had little time for the pomp and trappings of high office. From the beginning of his pontificate, he was determined to maintain the friendly, less formal style of his predecessor. Paul wanted the Papacy to be accessible, he was available. He ordered the *Acta Apostolicae Sedis* and the *Osservatore Romano* to drop his imperial titles and to refer to him simply as 'Holy Father'. Visitors were no longer told to kneel and kiss his hand. The Pope preferred people to choose their own form of greeting while he himself embraced those whom he knew. In 1968 he reformed the organization of the papal household and abolished many honorary positions and titles. Two years later he suppressed the Pontifical Armed Guard with the exception of the Swiss Guards.

In 1965 Paul VI created twenty-seven new cardinals and increased the membership of the Sacred College to a higher level than ever before. One hundred and three cardinals represented forty-three countries throughout the world and included three patriarchs of eastern rites, three prelates from Communist countries and an African. Pope Paul made the College of Cardinals more representative of the Church throughout the world. By the fifteenth year of his pontificate almost half of the cardinals came from the Third World. Pope Paul had appointed forty-six cardinals from the developing nations and there were cardinals as residential bishops in almost every country in which the Church was operating including Korea, Sri Lanka and even Western Samoa. Incidentally Pope Paul appointed 100 of the 111 cardinals who were eligible to vote for his successor. There were 27 Italian Cardinals, another 29 Europeans, 12 Africans, 19 Latin Americans, 11 North Americans and 13 Cardinals from Asia and Oceania. Furthermore, in November 1970, Paul announced that cardinals over eighty would no longer take part in the conclaves to elect popes or even hold active positions within the central government of the Church. This decision effectively reduced the number of voting members in the Sacred College by twenty-five of whom eleven were Italians. This was also the first restriction placed on the cardinals' right to elect the popes since that right had been confirmed by the Third Lateran Council in 1179.

Pope Paul was also concerned to give tangible expression to the doctrine of episcopal collegiality. He made an early and typically symbolic move when he allowed all bishops to wear the *mozzetta* in his presence as an illustration of his desire to appear as a bishop among his episcopal colleagues. In November 1963 an apostolic letter granted many faculties and privileges to the bishops which enhanced their dignity and enabled them to carry out more effectively their pastoral duties. At the same time, the Pope was extremely sensitive about the prerogatives of the Papacy and was always careful not to modify them. His determination to accept the doctrine of collegiality – clearly manifested in his public audiences when bishops present shared the platform with him – was always balanced by his determination to exercise the potential and the leadership of the Roman Pontiff. At the first opening of the Synod of Bishops on 29 September 1967, he not only made the point that he too was one of the bishops by con-celebrating with the rest, but he reminded the other bishops of papal primacy by kissing the foot of and placing a candle before the statue of St Peter.

The establishment of the Synod of Bishops had been one of the most promising moves made during the Council, though it was explicitly stated that this was merely a consultative body to provide 'more effective assistance to the supreme pastor of the Church'. The bishops themselves were careful to try to balance the declaration of episcopal collegiality with the claims of papal primacy. In theory at least, nothing said by the Fathers about collegiality at the Second Vatican Council contradicted what had been decreed about the position of the Pope at the First. In a *motu proprio*, Pope Paul declared that the Synod should be a permanent central ecclesiastical institution representing all the Catholic bishops, normally acting as a consultative body but with authority to make decisions when this power had been conferred by the Pope who must also confirm all its decisions. Once again, in other words, papal prerogatives were not to be sacrificed to the claims of collegiality.

On 25 July 1968 the Pope published *Humanae Vitae*, his long-awaited statement on artificial birth control, in which he first condemned the use of abortion or direct sterilization as means of contraception and then went on: 'Similarly excluded is every action which, either in anticipation of the conjugal act, or in its accomplishment, or in the development of its natural consequences, proposes, whether as an end or as a means, to render procreation impossible'. Although the encyclical manifested positive qualities, which were too often ignored at the time, and can now be seen in a different perspective from that prevailing at the time, publication of *Humanae Vitae* undoubtedly occasioned the gravest crisis in the pontificate of Paul VI.

The euphoria aroused by the Council had led Catholics to expect a different approach from Paul VI than that adopted by Pius XII and his predecessors. Open debate, the acceptance of doctrinal development, a wide ranging process of consultation particularly among the subjects of the encyclical – the married laity – were all confidently expected and just as confidently denied. The expectations of a change in attitudes and methods had been further strengthened by the abolition of the Index, but above all by the Council's formally conceding the principle for which the Liberal Catholics of a previous generation had been condemned, namely liberty of conscience. On these grounds it was confidently assumed that, on matters which touched them so intimately, the laity would be brought fully into the decision-making process. There was consultation, though much of it took place in secret and was subsequently 'leaked' to the press rather than communicated publicly. An advisory Commission on Population and Family Life had been set up by John XXIII in 1963. This was confined to theologians but was enlarged by Pope Paul to include sixteen cardinals and bishops under the Presidency of Cardinal Ottaviani. After months of argument a majority reported in favour of change, a minority – headed by the President – did not. Pope Paul, who had previously withdrawn the question of contraception from the floor of the Council, was forced to resolve the impasse, and the result was *Humanae Vitae*.

Publication of *Humanae Vitae* dramatically raised the crucial and significant issues of ecclesiastical infallibility, the rights of conscience and the responsibilities of Christian love in marriage. Critics of the Pope insisted that his teaching was not binding on the faithful, while his defenders maintained that he had simply expressed the traditional and irrevocable teaching of the Church. Theologians like Karl Rahner and Bernard Häring claimed that *Humanae Vitae* was not infallible and could be reversed. Supporters of the Pope maintained that although the encyclical was not in the form of an *ex cathedra* statement, its teaching had always been considered an essential part of Christian morality; a point which was inevitably challenged by their opponents. According to the Scandinavian bishops, the crucial question was that of conscience: 'One is never allowed to go against one's own conviction. If someone has really done his best to find the right norms, the application of these norms under all circumstances is, in each special case, the person's own responsibility. No one, including the Church, can absolve anyone from the obligation to follow his conscience and from the responsibility for his actions'.

Catholics also found themselves divided on the nature of Christian love in marriage. Critics of the Pope accused him of over-emphasizing the significance of biology and under-emphasizing the significance of the population problem. His supporters concentrated on the responsibilities of Christian love and the inevitable dangers involved in the exploitation of sexual gratification for its own sake.

But, in spite of the Pope's responsibility for the publication of *Humanae Vitae*, two other important points must always be borne in mind in assessing the action of Paul VI. His deep concern with the injustice of the distribution of resources was totally genuine and he was always conscious of the need for development as the way to peace. Furthermore he was prepared to tolerate a wide latitude of humane and psychological considerations when dealing with the problems of married people and religious even to the extent of tolerating the dissolution of impossible conjugal situations or granting dispensations from vows of celibacy.

However, in 1968 the leader writer of *The Times* described the exercise of the papal prerogative in *Humanae Vitae* as 'pre-conciliar in its individuality' and the grounds for rejecting the majority report of the Commission were not argued, but merely asserted. Yet what was overlooked at the time was the depth of the strongly held differences of opinion and the real difficulties in the face of any real 'solution'. The grounds chosen by Paul for rejecting the majority report were that there was 'no full concordance concerning the moral norms', that is, that disagreement about moral presuppositions was so deep that no consensus could be said to have emerged. In the light of subsequent events in moral theology and other fields this may now seem to have been a not unreasonable conclusion to draw. Since the issue was too confused for settlement, it was best to re-state the existing views and then let matters work themselves out. However this seemed small comfort for the laity and the subsequent uproar rocked the Church. In the longer term, the unintended effect of *Humanae Vitae* has been to put the emphasis where it truly belongs – upon the consciences of individual Catholics. Indirectly the effect of the crisis was what one Protestant observer has called 'an ecumenical boon', since it awakened Protestants to the fact that lay Catholics were prepared to follow their consciences and that their bishops were in the event prepared or forced to allow them to do so.

The fact that *Humanae Vitae* was published in 1968, the year following the first Synod and the year before the one due to be held in 1969, inevitably raised the further question whether the Pope should not have sought the advice or even the approval of the bishops. The need to re-examine the exercise of papal authority within the Church was an issue of immediate concern to Paul's old friend, Cardinal Leo Josef Suenens, Archbishop of Malines, and the subject of his famous book *Co-responsibility in the Church* which was published in 1968. At the subsequent Synod, the Pope appealed for unity. He accepted that collegiality was co-responsibility but he also emphasized that the Pope's duty to respect the rights of the bishops must be balanced or matched by their duty to recognize the supremacy of the Pope.

At first the Synods met every two years in 1967, 1969 and 1971 and then every three years in 1974 and 1977. In 1967 the bishops discussed the revision of canon law, doctrine, liturgy, seminaries and mixed marriages. The Synod in 1969 dealt with the aftermath of *Humanae Vitae*. In 1971 the bishops dealt with the priesthood, justice in the world and the promotion of the work of the Pontifical Justice and Peace Commission. The early agendas, which were too crowded, proved unworkable and so the bishops began to concentrate on specific themes such as evangelization in 1974 and catechesis in 1977. It is perhaps not surprising that commentators have proved to be somewhat mixed in their opinions on the Synods and only that on the subject of catechesis seemed to win general approval, though even that Synod did not pass without some criticisms. Perhaps as a reaction against the wider situation in the Church, Paul VI tended to keep the Synods firmly under his own control and endorsed or rejected recommendations more or less as he pleased. In 1974, for example, the bishops wanted to discuss the family but eventually had to turn their attention to the subject of evangelization. Although the sense of crisis following the publication of *Humanae Vitae* quickly passed and in spite of subsequent detailed discussions, the inevitable tension and even the possibility of conflict between the claims of the Pope and the demands of the bishops, between papal authority and episcopal collegiality, had not yet been resolved.

Some commentators would seem to suggest that the conflict between freedom and authority in the Catholic Church only assumed serious proportions following the Second Vatican Council and during the controversies over *Humanae Vitae*. But the exercise of ecclesiastical authority has always been deeply influenced by contemporary society. The exercise of that authority during the nineteenth century became increasingly centralized, clerical and even personal as the development of Ultramontanism effectively destroyed support for Gallicanism or Febronianism, movements which had maintained that ecclesiastical affairs should be kept as

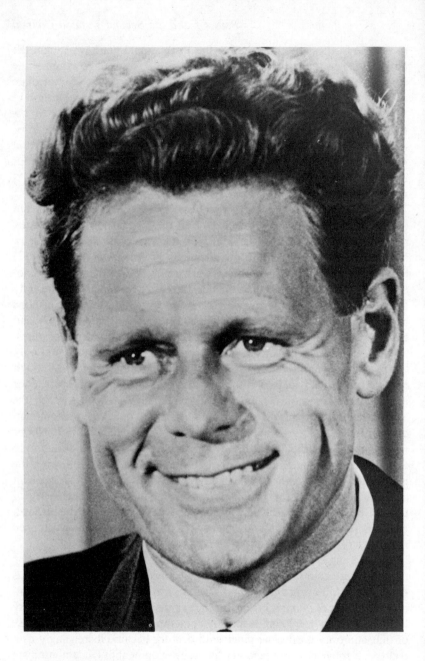

Professor Hans Küng

far as possible under local civil or episcopal control. In view of the intense nationalisms of the nineteenth and twentieth centuries, Ultramontanism proved to be of positive help to the Church in spite of its more obvious negative characteristics. However, by the time of the Second Vatican Council there was a new emphasis on internationalism as well as decentralization in religious as well as political circles and the threat of emerging national churches seemed somewhat remote. The development of easier communications coupled with the growth of the Catholic population – from a hundred million in 1900 to almost six hundred million in 1960 – reduced the necessity as well as the desirability of interminable consultations with Roman officials except on the most serious and important issues. This was the background to the doctrine of episcopal collegiality accepted in the Council's *Constitution on the Church*. Bishops were not simply papal delegates but shared divinely guaranteed rights within their dioceses in full communion with their fellow bishops and especially with the Bishop of Rome.

In view of the fact that the size of the Catholic Church in Holland is less than that in the metropolitan area of New York City, the Dutch Church and 'those Dutch Catholics' proved to be far more significant in the life of the Church during the 1960s than either their numbers or their history would seem to justify. *The New Dutch Catechism for Adults*, published in 1964, attempted to present contemporary theological scholarship in a popular way and was an immediate success. The authors consciously adopted a liberal and ecumenical approach as they attempted to present the Christian understanding of creation, miracles and original sin and to reformulate such Catholic beliefs as the sacrifice of the Mass and the Real Presence. More conservative Dutch Catholics immediately questioned the orthodoxy of this Catechism and although the Dutch bishops defended their theologians, the inconclusiveness of the dialogue between their representatives and the Roman authorities only served to exaggerate the misunderstandings between them.

In 1965 the Pope published an encyclical, *Mysterium Fidei*, which was a restatement of the Church's teaching on the Eucharist and the Real Presence. The Pope seems to have shared the fears of the Roman authorities that contemporary Dutch theologians were threatening the integrity of the faith. However, many Catholics throughout the world regarded this encyclical as a discouraging document, exaggerated in its fears, old-fashioned in its content and even unfair in some of its implications. Furthermore the encyclical was published the week-end before the opening of the fourth session of the Council at a time when many of the Fathers were hoping for more positive papal leadership after the depressing end to the previous session. As the prelates assembled for the last session of the Council, the Dutch bishops were able to read in the Italian press that the Pope had 'condemned' Holland. The Dutch bishops were also aware of the fact that this interpretation of the Pope's encyclical had been inspired by those who deliberately wanted to convey precisely that impression.

The actual details of negotiations between the Dutch bishops and the Roman authorities are still not entirely clear and the same is true of the process by which the *imprimatur* originally granted for the German and English translations of the Catechism was subsequently rescinded. However the bishops' defence of the Catechism was based on the necessity of finding new formulations of an unchangeable faith and on the right of Dutch bishops to explain that faith to the Dutch people. Similarly the Cardinals who examined the Catechism did not only question the language used to describe different theological doctrines, but also demanded that: 'the new Catechism clearly recognize that the teaching authority and the power of ruling in the Church is given directly to the Holy Father and to the Bishops joined with him in hierarchical communion, and that it is not given first of all to the people of God to be communicated to others. The office of Bishops, therefore, is not a mandate given them by the people of God, but is a mandate received from God Himself for the good of the whole Christian community'. Some time previously, the First Plenary Assembly of the Dutch Pastoral Council had called for structures and procedures that would have restricted clerical and Roman authority.

It was perhaps fitting that the Church should have been led by a Pope-theologian at a time when Catholics were beginning to recognize and appreciate the distinct rôle of scholars and theologians in the life of the Church. Theologians came into prominence during the Second Vatican Council as lecturers in seminaries and professors in universities found themselves actively involved in the task of renewal and reform. Furthermore, it was impossible for theologians to work effectively without academic freedom, though not all examples of theological pluralism were compatible with either pastoral responsibility or traditional teaching. In 1966 the Pope himself addressed an International Congress on the Theology of the Second Vatican Council: 'The Council asks theologians to develop a theology which is no less pastoral than scientific; a theology that remains in close contact with patristic, liturgical and particularly with Biblical sources; a theology which always holds the teaching authority of the Church and especially that of the vicar of Christ in highest esteem; a theology which concerns humanity as seen in history and in concrete reality; a theology which is frankly ecumenical and sincerely Catholic'.

Pope Paul had already told theologians to keep their 'minds open to all the voices, all the needs and all the authentic values of our fast-evolving era', emphasizing the term 'authentic' to stress the importance of discernment as well as openness.

In 1969 the National Council of the Dutch Church voted in favour of the abolition of compulsory celibacy for the Catholic clergy and shortly afterwards Cardinal Suenens gave a celebrated newspaper interview in which he openly questioned Pope Paul's attitude towards celibacy and contraception. At the time many priests and nuns in America and Europe as well as the 'Third World' were publicly rejecting compulsory celibacy and some of them were confidently expecting a relaxation of the canonical rules. The number of priests and religious who left the active ministry in the ten years from 1960 to 1970 has had no parallel since the sixteenth century. The Roman authorities issued a series of statements between 1965 and 1970 re-affirming the value of the commitment to celibacy for priests of the Roman rite. But these statements as well as the Pope's own sixth encyclical, *Sacerdotalis Caelibatus*, published in June 1967, had failed to satisfy the opposition.

During the Second World War a number of priests, particularly those involved in military service, had contracted civil marriages. Pius XII had approved of their laicization and allowed their marriages to be blessed in Church, though they were no longer allowed to exercise their priestly ministry. At the same time, Pius XII was also prepared to allow convert married clergymen to be ordained to the Catholic priesthood. But in an encyclical published in 1954, the Pope repeated his support for the traditional Roman practice and in the following year sent a confidential document to bishops throughout the world in which he insisted that those who were to be ordained to the priesthood should be aware of what was involved in a life of celibacy. Several of the Fathers wanted to debate the subject during the Second Vatican Council but during the last session of the Council Paul VI simply announced that he intended to maintain the law of celibacy for the clergy of the Latin rite.

Meanwhile the Council attempted to lay down the principles governing the renewal of the religious life which would bring about a peaceful adjustment of the spirituality of the past to the spirit of the modern age. In the event, however, the Council seemed to be followed by a series of crises in the religious life which even threatened the very existence of some orders and congregations in various countries. One American archdiocese reported the loss of over a thousand nuns in five years and it is estimated that in 1969 6500 nuns left the religious life. Furthermore there was a sharp decline in the number of vocations in the Western World, though vocations in Communist countries and those of the Third World have sometimes remained at a remarkably and consistently high level.

At the same time, Catholic lay men and women were also experiencing difficulties in remaining faithful to their marriage vows. In the period before the Second World War increasing numbers of Catholics had divorced and been re-married by the civil authorities. These were then automatically barred from the sacraments unless they later separated from their partners or promised to live together as brother and sister. In this context, Pope Pius XI issued *Casti Connubii* in which he defended the indissolubility of Christian marriage as of divine law. During the Second World War the number of divorced Catholics increased as a result of hasty marriages, enforced separations and the migration of peoples as well as physical and psychological sufferings. In some places the number of divorces doubled in less than five years. Again one of the Fathers raised the issue during the Second Vatican Council but he promptly received the traditional answer and had to reaffirm his own acceptance of 'the immutable principle of the indissolubility of marriage'.

At the end of 1969 Pope Paul wrote to remind the Dutch bishops of their duty to act 'in harmony with the decisions of the Second Vatican Council' and 'to teach clearly and firmly that the generous practice of perfect chastity is not only possible but that it is a source of joy and sanctity'. Following a meeting with Pope Paul, Cardinal Alfrink reported that 'the Pope considers the reasons for maintaining a traditional link between priesthood and celibacy in the Latin Church are still valid'. Paul VI received strong support for his stand from bishops throughout the world and within three months a dozen different hierarchies had criticized the attitudes of the Dutch bishops and defended the actions of the Pope. Cardinal Bengsch of Berlin reminded the Dutch hierarchy that collegiality involved agreement with the Pope and with the other Catholic bishops: '. . . pressure exerted by a local church to go its own way affects *all* local churches, and frequently leads, among extremist groups, to an arrogance which has no respect for others. This causes harm, not only to the universal Church, but also to innumerable faithful in their personal Christian lives'.

Nevertheless in 1971 the National Federation of Priests' Councils in the United States voted in favour of the abolition of compulsory celibacy. The Congolese bishops and a meeting of European priests in Geneva supported the ordination of married men, and the Latin American Bishops' Council also called for abolition. The Pope retaliated by referring to 'a restless, critical, unruly, demolishing rebellion' and criticized that 'moral mediocrity' which pretended that 'it is natural and logical to break a long-premeditated promise'.

A third major issue, which seemed to some outside observers to threaten the essential unity between the church in Holland and the Holy See, was the appointment of two bishops who were well known for their opposition to recent developments in Holland and for their devoted loyalty to the See of Rome. But when Adrien J. Simonis was appointed as Bishop of Rotterdam, the Dutch bishops made it clear that they had accepted him 'into their college', while he in turn regretted 'that several of his remarks after his appointment might have given the impression that he desires to set himself against the Netherlands bishop-college'. At the consecration of Simonis, Cardinal Alfrink declared: 'We are going to consecrate a new bishop for the church in Rotterdam. We are going to take him into the Bishops' College of the universal Church. . . . The Bishops' College is not conceivable without the Bishop of Rome, the Pope, who is placed at the head of the College of Bishops'. The Cardinal ended his personal welcome to Simonis with the words: 'In a collegial government, the contribution of each of the members has its own separate value. I can assure you that the bishops are ready to accept you with your contribution. Our mutual task will be to preserve the church in the Netherlands in the present situation in unity with the universal Church, which is not conceivable without the successor of the Apostle Peter'.

However, this explanation of collegiality and profession of loyalty to the Pope does not seem to have satisfied the Roman authorities because when Jan Gijsen was appointed Bishop of Roermond, Paul VI decided to consecrate the new bishop in St Peter's and insisted that the reluctant Alfrink should also attend as co-consecrator. Gijsen himself was more extreme than Simonis and seems to have been prepared for the possibility of a schism in the Netherlands. On at least one occasion he stated that, if it were necessary, he would inform his people of those churches where they might no longer hear Mass and those priests who could no longer be regarded as Roman Catholics. On the other hand the appointment of Cardinal Willebrands, President of the Secretariat for Promoting Christian Unity, to succeed Cardinal Alfrink when the latter retired on his 75th birthday was universally welcomed by all sides. Willebrands was a moderate progressive who pledged himself to follow his predecessor's policy of being a bishop above parties. Of course some of the difficulties which have plagued the Dutch Church have not yet been satisfactorily solved. In November 1977 the Pope himself told the Dutch hierarchy: 'The life of the Church in your country has undergone deep perturbations – in spite of the teaching and repeated reminders of the Holy See – in the field of faith and morality, and also of liturgical and ecclesiastical discipline, all that being accompanied by many defections of priests who have not succeeded in remaining faithful to their commitments'. However, the immediate threat of a schism, if such a threat ever really existed, had undoubtedly receded somewhat by the end of Pope Paul's pontificate.

Pope Paul was perhaps most immediately successful in identifying the Church with the cause of justice and peace, though that process had been developing for some time, especially following the publication of Leo XIII's social encyclicals. In spite of inevitable difficulties, Paul VI firmly committed the Church to the social apostolate as part of its mission to advance the Kingdom of God on earth. As the Synod of Bishops declared in 1971: 'Action on behalf of justice and participation in the transformation of the world fully appears to us as a constitutive dimension of the preaching of the Gospel, or, in other words, of the Church's mission for the redemption of the human race and its liberation from every oppressive situation'.

The identification of the Church with the demands of the nations of the Third World obviously reflected the fact that the number of Catholics in the Third World will quickly and even substantially exceed the number of Catholics in Europe and North America. But the Pope was also expressing his genuine hopes and fears when he warned that if the expectations of the developing nations were denied, this would have fatal consequences for the causes of international progress, peace and the very future of mankind. In January 1967 he established on an experimental basis what eventually became the Pontifical Commission for the Laity and the Pontifical Commission for Justice and Peace. His most celebrated appeal for social justice was made in the encyclical *Populorum Progressio* which was published in the following March. Here the Church was acting as the keeper of the world's conscience where the emerging countries of the Third World were concerned. The encyclical denounced the inequitable distribution of wealth and power, and declared that the surplus wealth of the rich must be used for the benefit of the poor and the dispossessed. To reinforce this point, Paul had some three years before in 1964 made a typically symbolic gesture. He had placed a tiara given to him by the people of Milan at the time of his election on the altar of St Peter's announcing that he would sell it and give the money to the poor. Cardinal Spellman was the purchaser.

Pope Paul's appointments of bishops in African, Eastern and Latin American countries were usually distinctly 'progressive' and he himself consistently condemned the use of torture or official forms of repression by secular governments as well as all types of terrorism. Governments that supported or tolerated political, economic or social exploitation were simply unjust. In 1969 the Pope created Archbishop Stephen Kim of Seoul a Cardinal and publicly gave his support to Kim in the latter's conflict with

President Park. However Paul was not always supported in these policies by local bishops. In 1971 the Archbishop of Sao Paulo was removed from his post and given a curial appointment in Rome – a move which was interpreted as a sign of the Pope's disapproval of the Archbishop's support for the Brazilian Government. At the same time the Pope also spoke out against the torture of political prisoners and the Paraguayan Minister of the Interior and Chief of Police were excommunicated.

The Pope's double concern for justice and peace found its focus in the United Nations, whose Secretary General U Thant he welcomed to Rome and whose Assembly he addressed on the feast of St Francis of Assisi, 4 October 1965. U Thant himself recorded that he had been deeply moved by the Pope's address which, he claimed, 'was of historic importance and left a lasting impression on all the diplomats present, to whatever religion they belonged'. Paul VI was the first Pope to travel outside Italy since Pius VII who had been taken into captivity by Napoleon in 1809 and at the end of his journey to the Far East in 1970 he had travelled almost 70,000 miles, more than all his predecessors combined. All these journeys were designed to enable the papacy to play a vital rôle in contemporary politics by urging conciliation and agreement on the nations, rather than, as in the past, by taking or supporting particular sides. When he was once asked by two American correspondents whether he was prepared to go to Red China, he replied that he was prepared to go anywhere if it would contribute to the cause of peace.

In January 1964 Paul VI visited both Israel and Jordan when he made a pilgrimage to the Holy Land. On learning that the Israeli President was to deliver a speech at the Mandelbaum Gate, contrary to agreements previously made, the Pope took the opportunity of defending the memory of his predecessor, Pius XII. At the end of the same year he went to the International Eucharistic Congress in Bombay where he again demonstrated his concern for the poor of the world. In May 1967 he visited the shrine of Fatima in Portugal, a visit which was criticized on theological and political grounds as well as endorsed for many of the same reasons. Right-wing clericals publicly interpreted the visit as a return to the extreme Mariology and intransigent opposition to Communism which they associated with Pius XII. Left-wing commentators did not ignore the fact that Portugal was fighting a colonial war in Africa and claimed that Portugal seemed an odd place to pray for peace in Vietnam. Such criticisms, however, deliberately ignored the fact that the Pope was always careful to avoid endorsing extreme theological opinions on the position of Our Lady, had already clearly criticized the exploitation of others, and was much more moderate in his attitudes to Communism than many of his contemporaries, Catholic and non-Catholic alike. Only a few commentators seemed to appreciate that he might have gone to Fatima as an act of religious devotion or in order to show his affection for Portuguese Catholics.

In July 1968 the Pope went to Africa where he condemned the evils of racism and asserted that: 'The path of civilization leads towards the recognition of the equality of all men'. In August of the following year he presided at a meeting of African bishops in Uganda and spoke of his determination to assist the economic development of the African nations. He also took the opportunity to appeal for peace to representatives from Biafra and Nigeria. In August 1968 he attended the International Eucharistic Congress at Bogotá in Colombia where he urged the Church to become more active in meeting social needs. On the fiftieth anniversary of the International Labour Organization in 1969, the Pope went to Geneva to plead for a recognition of the dignity of labour, urging delegates to ensure that workers not only participated in the fruits of their labour, but in the social and economic responsibilities on which their futures depended. He also took the opportunity to visit the headquarters of the World Council of Churches and spoke of 'a truly blessed encounter, a prophetic moment, dawn of a day to come and yet awaited for centuries'.

Towards the end of 1970, Pope Paul made an extensive tour of the Far East and Australia. He conferred with the Shah of Iran, personally expressed his sympathies for the victims of cyclones and tidal waves in East Pakistan, and appealed to the rest of the world for help. He attended the first conference of Pan-Asian bishops at Manila where he also visited the slums and when an attempt was made on his life by a madman. At Sydney he attended the first Pacific Episcopal Conference. The Pope also visited Samoa, Sri Lanka, Indonesia and Hong Kong – not Taiwan incidentally – from where he broadcast to the people of China.

For Pope Paul, the diplomatic machinery of the Vatican was a means of presenting the claims of conscience and morality in the world at a time when the claims of power politics normally prevailed. His almost frenzied activities in support of justice and peace would seem to show that he was determined to avoid the accusation that the Holy See was 'silent', the accusation from which he had defended the memory of Pius XII. While maintaining a strict diplomatic neutrality, Pope Paul made many public appeals and used all the diplomatic means at his disposal in an effort to end conflicts and to establish justice and peace. In the year in which he died, he sent a personal message to the delegates of the special assembly on disarmament at the United Nations in which he declared: 'The Holy See is not a world power, but if you ever think that the Holy See can help overcome the obstacles blocking the way to peace, it will not shelter behind the argument of its "non-temporal" character, nor shy away from its responsibilities'.

The Pope's attitudes became most clearly apparent during the conflict in Vietnam. One of his most significant early moves occurred in August 1963 when the Roman Catholic President, Ngo Dinh Diem, was persecuting the Buddhists. Receiving Vietnamese students in audience, he reminded them that the unity of the Church 'does not ignore the rights, the merits, the characteristic aspects of the country . . . does not suffocate the genius of the people to which it addresses itself'. In February 1964 he wrote to the Vietnamese bishops expressing his hopes for peace. He again pleaded for peace in June 1966, the same year in which Cardinal Spellman had seemed to appeal for a holy war in a sermon preached to American servicemen on Christmas Day. In December of the following year the Pope discussed the possibility of peace initiatives with President Johnson at the Vatican and in May 1968 he revealed that the Vatican had been offered as a site for possible peace talks. The Pope did not fear to condemn the American bombing of North Vietnam and he entrusted a personal message appealing for a truce to the leader of the Italian Communist Party when the latter was about to visit Hanoi. In June 1971 he promised to continue to work for peace especially in Vietnam and the Middle East. Paul met the President of South Vietnam in 1973 and the representatives of the Viet Cong and North Vietnam attending the Paris peace talks. In April 1974 he urged that the peace efforts should be continued and in March of the following year pleaded for relief for the suffering Vietnamese.

In August 1969 Pope Paul pleaded for peace in Northern Ireland and expressed his concern about the explosive situation in the Middle East where he was concerned to secure the International status of Jerusalem. In 1971 he denounced the sentences of death and life imprisonment imposed on 164 people in African Guinea and offered to mediate in the conflict between India and Pakistan. In September 1972 he expressed his sorrow at the murder of the Israeli Olympic athletes in Munich and the deaths of the Arab guerrillas. He appealed to the world to help the victims of drought in Africa during 1973 and expressed his horror at the killing of some 400 people in Mozambique. In the following year he was concerned over the conflict in Cyprus, while in January 1975 he warned the world against the dangers of relying on an atomic 'balance of terror' and in October he condemned the mounting campaign of violence in Spain. During the last year of his pontificate he offered himself in exchange for 86 hostages held in a Lufthansa aircraft at Mogadishu airport. He also offered himself as a substitute hostage for the former Italian Premier, Aldo Moro, and appealed for the life of an 11-year-old boy who had been kidnapped in Sardinia.

Pope Paul himself later presided at the Requiem Mass of Aldo Moro when Enrico Berlinguer made his first appearance in church since becoming leader of the Italian Communist Party.

Even before he became Pope, when Monsignor Montini was an official under-secretary at the Secretariat of State, he believed that one of the aims of Vatican diplomacy was not to secure a privileged position for the Church, but the freedom needed in order for the Church to be able to operate. In 1964 Pope Paul signed a *modus vivendi* with Tunisia. This was the first agreement between the Holy See and a nation which recognized Islam as the official religion of the state. By the tenth anniversary of his election some seventy nations had established diplomatic relations with the Vatican, almost double the number when he first became Pope. At the same time the Holy See was being kept informed of developments throughout the world by thirty-six nuncios, thirty-six pro-nuncios, sixteen apostolic delegates and a *chargé d'affaires*.

Similarly the number of State Visits to the Vatican increased over the years. There were ten State Visits during the pontificate of Pius XI, twenty-six during that of Pius XII, thirty-four during the reign of Pope John and over ninety during that of Pope Paul. Paul's visitors included Presidents Podgorny and Tito as well as Presidents Johnson, Nixon and Ford. It is of course far too soon to determine if commensurate results will follow from the Pope's great and exhausting efforts. What is certain is the growing respect and affection with which this shy, yet determined man – so different from the spacious, outgoing personality of his predecessor – came to be regarded by more perceptive commentators throughout the world. Pope Paul was willing to take risks in his efforts to improve the position of the Church as well as in his pursuit of peace. But it was perhaps in his dealings with the Communist régimes of Eastern Europe that he showed the greatest courage and where it must be hoped that his statesmanship will prove both immediately and obviously effective.

By 1963 some tentative moves had already been made in an effort to improve relations between the Church and the Communist powers. Pope John had distinguished the error to be condemned from its sincere adherents in establishing contacts with Communist diplomats. Pope Paul followed the same policy in order to advance the cause of peace and to improve the conditions under which millions of Catholics were living under Communist domination. The first ever agreement with a Communist state was signed with Hungary in September 1964. This agreement gave the Holy See greater freedom in the appointment of bishops and modified the oaths of loyalty imposed on priests. In 1965 the Holy See came to an agreement with the Czech Government and the Pope met the Russian

Foreign Minister, Andrei Gromyko. In the same year the Pope proposed that China should be admitted to the United Nations and two years later suggested to diplomats from Taiwan that they should make diplomatic contacts with mainland China. Although the Pope was not allowed to visit Poland in 1966 for the celebrations marking the advent of Christianity in 966, the Holy See did succeed in re-establishing diplomatic relations with Hungary.

The Pope was also successful in gaining a few concessions for Catholics in Russia and Yugoslavia. In 1967 President Podgorny of the Soviet Union became the first Communist Head of State to have an audience with the Pope who again met with Foreign Minister Gromyko in 1966, 1970 and 1974. Yugoslavia renewed diplomatic relations with the Vatican in 1970 and in the following year Tito paid an official visit to the Pope. The President of Rumania met the Pope in 1973 and during the same year the Polish Foreign Minister visited the Holy See. At the same time arrangements were being made for the first episcopal appointments in Czechoslovakia for almost twenty-five years. Paradoxically, relations with Communist powers seemed to be improving as they deteriorated with some traditionally 'Catholic' countries in Europe and South America where the Pope was supporting local efforts to promote social justice and to secure ecclesiastical independence from the State. The policies of the Pope were also in danger of alienating some old opponents of Communism exemplified dramatically in the case of Cardinal Mindszenty.

Pope Paul had decided that for the sake of Catholics in Hungary, it was better to take a less intransigent and more cooperative stand in relations with the Communist authorities. Mindszenty who not unnaturally believed that persecution followed from 'the essential nature and internal organization' of Bolshevik ideology found it impossible to sympathize with this new approach. When the Pope asked the Cardinal with 'bitter reluctance' to resign his archbishopric in view of 'the pastoral necessities' of the archdiocese, Mindszenty refused. In December 1973, the Pope informed the Cardinal of his deep appreciation and gratitude for his services to the Church, but felt obliged to declare that his see was now vacant. The Pope's treatment of Mindszenty has been contrasted with his opposition to the growth of the Communist Party within Italy. In May 1976 the Pope asked Italian Catholics not to vote for Communist candidates in the forthcoming national elections, though at the beginning of the following year he proved willing to receive in audience the first Communist mayor of Rome.

Yet this contrast is of the essence of the problem which Paul spent his life as Pope trying to resolve. The Pope is not merely an ecclesiastical Secretary-General of an early form of the United Nations. He is primarily a bishop. Herein lies the strength of the papacy – that its authority derives from a local office pastorally exercised. It is the Pope with whom Roman Catholics are in communion, not his administration. No pope in modern times has been more aware of this dual and seemingly conflicting role than Paul VI. It leads, even for a non-Italian to a special relationship to a particular diocese – Rome – as well as to its bishop. This is what leads to such remarks as that we cannot understand Italy without the Papacy any more than we can understand the Papacy without taking into account the problems which are peculiar to contemporary Italy in general and to Rome in particular. Far from conceiving the Papacy as primarily an exercise in statesmanship, Paul held that a healthy local church was as much a matter of urgent concern to him as to any parish priest. Ecclesiastical reform, by enabling the Pope to be a better bishop, would also enable him to achieve the right balance as papal statesman. This conception elucidates Paul's order of priority in the internal reforms which he initiated.

Pope Paul himself made no secret of the fact that he found it difficult to carry the burdens of his high office. In 1969 a prelate complained of the confusion and uncertainty that seemed to be affecting Catholics everywhere and Paul responded by musing in public: 'This remark made Us think. Were We ourself overcome by loss of confidence? "I am a man", and there would be nothing strange about such an event. Peter, or rather Simon was weak and inconstant, with alternating moods of enthusiasm and fear. In that case, We, too, should need to throw ourselves at Christ's feet and with deep humility repeat Peter's words, "I am a sinful man", but also say with immense love, "You know that I love You"; and then have to make a humble apology for Ourself to Our Brothers and Our Children, with no other purpose than to cancel in them any impression they may have had of the kind mentioned before and to assure them of all the interior certainty with which the Lord deigns to strengthen Our ministry'.

On the day before his coronation as pope, Cardinal Montini went to say farewell to the people of Milan where, it is said, he asked them in tears: 'What will become of me?' In due course, as pope, he would describe himself as 'a useless servant' and look forward to his death as a 'providential solution . . . so that others may succeed, stronger and not bound by the present difficulties': 'Why did you call me, why did you choose me – so unfit, so reluctant, so poor in mind and heart? My election indicates two things: my smallness and your merciful and powerful freedom, which was not even stopped by my infidelity, my wretchedness, my capacity to betray you. . . . Therefore, I pray that the Lord will give me the grace to make of my approaching death a gift of love to the Church'. After expressing his love for the Church which he said motivated his service, the Pope went on:

'But I wish that the Church knew this, and that I had the power to communicate it as a confidence from the heart'.

It is not difficult to paint a black picture of the pontificate of Paul VI. In the United States alone it has been estimated that some 10,000,000 Catholics ceased to attend Sunday Mass regularly and that there was a more marked decline among those young Catholics who had received a complete Catholic education. The number of children educated in Catholic schools dropped by two million, the number of baptisms by almost half a million and the number of converts by about 50,000. According to one survey conducted in 1976, three out of four Catholics approved of sexual intercourse for engaged couples, eight out of ten approved of contraception, seven out of ten of legalized abortion, while four out of ten did not believe that the Pope was infallible.

It also seems to be true that the Pope's momentum and drive dramatically declined during the later years of his pontificate. This was only partly the inevitable effect of old age and a long pontificate. Other factors were the increasing influence of particular members of Congregations and the Pope's own natural reaction to such unwelcome prospects as the movement in favour of the ordination of women which threatened to divide further the Protestant west from the Orthodox east. But those contemporaries who forget the optimism and achievements of Paul's earlier pontificate and simply remember the ageing Pope with his sorrows and premonitions also tend to forget the dramatically changed circumstances in the rest of the world. The 1960s had become the 1970s. The 'flower children' had become middle-aged drug addicts, sexual liberation had turned into sexual licence, youthful idealism had turned into radical terrorism, hopes of peace had been followed by a series of wars, and the major powers continued to accumulate improved and more powerful methods of destruction. Meanwhile the Church itself had seemed racked by dissensions and defections. As for Paul, 'In an age of war, he was a man of peace; in an age of bitterness and cynicism, a man of hope; in an age of disbelief, a man of faith'.

In 1978, as the Pope was approaching the end of his life, Oscar Cullman wrote a judicious appraisal of Paul's pontificate in which he maintained: 'People have often been unjust in his regard; some years ago certainly more than today. In the first place it is necessary to reject the one-sided way of comparing him with John XXIII, as if all the light were on John XXIII's side and all the shade on his side; as if the prophetic work of the former, whose merits are certainly great, had been destroyed by his successor's reactionary attitude. This over-simple cliché, which will certainly not be confirmed by the judgment of history, does not correspond to the reality at all. It does not take into account the different charisms of these two popes, and it is a mistake to contrast them in this way. It was, for example, the merit of John XXIII to have convened the Council, but it was the merit of Paul VI to have brought it successfully to a conclusion in spite of extraordinary difficulties which his predecessor had not foreseen. . . . Those who reproach the sovereign pontiff for not going far enough in the reforms, forget too quickly the bold initiatives that he has taken. They are forgotten all the more easily in that he does not surround them with sensational propaganda. He dislikes all demagogy. These initiatives prove that he does not lack imagination and that it is false to deny his prophetic spirit. In spite of the absence of spectacular publicity, he has often astonished not only members of the Church, but also the world, with the boldness of his prophetic acts: his intervention at the UN, his journeys to Palestine and other distant countries, internal reforms in the Curia, liturgical changes and innumerable measures which bear witness to his openness, the establishment of relations with unbelievers, his diplomatic activity, but above all his achievements in relations with other Christian Churches'.

Even many of those who have been critical of Pope Paul VI would admit that if he had not written *Humanae Vitae* and if he had resigned when he was seventy-five, he would have gone down as one of the greatest popes in history. But this is to ignore the fact that the same conscientiousness that forced him to promote the work of reform also forced him to publish *Humanae Vitae* and to continue in office until his death. The Pope's greatest achievements were to ensure that the revolution begun by his predecessors could not possibly be reversed by his successors and his implementation of the decrees and constitutions of the Second Vatican Council, particularly those governing liturgy, collegiality and ecumenism. At the same time and in spite of tensions in Holland and South America, he succeeded in preserving the essential unity of the Church. Some of his internal reforms of the Church have proved to be of increasing benefit, while his ecumenical endeavours were also fruitful on the whole. His journeys were not mere gestures, his statements especially on social reform were often prophetic and he secured a modest improvement in the conditions of those Christians living behind the Iron Curtain.

It will always be debatable to what extent Pope Paul acted in accordance with his own awareness that the Church must not be expected to provide instant automatic answers to contemporary problems which were often so difficult and constantly changing: 'Burning questions are also complex ones. Simple honesty demands that they be considered without haste. We should have respect for the complexity of things, listen, weigh them. If the past teaches us anything, it is that it is better to wait, to risk disappointing the impatient, than to make hasty improvisations. And the higher the authority, the more it must wait. It is easy to study, difficult to decide'.

In practice Pope Paul was very cautious and reserved in the exercise of his authority and he carefully avoided using the ultimate sanctions even under some extreme provocations. Paul suffered Hans Küng as he suffered Archbishop Lefebvre and as he himself said of the latter: 'Our predecessors to whose discipline he presumes to appeal would not have tolerated a disobedience as obstinate as it is pernicious for so long a period as we have so patiently done'. On another occasion Pope Paul remarked: 'A pope must be neither a reactionary nor a progressive. He must be a pope – that's all'.

Paul VI always remained an essentially shy and even retiring person. After fifteen years as Pope when he had given more than 700 general audiences, he could still confess: 'It is with humble trepidation and ardent prayer that we always come to the audience, with one anxious question in our heart: "will we have the grace . . . to touch just one person, to lead him to interior reflection and set him on the path of religious authenticity and Christian fidelity?"'

His pastoral and charitable works reflected this unassuming character. Carlo Falconi, a former priest, once recalled a visit made to him in 1950 by Montini who, 'had come to see me knowing that I was alone on Christmas Eve when solitude is particularly hard to bear. As to the step I had taken in leaving the Church, he passed no judgment on me, and in any case, he added, we could have a talk later on if I wished . . . ever since I have continued to be half-moved, half-irritated at my recollection of those few minutes: moved because of the gesture, prompted as it was by no thought of publicity, and irritated because of the pretences and contradictions in which at a certain point Montini had become involved'.

It has been said of Pope Paul's death that: 'There was a perfect match between his life and his dying: both were an expression of trust and self-giving. There was no more he could do for the 'apostolic Church' he had served'. The Pope's will, written at the beginning of the third year of his Pontificate, was a prayer of gratitude in serene and confident faith for all the natural and supernatural gifts he had received and particularly for his family and his friends. In his will he appears essentially as 'a man of the Church', not the institution but the people of God, and a firm supporter of the essential brotherhood of man. The Pope requested that his funeral and his tomb should be simple. He asked to be interred below the floor of the basilica rather than in a sarcophagus and he approved of the placing and the design of his tomb before his death: 'I would like it to be in real earth with a humble sign indicating the place and inviting Christian mercy. No monument for me'.

Metropolitan Nikodim of Leningrad celebrated a short liturgy for the dead before the body of the Pope in St Peter's. Paul was buried in a simple wooden coffin beside which was a single candle, a symbol of Christ the light of the world. The funeral rites were broadcast live to some forty-eight nations. There were official delegations from ninety-five nations including representatives from Poland, Hungary and Eastern Germany. Kurt Waldheim, Secretary General of the United Nations, was also present. There were delegates from thirteen other Christian Churches, including representatives of the Greek and Russian Orthodox Churches, the Rumanian and Bulgarian Orthodox Churches, the Archbishop of Cyprus, the Coptic Patriarch of Alexandria, the Old Catholic Union of Utrecht, and the retired Archbishop of Canterbury, Michael Ramsey, who wore the ring that Pope Paul had given to him in 1966.

Pope Paul emphasized not the political or the ecclesiastical dignity of the Papacy but his role as the 'Servant of the servants of God'. And the chief form of papal service anticipated by Pope John and developed by Pope Paul may well be to stand not only for the unity of Catholics, or even of Christians, but of all men; the Pope's function being to increase unity throughout the world so that all men may be one in Christ. Such an aim certainly would account for the immensely wide range of Paul's interests, travels and activities. But whether or not this rôle is best undertaken in the form Paul adopted, or whether it can even be undertaken successfully at all, is a question which still remains to be resolved.

Pope John Paul I

Conclusion
Pope John Paul I

As a result of improvements in communications, the Synods of Bishops and their participation in the central government of the Church, many of the Cardinals who met in Conclave in August 1978 were more familiar with each other and more independent of the 'Roman' Cardinals than most of their predecessors. Albino Luciani was personally charming, friendly and attractive. He had pastoral experience as well as the common touch and this simple, holy and pastoral man won the support of 'liberal' and 'conservative' Cardinals alike. But what was not appreciated at the time was the fact that if the Patriarch of Venice was the best of the Italian candidates for the Papacy, was it not time for the Cardinals to begin to look beyond the ranks of the Italians?

The new Pope himself explained his choice of name: 'Pope John had wanted to consecrate me with his own hands here in the basilica of St Peter's. Then, though unworthy, I succeeded him in the cathedral of St Mark – in that Venice that is still filled with the spirit of Pope John. The gondoliers remember him, the sisters, everyone. On the other hand, Pope Paul not only made me a cardinal but some months before that, in St Mark's Square, he made me blush in front of 20,000 people, because he took off his stole and placed it on my shoulders. I was never so red-faced. Furthermore, in the fifteen years of his pontificate, this pope showed not only me but the whole world how he loved the Church, how he served it, worked for it, and suffered for this Church of Christ. And so I took the name "John Paul"'.

Since his death of a heart attack on 28 September after only thirty-four days in office, it has been possible for commentators to come to very different conclusions about the sort of Pope that John Paul I might have been. He issued no encyclicals or major publications and his earlier book, *Illustrissimi*, was dismissed by several commentators as 'Readers Digest Catholicism'. He made no major changes in the Curia and never even celebrated Mass as Pope on the high altar of St Peter's. At the same time, 'the smiling Pope' captivated papal audiences, especially children, by his humility, modesty and joyful confidence; qualities which also endeared him to people throughout the world.

Luciani had felt more at home in the country diocese of Vittorio Veneto than he did in the archdiocese of Venice where he lived simply and dispensed with pomp and ceremony. As Patriarch he personally visited the remote country parishes in his archdiocese and disposed of valuable jewels for the benefit of the poor. Luciani was widely regarded as being rather conservative in his theological attitudes and approach. However, he advised Paul VI that there should be further study and discussion before the publication of *Humanae Vitae* and he also opposed the referendum on divorce, though in both cases he loyally supported the decisions of the Pope and the other Italian bishops. As Patriarch of Venice, however, he himself never vetoed the decisions of his priests in senate. He was more familiar with contemporary theologians and nineteenth-century writers like Rosmini than many of the other Cardinals and wrote to congratulate Hans Küng on the publication of *On Being a Christian*. When Luciani was questioned about the birth of the first test-tube baby, he first congratulated the child and her parents before recalling Pius XII's opposition to artificial insemination and expressing his own reservations over experiments on human beings: 'I send the most heartfelt congratulations to the English baby girl whose conception took place artificially. As far as her parents are concerned, I have no right to condemn them. If they acted with honest intentions and in good faith, they could even be deserving of merit before God for what they wanted and asked the doctors to carry out'.

John Paul I refused to use the tiara, a symbol of secular as well as religious authority, and he described his first Papal Mass as the inauguration of his ministry as supreme pastor rather than a coronation. He rejected the use of old titles like 'Head of the Church' or 'Vicar of Christ' in favour of 'Pope' or 'Bishop of Rome', and he avoided the use of the majestic plural. The new Pope also tried to avoid using the portable throne until pilgrims began to complain that they could not see him. But in spite of the immediate impact which the new Pope made, there were those who suggested that he was out of his depth, that his attractive smile disguised a basic sense of insecurity or even helplessness. When he died of a heart attack on 28 September, it was even suggested that the Lord might have spared his Church from disaster by the early demise of the Pope. But this is to ignore Pope John Paul's explicit determination to continue the work of his predecessors and the extent to which he was influenced by the pastoral programme of Paul VI. Pope John Paul was committed to implementing the decrees of the Second Vatican Council, promoting ecumenism 'without hesitation', reforming canon law, accepting the implications of collegiality, working for development and progress, justice and peace, and the evangelization of the world. And it is only with such a programme that Catholics will be able to deal with the problems facing the Church in the last two decades of the twentieth century.

During the Second Vatican Council, the Fathers failed to deal adequately with many contemporary problems or only partially solved them because they themselves and the ideas with which they were inspired were neither fully developed nor matured. Meanwhile the intransigence of others to some extent hindered the work of reform. Nevertheless, Church leaders will not now be able to reverse the work of the Council and in particular its decrees on the liturgy, ecumenism and collegiality. For better or worse the Second Vatican Council will have a greater positive influence on the Church and the World than the first Council of that name and will ultimately prove to have had as great an impact on the history of the Church as the Council of Trent.

Several factors in contemporary society have proved hostile to the development if not to the very existence of Christianity and Catholicism: the social and economic problems of industrialization; the abuse of the world's resources threatening future generations with catastrophe as well as the poor and the deprived of this generation; the Communist domination of traditionally Catholic countries in Eastern Europe; the danger of nuclear war and destruction; the growth of scepticism and secularism, religious indifference and materialism. Of course the Church itself must accept some of the responsibility for creating this hostile climate of opinion. The political successes of Communism, for example, occasionally resulted from the failure of Christians to put into practice the social demands of the Gospel of Christ who told his followers to love their neighbours as well as their Father in heaven. The Catholic Church was slow to recognize the force of secular political developments and the Popes were simply content to reject liberalism until Leo XIII, to condemn Socialism until Pius XI and to denounce Communism until John XXIII.

Roman Catholicism embraced a smaller proportion of mankind in the middle of the twentieth century than it had in 1914, as a result of the population explosion in the East and political, social and economic developments in the West. Meanwhile the gap between practising and non-practising Catholics continued to widen. However, practising Catholics in the twentieth century were probably more active and devoted than most of their predecessors, while new Catholic movements and organizations attempted to meet the problems and the challenges of the age. The renewed appreciation of scripture, the liturgical movement, pastoral and catechetical initiatives, spiritual and devotional developments were all signs of a deeper and richer Christian life. Furthermore the amount of sheer space devoted by the secular media to matters spiritual and religious would seem to suggest that men and women in the contemporary world are not entirely indifferent to such issues. If nothing else, they are apparently aware of the contrast between their secular preoccupations with the things of this world and a sacred dimension where the Spirit of God might yet be found.

There are those who would argue that a Catholic crisis of faith in the authority of the Church as the infallible teacher of divine revelation – like the Protestant crisis of faith in biblical authority as the revealed Word of God – has given rise to a form of Pentecostalism as an answer to the psychological need for reassurance that the Church is still a safe guide on the road to salvation. But such a view, patterned as it is on the history of the early Church, would seem to ignore the fact that the moral prestige of the Papacy has risen at a time when the concept and understanding of infallibility has already been qualified and modified. The Papacy was stronger and more influential during the second half of the twentieth century than it had been at the beginning. The triumph of Ultramontanism in the nineteenth century had so united the Church administratively, theologically and spiritually that it could maintain that unity in spite of two world wars. The eventual solution of the Roman Question then freed the Papacy from the embarrassments of political authority and national politics so that the popes were free to devote their time to promoting their spiritual and moral influence. The popes who led the Church in the twentieth century have certainly proved to be both able and determined in promoting that spiritual and moral influence, not just within the Church but throughout the world. Only time can tell, however, to what extent and in what ways their efforts and the efforts of their successors will meet with success.

It is of course also impossible to foretell how the election of such a striking personality as the Polish Pope John Paul II will ultimately affect the future development of the Church. There are those who already see in him another Pius IX and others for whom he might yet prove to be the 'acceptable face' of Ultramontanism. He is clearly an attractive, intelligent man who is very familiar with many of the problems, particularly some of the political problems, facing the contemporary papacy yet at the same time he seems curiously unsympathetic and even comparatively indifferent to many other important issues that have been discussed and argued by Catholics over the last few decades. Pope John Paul II seems to have no intention of reducing the traditional prerogatives – as opposed to the elaborate ritual or historic titles – of the Bishop of Rome. But it is difficult to see how he could or would wish to reverse the policies of his immediate predecessors though he could certainly defer and easily modify them. On the whole it would seem that the most likely prospect over the next few years is that the policies associated with Pope John and Pope Paul will indeed continue to be pursued by Pope John Paul but in a more measured way; balanced with, perhaps even subordinated to, his own interests and initiatives, and stamped with the force of his own personality and authority.

Select bibliography

*Abbott, W. M., Gallagher, J. (Eds) *The Documents of Vatican II* (London, 1966).

Algisi, L., *John the Twenty-third* (London, 1963).

Alix, C., *Le Saint-Siège et les Nationalismes en Europe* (Paris, 1962).

Anon, *A Tribute to Pope Paul VI* (Woking, 1978).

Anon (Ed.), *Church and State in Spain* (Madrid, 1962).

Anon (Ed.), *The Worker-Priests. A Collective Documentation* (London, 1956).

A New Catechism. Catholic Faith for Adults (London, 1967).

Aradi, Z., Derrick, M., Woodruff, D., *John XXIII Pope of the Council* (London, 1961).

*Aubert, R., and others, *The Church in a Secularized Society* (London, 1978)

Barry, C. J. (Ed.), *Readings in Church History: The Modern Era 1789 to the Present* (Westminster, 1965).

Baum, G., *That they may be one: A Study in Papal Doctrine, Leo XIII–Pius XII* (London, 1958).

Beales, A. C. F., *The Catholic Church and International Order* (London, 1941).

*Bell, Bishop G. K. A., *The Church and Humanity (1939–1946)* (London, 1946).

Bevan, R. J. W. (Ed.), *The Churches and Christian Unity* (London, 1963).

*Binchy, D. A., *Church and State in Fascist Italy* (Oxford, 1941).

Blauw, J., *The Missionary Nature of the Church* (London, 1962).

*Blet, P., Graham, R. A., Martini, A., Schneider, B. (Eds), *Actes et Documents du Saint Siège relatifs à la Seconde Guerre Mondiale* (Libreria Editrice Vaticana, 1965ff), 9 vols to date.

Bosanquet, M., *The Life and Death of Dietrich Bonhoeffer* (London, 1968).

Bosworth, W., *Catholicism and Crisis in Modern France: French Catholic Groups at the Threshold of the Fifth Republic* (Princeton, 1962).

Bourdeaux, M., *Land of Crosses: The struggle for religious freedom in Lithuania, 1939–1978* (Devon, 1979).

Brenan, G., *The Spanish Labyrinth: An Account of the Social and Political Background of the Spanish Civil War* (Cambridge, 1960).

Brennan, A., *Pope Benedict XV and the War* (London, 1917).

Brown, R. M., *The Ecumenical Revolution: An Interpretation of the Catholic-Protestant Dialogue* (London, 1969).

Bühlmann, W., *The Missions on Trial* (Slough, 1978).

Cadet, J., *Le Laicat et le Droit de l'Église* (Paris, 1963).

*Carsten, F. L., *The Rise of Fascism* (London, 1967).

Cassels, A., *Fascist Italy* (London, 1969).

*Chadwick, O., 'The Papacy and World War II', *Journal of Ecclesiastical History*, vol 18 (1967).

―― 'The Papacy and World War II: Further Documents', *Journal of Ecclesiastical History*, vol 19 (1968).

―― 'The Present Stage of the "Kirchenkampf" Enquiry', *Journal of Ecclesiastical History*, vol 24 (1973).

―― 'Weizsacker, the Vatican, and the Jews of Rome', *Journal of Ecclesiastical History*, vol 28 (1977).

Chinigo, M. (Ed.), *The Teachings of Pope John XXIII* (London, 1967).

*Cianfarra, C. M., *The War and the Vatican* (London, 1945).

'Civis Romanus', *The Pope is King* (London, 1929).

263

Clancy, J. G., *Apostle for our Time, Pope Paul VI* (London, 1963).

Clonmore, Lord, *Pope Pius XI and World Peace: An Authentic Biography* (London, 1938).

*Coleman, J. A., *The Evolution of Dutch Catholicism, 1958–1974* (Berkeley and Los Angeles, 1978).

Congar, Y. M. J., *Divided Christendom* (London, 1939).

*Congar, Y. M. J., Küng, H., O'Hanlon, D. (Eds), *Council Speeches of Vatican II* (London, 1964).

Connolly, J. M., *The Voices of France, A Survey of Contemporary Theology in France* (New York, 1961).

Constantine, Prince of Bavaria., *The Pope: A Portrait from Life* (London, 1954).

*Conway, J. S., *The Nazi Persecution of the Churches 1933–45* (London, 1968).

Conzemius, V., *Églises chrétiennes et totalitarisme national-socialiste: un bilan historiographieque* (Louvain, 1969).

Crossman, R. (Ed.), *The God that Failed: Six Studies in Communism* (London, 1950).

Curtiss, J. S., *The Russian Church and the Soviet State, 1917–1950* (London, 1953).

*Daniel-Rops, H., *A Fight for God, 1870–1939* (London, 1966).

—— *Our Brothers in Christ* (London, 1967).

*Dansette, A., *Destin du catholicisme français 1926–1956* (Paris, 1957).

—— *Religious History of Modern France* 2 vols (Freiburg, Edinburgh, London, 1961).

De Fabrègues, J., *Charles Maurras et son Action Française* (Paris, 1966).

Deroo, A., *L'Épiscopat Français dans la mêlee de son temps 1930–1954* (Lille, 1955).

Diamant, A., *Austrian Catholics and the First Republic: Democracy, Capitalism and the Social Order 1918–1934* (London, 1960).

Domenach, J. M., de Montvalon, R., *The Catholic Avant-Garde: French Catholicism since World War II* (New York, 1967).

Donohoe, J., *Hitler's Conservative Opponents in Bavaria 1930–1945. A Study of Catholic Monarchist and Separatist Anti-Nazi Activities* (Leiden, 1961).

Dudon, P., *L'Action de Benoit XV pendant la guerre* (Paris, 1918).

Duquesne, J., *Les Catholiques français sous l'occupation* (Paris, 1965).

*Ehler, S. Z., Morrall, J. B. (Eds), *Church and State through the Centuries. A Collection of historic documents with commentaries* (London, 1954).

Eppstein, J., *Has the Catholic Church Gone Mad* (London, 1971).

*Falconi, C., *Pope John and His Council: A Diary of the Second Vatican Council, September–December 1962* (London, 1964).

—— *The Popes in the Twentieth Century From Pius X to John XXIII* (London, 1967).

—— *Silence of Pius XII* (London, 1970).

Fey, H. E., *The Ecumenical Advance: A History of the Ecumenical Movement, 1948–1968* (London, 1970).

Fischer, H. G., *Evangelische Kirche und Demokratie nach 1945* (Lübeck, 1970).

Fletcher, W. C., *The Russian Church Underground 1917–1970* (Oxford, 1971).

*Fontenelle, R., *His Holiness Pope Pius XI* (London, 1939).

Foss, W., Gerahty, C., *The Spanish Arena* (London, nd).

Frey, A., *Cross and Swastika: The Ordeal of the German Church* (London, 1939).

Friedländer, S., *Pius XII and the Third Reich* (London, 1966).

Gallin, M. A. *The German Resistance: Ethical and Religious Factors* (Washington, 1961).

Galter, A., *The Red Book of the Persecuted Church* (Dublin, 1957).

*Gollwitzer, H., Kuhn, K., Schneider, R. (Eds), *Dying We Live: The Final Messages and Records of the Resistance* (New York, 1961).

Goodall, N., *Ecumenical Progress: A Decade in the Ecumenical Movement 1961–1971* (Oxford, 1972).

Goodall, N., *The Ecumenical Movement: what it is and what it does* (Oxford, 1961).

*Graham, R. A., *Vatican Diplomacy: a Study of Church and State on the International Plane* (Princeton & London, 1960).

—— 'Vatican Radio between London and Berlin 1940–41', *The Month*, n.s., vol. 9 (1976).

Graml, H., Mommsen, H., Reichhardt, H. J., Wolf, E., *The German Resistance to Hitler* (London, 1970).

*Greeley, A. M., *Crisis in the Church: A Study of Religion in America* (Chicago, 1979).

—— *The Making of the Popes 1978. The Politics of Intrigue in the Vatican* (Kansas, 1979).

Guilmot, P., *Fin d'une Église cléricale? Le débat en France de 1945 à nos jours* (Paris, 1969).

*Guitton, J., *The Pope Speaks* (London, 1968).

Gurian, W., *Hitler and the Christians* (London, 1936).

*Gwynn, D., *The 'Action Française' Condemnation* (London, 1928).

—— *The Catholic Reaction in France* (New York, 1942).

—— *The Vatican and the War in Europe* (Dublin, 1941).

*Haecker, T., *Journal in the Night* (London, 1949).

Halecki, O., Murray, J. F., *Pius XII: Eugenio Pacelli, Pope of Peace* (New York, 1954).

*Hales, E. E. Y., *Pope John and his Revolution* (New York, 1965).

—— *The Catholic Church in the Modern World* (London, 1958).

Halperin, S. W., *Mussolini and Italian Fascism* (Princeton, 1964).

Hanquet, K., *Le Pape Benoit XV* (Brussels, 1922).

*Hardon, J. A., *Christianity in the Twentieth Century* (New York, 1972).

Häring, B., *Embattled Witness: Memories of a Time of War* (London, 1977).

Hartley, T. J. A., *Thomistic Revival and the Modern Era* (Toronto, 1971).

Hatch, A., Walshe, S., *Crown of Glory: The Life of Pope Pius XII* (New York, 1957).

Hayward, M., Fletcher, W. C. (Eds), *Religion and the Soviet State: A Dilemma of Power* (New York, Washington, London, 1969).

*Hebblethwaite, P., *The Year of Three Popes* (London, 1978).

Hennesey, J., 'American Jesuit in Wartime Rome: The Diary of Vincent A. McCormick, S.J., 1942–1945', *Mid-America: An Historical Review*, vol. 56 (1974).

Hinsley, Cardinal A., *The Bond of Peace and other war-time addresses* (London, 1941).

Hlond, Cardinal A., *The Persecution of the Catholic Church in German-occupied Poland* (London, 1941).

Hoare, F. R., *The Papacy and the Modern State* (London, 1940).

*Hochhuth, R., *The Deputy* (New York, 1964).

Holmes, J. D., 'Pope Pius XII: Impressions of a Pontificate', *Clergy Review*, vol. LXI (1976).

—— 'The Church in the First Half of the Twentieth Century: An Historiographical Survey', *Clergy Review*, vol. LVIII (1973).

Hughes, P., *Pope Pius the Eleventh* (London, 1937).

Hyde, D., *I Believed: The Autobiography of a former British Communist* (London, 1951).

*Jemolo, A. C., *Church and State in Italy, 1850–1950* (Oxford, 1960).

*John XXIII, Pope, *Journal of a Soul* (London, 1965).

—— *Mission to France, 1944–1953* (London, 1966).

—— *My Bishop: A Portrait of Mgr Giacomo Maria Radini Tedeschi* (London, 1969).

Johnson, H., *The Papacy and the Kingdom of Italy* (London, 1926).

—— *Vatican Diplomacy* (Oxford, 1933).

Kaiser, R., *Inside the Council: The Story of Vatican II* (London, 1963).

*Kelly, G. A., *The Battle for the American Church* (New York, 1979).

Kelly, M., *Pioneer of the Catholic Revival: The ideas and influence of Emmanuel Mounier* (London, 1979).

Kerkvoorde, A., Rousseau, O., *Le mouvement théologique dans le monde contemporain: liturgie, dogme, philosophie, exégèse* (Paris, 1969).

Kolarz, W., *Religion in the Soviet Union* (London, 1961).

Lampart, B., *Ecumenism: Theology and History* (London, 1967).

Lapide, P. E., *The Last Three Popes and the Jews* (London, 1967).

Latourette, K. S., *Christianity in a Revolutionary Age*, vols IV, V (Exeter, 1970).

—— *History of the Expansion of Christianity*, vol. VII (Exeter, 1971).

Laures, J., *The Catholic Church in Japan: A Short History* (Westport, 1970).

Leeming, B., *The Churches and the Church* (London, 1960).

—— *The Vatican Council and Christian Unity* (London, 1966).

LeGuillou, M. J., *Mission et Unité* (Paris, 1961).

Lewy, G., *The Catholic Church and Nazi Germany* (London, 1964).

Liénart, Cardinal M. E., *Vatican II* (Lille, 1976).

Loew, J., *Journal d'une Mission ouvrière 1941–1959* (Paris, 1959).

—— *Mission to the Poorest* (London, 1951).

Lunn, H. S. (Ed.), *United Christian Front* (Cambridge, 1938).

MacGregor-Hastie, R., *Pope Paul VI* (London, 1966).

*Mariaux, P. W., *The Persecution of the Catholic Church in the Third Reich* (London, 1940).

Maritain, J., *The Peasant of the Garonne: An Old Layman Questions Himself about the Present Time* (London, 1968).

Mauriac, F., and others, *Communism and Christians* (London, 1938).

McKenzie, J. L., *Roman Catholic Church* (London, 1969).

Mecham, J. L., *Church and State in Latin America* (London, 1966).

*Messenger, E. C. (Ed.), *Rome and Reunion: A Collection of Papal Pronouncements* (London, 1934).

Meyer, J. A., *The Cristero Rebellion: the Mexican People between Church and State, 1926–1929* (Cambridge, 1976).

'Michael Serafian', *The Pilgrim Pope Paul VI, the Council and the Church in a Time of Decision* (London, 1964).

Micklem, N., *National Socialism and the Roman Catholic Church* (Oxford, 1939).

—— *The Theology of Politics* (Oxford, 1941).

*Mindszenty, Cardinal J., *Memoirs* (London, 1974).

*Molony, J. N., *The Emergence of Political Catholicism in Italy Partito Popolare 1919–1926* (London, 1977).

Moody, J. N. (Ed.), *Church and Society: Catholic Social and Political Thought and Movements 1789–1950* (New York, 1953).

Moore, T. E., *Peter's City: An Account of the Origin, Development and Solution of the Roman Question* (London, 1929).

Murphy, F. X., *John XXIII: The Pope from the fields* (London, 1959).

Murray, J. C., *We Hold These Truths. Catholic Reflections on the American Proposition* (London, 1961).

Newman, L. I., *A 'Chief Rabbi' of Rome becomes a Catholic. A Study in Fright and Spite* (New York, 1945).

*Nichols, P., *The Politics of the Vatican* (London, 1968).

*Nolte, E., *Three Faces of Fascism* (New York, 1969).

O'Neill, C. (Ed.), *Ecumenism and Vatican II* (Milwaukee, 1964).

*Padellaro, N., *Portrait of Pius XII* (London, 1956).

Pallenberg, C., *Inside the Vatican* (New York, 1960).

Paul, H. W., *The Second Ralliement: the Reapprochement between Church and State in France in the Twentieth Century* (Washington, 1967).

Paul VI, Pope, *The Church* (Dublin, 1964).

Payne, S. G., *Falange: A History of Spanish Fascism* (Stanford, 1961).

Pelikan, J., *The Riddle of Roman Catholicism: Its History, Its Beliefs, Its Future* (London, 1960).

Pernot, M., *Le Saint-Siège, l'Église catholique et la Politique mondiale* (Paris, 1924).

Perrin, H., *Priest and Worker* (London, 1964).

Philips, G., *The Role of the Laity in the Church* (Cork, 1956).

*Pius XI, Pope, *Twelve Encyclicals* (London, 1943).

Pollock, R. C. (Ed.), *The Mind of Pius XII* (London, 1955).

Portmann, H., *Cardinal von Galen* (London, 1957).

Poulat, É., *Naissance des prêtres-ouvriers* (Paris, 1965).

*Purdy, W. A., *The Church on the Move: The Characters and Policies of Pius XII and John XXIII* (London, 1966).

Ramati, A., *While the Pope Kept Silent* (London, 1978).

Randall, Sir A., *Vatican Assignment* (London, 1957).

*Rankin, C. (Ed.), *The Pope Speaks* (London, 1941).

Raven, C. E., *War and the Christian* (London, 1938).

Regan, R., *Conflict and Consensus: Religious Freedom and the Second Vatican Council* (New York, London, 1967).

*Rhodes, A., *The Vatican in the Age of the Dictators, 1922–1945* (London, 1973).

*Riesterer, P., *Father Rupert Mayer, SJ* (London, nd).

Rogger, H., and Weber, E. (Eds), *The European Right* (London, 1965).

*Rope, H. E. G., *Benedict XV: The Pope of Peace* (London, 1941).

Rossini, G., *Il Movimento cattolico nel periodo fascista* (Rome, 1966).

Rouse, R., Neill, S. C. (Eds), *A History of the Ecumenical Movement, 1517–1948* (London, 1954).

Sartory, T., *The Oecumenical Movement and the Unity of the Church* (Oxford, 1963).

Schall, J. V., *The Sixth Paul* (Ohio, nd).

Schillebeeckx, E., *Vatican II: The Real Achievement* (London, 1966).

Second and Third Reports on the Communist Atrocities issued by the Committee of Investigation appointed by the National Government at Burgos (London, 1937).

**Selected Papal Encyclicals and Letters 1928–1932* (London, 1933).

Sereny, G., *Into that Darkness* (London, 1974).

Sforza, C., *Contemporary Italy: Its Intellectual and Moral Origins* (New York, 1944).

Siefer, G., *La Mission des Prêtres-ouvriers: Les faits et consequences* (Paris, 1963).

Smit, J. O., *Pope Pius XII* (London, 1950).

Spadolini, G., *Il Cardinale Gasparri e la Questione Romana (con brani delle memorie inedite)* (Florence, 1972).

Spellman, Cardinal F. J., *Action this Day: Letters from the Fighting Fronts* (London, 1944).

Stroyen, W. B., *Communist Russia and the Russian Orthodox Church* (Washington, 1967).

Sturzo, L., *Church and State* (London, 1939).

Suenens, Cardinal L. J., *Co-responsibility in the Church* (London, 1968).

Sutherland, H., *Spanish Journey* (London, 1950).

Sweeney, F. (Ed.), *The Vatican and World Peace* (Gerards Cross, 1970).

Tavard, G. H., *Two Centuries of Ecumenism* (London, 1960).

Taylor, M. C. (Ed.), *Wartime Correspondence between President Roosevelt and Pope Pius XII* (New York, 1947).

Teresia de Spiritu Sancto, Sister, *Edith Stein* (London, 1952).

*The Pope and the People Select Letters and Addresses on Social Questions (London, 1950).

Thils, G., *Histoire Doctrinale de Mouvement Oecuménique* (Louvain, 1955).

*Thomas, H., *The Spanish Civil War* (London, 1965).

Thomas, L., *L'Action Française devant l'Église. De Pie X à Pie XII* (Paris, 1965).

Timasheff, N. S., *Religion in Soviet Russia 1917–1942* (London, 1943).

Townsend, W. and L., *The Biography of His Holiness Pope Pius XI* (London, 1930).

Trevor, M., *Pope John* (London, 1967).

Utley, T. E., Stuart Maclure, J. (Eds), *Documents of Modern Political Thought* (Cambridge, 1957).

Van den Heuvel, J., *The Statesmanship of Benedict XV* (London, 1923).

Van Hecken, J. L., *The Catholic Church in Japan since 1859* (Tokyo, 1963).

Van Lierde, P. C., *The Holy See At Work: How The Catholic Church is Governed* (New York, 1962).

Villain, M., *Unity: A History and Some Reflections* (London, 1963).

Vistalli, F., *Benedetto XV* (Rome, 1928).

*Von Aretin, K. O., *The Papacy and the Modern World* (London, 1970).

Von Hildebrand, D., *Trojan Horse in the City of God* (Chicago, 1967).

Von Loewenich, W., *Modern Catholicism* (London, 1959).

Vorgrimler, H., *Karl Rahner: His Life, Thought and Work* (London, 1965).

Weber, E., *Action Française* (Stanford, 1962).

Webster, R. A., *Christian Democracy in Italy, 1860–1960* (London, 1961).

Wilkinson, A., *The Church of England and the First World War* (London, 1978).

Willam, F. M., *Vom jungen Angelo Roncalli zum Papst Johannes XXIII* (Innsbruck, 1967).

*Williamson, B., *The Story of Pope Pius XI* (London, 1931).

—— *The Treaty of the Lateran* (London, 1929).

Wiskemann, E., *Fascism in Italy: its Development and Influence* (London, 1970).

Woodlock, T. F., and others, *Democracy, should it survive?* (London, 1946).

Wright, G., *The Ordeal of Total War* (New York, 1968).

'Xavier Rynne', *Letters from Vatican City: Vatican Council II (First Session): Background and Debates* (London, 1963).

—— *The Second Session: The Debates and Decrees of Vatican Council II, September 29 to December 4, 1963* (London, 1964).

—— *The Third Session: The Debates and Decrees of Vatican Council II, September 14 to November 21, 1964* (London, 1965).

—— *The Fourth Session: The Debates and Decrees of Vatican Council II, September 14 to December 8, 1965* (London, 1966).

Zahn, G. C., *German Catholics and Hitler's Wars: A Study in Social Control* (London, 1962).

—— *In Solitary Witness* (London, 1966).

Zatko, J., *Descent into Darkness: The Destruction of the Roman Catholic Church in Russia 1917–1923* (Notre Dame, 1965).

Index